WOMEN'S WRITING IN ENGLISH:
MEDIEVAL ENGLAND

Women's Writing in English

Series Editor:
Gary Kelly, Professor of English, University of Alberta, Canada

Published titles:
Anthea Trodd, *Women's Writing in English: Britain 1900–1945*
Laurie A. Finke, *Women's Writing in English: Medieval England*

Women's Writing in English: Medieval England

Laurie A. Finke

Longman
London and New York

Addison Wesley Longman Limited
Edinburgh Gate
Harlow
Essex CM20 2JE
United Kingdom
and Associated Companies throughout the world.

Published in the United States of America
by Addison Wesley Longman Inc., New York

First published 1999

ISBN 0-582-25939-8   CSD
ISBN 0-582-25940-1   PPR

Visit Addison Wesley Longman on the world wide web at
http://www.awl-he.com

British Library Cataloguing-in-Publication Data

A catalogue record for this book is available from the British Library

Library of Congress Cataloging-in-Publication Data

Finke, Laurie A.
  Women's writing in English : medieval England / Laurie Finke.
    p. cm. — (Women's writing in English)
  Includes bibliographical references and index.
  ISBN 0-582-25939-8 (CSD). — ISBN 0-582-25940-1 (PPR)
    1. English literature—Middle English, 1100–1500—History and
  criticism.   2. English literature—Old English, ca. 450–1100—
  History and criticism.   3. English literature—Women authors—
  History and criticism.   4. Women and literature—England—History—
  To 1500.   5. Women—England—History—Middle Ages, 500–1500.
  I. Title. II. Series.
  PR113.F56   1999
  820.9'9287'0902—dc21   98–30636
                                                                  CIP

Set by 55 in 10/12 pt Bembo
Produced by Addison Wesley Longman Singapore (Pte) Ltd.,
Printed in Singapore

Contents

General Editor's Foreword

Women's Writing in English provides a comprehensive survey of women's writing in English from the Middle Ages to the present, and from around the globe. Recent feminist scholarship and criticism have pointed out ways in which women's writing has been excluded from or marginalized in the literary canon. Accordingly, the volumes in this series consider not only literary kinds of writing, including fiction, drama, and poetry, but also non-literary kinds, in which women were often pioneers, ranging from religious devotion and conduct books to books for children, from journalism to popularizations of science, theology, history, political economy, and so on.

Each volume in the series is based on original research and opens with a section placing women and women writers in the economic, social, cultural, literary, and publishing conditions of their time. Subsequent chapters examine critically the work of individuals and groups of writers and various kinds of writing in the particular region or country during a specified period. There is discussion of both major and minor figures; of writers now securely placed in the literary canon as well as those writers less well known. Volumes close with substantial sections of reference information, including bibliographies, chronologies, and author biographies. Although the volumes have a broadly similar structure, the authors of individual volumes are free to develop lines of inquiry and critical argument as they see fit. Above all, we want the series to be used by students and teachers on a range of courses, including those concerned with women's writing itself, with established literary periods and genres, and with particular focuses in cultural studies, social history, education and writing for children.

Gary Kelly

Preface

To make this volume more accessible to the general reader, all quotations of medieval works are cited in translation. Wherever possible, I have used the best available translation. Where no translation exists, I have used the best available edition of the work and supplied my own translation. For texts which are unavailable in modern editions, I have supplied a translation of the manuscript. In translation, clarity is sometimes achieved at the cost of aesthetic effect and for the infelicities of my translations I apologize. I have endeavoured to make them as literal as possible. The interested reader will find listed in the bibliography either the manuscript or edition from which I have translated, as well as the manuscripts I consulted in my research.

Acknowledgements

We are grateful to the following for permission to reproduce copyright material:

Addison Wesley Longman Ltd for extracts from *Women's Writing In Middle English* edited by Alexandra Barratt, © Longman Group UK Limited 1992; David Campbell Publishers for extracts from *Anglo-Saxon Poetry* by R.K. Gordon (1937); Doubleday, a division of Bantam Doubleday Dell Publishing Group Inc. for extracts from *The Lyrics Of The Troubadour, Trouveres* by Frederick Goldin, Copyright © 1973 by Frederick Goldin; W.W. Norton & Company Inc. for extracts from *The Women Troubadours* by Meg Bogin (1980); Oxford University Press for an extract from *Religious Lyrics Of The 14th Century* (second edition) by Carleton Brown and extracts from *Paston Letters and Papers Of The 15th Century, Volumes I & II* by Norman Davis (1976); Penguin Books Inc. for extracts from *Revelations Of Divine Love* by Julian of Norwich, translated by Clifton Wolters (1966) and *The Book Of Margery Kempe*, translated by B.A. Windeatt (1985).

Abbreviations

ANTS	Anglo-Norman Text Society
BL	British Library
BN	Bibliothèque Nationale
CUL	Cambridge University Library
EETS	Early English Text Society
MS	manuscript
f.	folio
r.	recto
v.	verso

Introduction

To modern readers encountering Christine de Pizan's fifteenth-century allegory, *The Book of the City of Ladies*, for the first time, the extensive architectural metaphor of building a city 'from foundation stone to turrets and towers' (Quilligan, *Allegory* 3) used to describe Christine's history of women may seem merely heavy-handed, just another wooden medieval allegory. But metaphors, as George Lakoff and Mark Johnson have shown, are never merely decorative; they are habits of mind. 'Our ordinary conceptual system, in terms of which we both think and act, is fundamentally metaphoric in nature' (Lakoff and Johnson, *Metaphors* 3). Like Christine, Lakoff and Johnson recognize the extent to which we organize arguments through architectural metaphors: 'What is the *foundation* for your assertion?' 'You need to *buttress* your argument with *solid* evidence.' 'You need to *construct* a *strong* argument.' 'That statement is without *foundation*' (46). The centrality of these metaphors to our most ordinary ways of thinking about the rhetorical task of persuasion should prompt us to rethink the appropriateness of Christine's allegory to the task of recovering women's lost literary traditions.

The city has always been for the west the paradigmatic symbol of culture. Christine's revisionary history plays on that connection between architecture and argument, city and culture, using the image of building the city to describe – and literally to create – women's textual authority (Quilligan, *Allegory* 83). The entire first section of the *City of Ladies* is devoted to female city builders like Semiramis (Babylon) and Dido (Carthage) and those women who founded cultural institutions.[1] The city is an apt figure for culture because it recognizes the collectivity of culture. It encompasses not only the monumental work of individuals, but the collective symbol-making activity of all its inhabitants. For this reason I invoke Christine's image of city building as a fitting description for a study of women writers in medieval England. Like Christine, I have begun with the premise that a

1

thorough revision of our literary and historical traditions, and the assumptions on which they are based, is necessary before those traditions can begin to articulate women's experiences of the past (Quilligan, *Allegory* 3).

The task of recovering the cultural contributions of women who wrote in English during the Middle Ages, then, requires some comment, particularly given beliefs about the scarcity of women's writing, even among those who are engaged in the work of recovering it. In the multivolume *History of Women* series published by Harvard's Belknap Press under the editorship of French historians Georges Duby and Michelle Perrot, the volume devoted to the Middle Ages is entitled *Silences of the Middle Ages*, suggesting the insignificance of women as historical subjects during the period and hence the insurmountable difficulties of recovering their lost lives. Alexandra Barratt in her anthology of women's writing in Middle English remarks on the 'lamentable dearth of Middle English women writers' and asks, reasonably enough 'How can a selection of women's writing in Middle English fill a whole book?' (Barratt, *Women's Writing* 1). Such conventional wisdom points to the methodological issues at stake in recovering medieval women's lives and writing. If women were so effectively silenced in the Middle Ages, how can our research recover information about them?

A conventional answer might argue that the vast majority of women were effectively silenced during the whole of the Middle Ages (as were the vast majority of men). The rare woman who did produce writing was unique; she had somehow managed to transcend the limitations of her sex. I hope, however, to take a different approach in this social history of medieval women's writing in England. Drawing upon Christine's architectural metaphor for the collective act of culture building, I will not survey women's writing during this period as the product of a few exceptional geniuses. Rather I will situate such writing in the context of the collective and shared cultural experiences of particular groups of women at specific moments in history, examining how the cultural experiences of the women who produced it helped shape larger currents in medieval culture and history. Mine is not, however, a separatist city of ladies. Women's literary activities did not emerge primarily from within a 'separate sphere' set apart from men's literary activity (in spite of stereotypic images of cloistered nuns), but were an integral part of medieval culture, existing in dialogic relations of both resistance and collaboration with other (male) cultural productions.[2]

I begin, then, from three related, if contradictory assumptions:

- Medieval women were oppressed by the institutions, practices and values of a patriarchal culture.

- Medieval women could perceive and resist that oppression. They might lack the resources to make public their resistance, so that it might manifest itself through more indirect means, requiring a very different methodological approach on the part of the literary historian to uncover it.
- From the above two assumptions it follows that medieval women participated fully, if not equally, in the making of their cultures.

These assumptions, I will show, produce a very different view of the woman writer from that of the lone genius rising above her sex. They suggest that the mere fact of oppression alone is not enough to silence women as a group. However oppressed by patriarchy, however subordinate to men, women have always resisted their oppression, although their resistance might remain invisible to historians because what we see in any historical record is a function of what we expect to see.[3] Our sense of the Middle Ages as primarily masculine turf has been largely produced by the kinds of histories that have been written about it. The questions that, in the past, have guided research about the Middle Ages have rendered women invisible because they assume that any resistance to male domination would take the same forms as those favoured by the dominant; they assume resistance will be marked by an open, public declaration of the intention to resist. But resistance to oppression most often expresses itself in ways that do not yield readily to traditional research methods precisely because the forms such resistance takes are rarely so public and overt as the forms of domination.

To reformulate our understanding of women's contributions to medieval culture, then, we must locate the analysis of women as an oppressed group within a theory of oppression that describes a dialogic interplay between the oppression of the powerful and the resistance of the oppressed. Such a theory must assume neither that those who are oppressed are completely docile and powerless nor that they enjoy equal access to the resources for making their demands public. The discrepancy between the forms of domination and those of resistance has led James Scott to argue that traditional analyses of power from both the right and left obscure much of the dynamics of power – and especially the nature of the resistance to it – because they focus only on the public displays and records of power, what he calls the *public transcript* (Scott, *Arts of Resistance* 5). The public transcript records the interactions between the powerful and their subordinates only as an elaborate public mask. Interactions in the public transcript are rituals designed to legitimate the expectations of those who wield power and, as such, can represent only incompletely the complexities of power relations. Much analysis from the left (including feminist analyses), for instance, assumes that oppressed groups have more or less internalized their oppression, that they are victims of a 'false consciousness'. Scott argues, however, that public displays of conformity, deference and docility for the benefit of those in power that are generally cited as evidence of this false consciousness often mask covert defiance. In fact, the greater the disparity between dominant and subordinate, 'the more the public transcript of subordinates will take on a stereotyped, ritualistic cast. In other words, the more menacing the power, the thicker the mask' (Scott, *Arts of Resistance* 5). Only rarely do the powerless 'speak truth to power'.

Behind the scenes, however, and away from the surveillance of the dominant, the subordinate display a whole range of discourses and behaviours that contradict their public performance. Because they only rarely emerge in the public record, these events are rarely considered in analyses of subordination (including feminist analyses). These events and discourses Scott calls the *hidden transcript*. The hidden transcript might be marked by such everyday acts of resistance as sabotage, foot dragging, desertion, evasion, poaching or outright disobedience, as well as by symbolic and discursive gestures like complaints, curses and other rituals of verbal aggression, gossip, rumour and carnival. By positing this other realm of activity not subject to the surveillance of the dominant, Scott does not mean to suggest that what happens in the public transcript is necessarily false and what happens in the hidden transcript is necessarily true. He is not claiming 'the former as a realm of necessity and the latter as a realm of freedom' (Scott, *Arts of Resistance* 5). Nor does he suggest that the subordinate have the freedom to say 'what they really think' in the hidden transcript. The exercise of power cannot be so simply reduced to a binary equation. Both transcripts are performances, subject to whatever rules govern the speech communities for which they are intended. But as performances they are directed toward different audiences and operate under different constraints. It follows, then, that any analysis of the power relations between two unequal groups (like men and women) requires that we consider at least four very different sets of performances: those of the dominant and subordinate in the public transcript, the hidden transcript of the dominant,[4] and that of the subordinate.

Of course the point of a hidden transcript is its hiddenness. Designed to take place outside of the public scrutiny of those who wield power, it finds expression primarily in ephemera, in discourses that were not likely to be preserved for posterity. For this reason, it is always difficult for historians to uncover the hidden transcript, especially in a period like the Middle Ages for which the historical record even of the public transcript is fragmentary. This explains why we know so little about the resistance of women to their subordination during the Middle Ages and why we assume that there was virtually none. To uncover the hidden transcript requires an approach that examines archival texts as performances rather than as simple statements of historical fact. The researcher who approaches the evidence with a different set of assumptions about what it reveals, assumptions designed to interrogate archival texts for evidence of both public and hidden transcripts, may be able to reconstruct some of the rich interplay between the public and hidden performances that describes the relations between men and women. This is the premise of this book, which will argue that far from being an expression of a rare genius, the medieval woman writer provides us with some insight into the hidden transcript of women's resistance to patriarchy. At the same time, a closer attention to the texture of women's lives and their literacies will illuminate the collective nature of women's writing and its dialogic relations with the dominant culture.

By way of example let me briefly examine just one way by which the hidden transcript may find its way into the historical record of the Middle Ages. The most obvious route would be those moments in which 'the frontier between the hidden and public transcripts is decisively breached' (Scott, *Arts of Resistance* 202), when those who have been subordinated refuse even superficially to continue to be complicit in their oppression. Sometimes such breaks take the form of outright rebellion – even armed confrontation – but often they are somewhat less violent, though perhaps no less spectacular. In examining such events, it is important to remember that, though the rebellious words might be spoken by an individual, they are not simply the expression of one individual's subjective experience; rather they are meant to convey a collective and shared experience of domination. They express publicly what many have been saying privately, usually with some frequency. The collective sense of elation and even fear that accompanies such events is precisely what gives them their feeling of release. What is said is not electrifying because of its novelty; rather the words (or actions) shock, incite or elate because what has so often been expressed privately in the hidden transcript has, at last, become public.

My example is taken from the opening of *The Book of the City of Ladies*.[5] Students reading this text for the first time often describe the experience of reading the opening pages as affording them just the sense of release – of giving voice to the forbidden – I have been describing above. The book opens with Christine's deferential nod to the power of literary authority, a performance in the public transcript: 'One day as I was sitting alone in my study surrounded by books on all kinds of subjects, devoting myself to literary studies, my usual habit, my mind dwelt at length on the weighty opinions of various authors whom I had studied for a long time' (*City of Ladies* 3). Here is the literary equivalent of the curtsy, a public sign recognizing the social superiority represented by the 'weighty opinions' of the male authorities to whom she properly 'devotes' herself. This tone of deference continues as her attention wanders to a book of misogynist invective by an author named Matheolus. Though she immediately dismisses the book as 'not very pleasant for people who do not enjoy lies' (3), even such a brief encounter reminds Christine how pervasive – and persuasive – such misogyny is in the books to which she has so humbly devoted herself. Misogyny is clearly a performance in the public transcript: 'But just the sight of this book, even though it was of no authority, made me wonder how it happened that so many different men – and learned men among them – have been and are so inclined to express both in speaking and in their treatises and writings so many wicked insults about women and their behavior' (4). Even in the face of her own experience, Christine's public persona – the mask she adopts to present herself as a proper woman writer to her readers[6] – seems to have internalized the misogyny she finds in her reading:

> And so I relied more on the judgment of others than on what I myself
> felt and knew. I was so transfixed in this line of thinking for such a long
> time that it seemed as if I were in a stupor. Like a gushing fountain, a
> series of authorities, whom I recalled one after another, came to mind,
> along with their opinions on this topic. I finally decided that God formed a
> vile creature when He made woman, and I wondered how such a worthy
> artisan could have deigned to make such an abominable work which, from
> what they say, is the vessel as well as the refuge and abode of every evil
> and vice. As I was thinking this, a great unhappiness and sadness welled up
> in my heart, for I detested myself and the entire feminine sex, as though
> we were monstrosities in nature. (4–5)

Here in the public transcript, deference to authority and humility before the more powerful leads to internalized self-loathing. Or appears to. There are signs that this self-loathing is mostly a performance. To the modern ear, for instance, Christine's prose sounds excessively wordy. Like most formal tokens of deference extracted from the subservient by the powerful, Christine's performance is marked by circumlocution, euphemism, excessive repetition ('the vessel as well as the refuge and abode of every evil and vice'), and exaggerated politeness ('like a gushing fountain'). These self-effacing strategies account for much of what feels 'artificial' or 'flowery' to us in Christine's prose. Placed in the context of an encounter with power (it is worth noting that Christine's primary audience and patrons were the most powerful aristocrats in Europe, the French royal family) her stylistic choices become more dynamic, less merely conventional.

Even as she speaks these formulae of the public transcript, brief glimpses of the hidden transcript that lies behind this public performance ironically undercut her words:

Thinking deeply about these matters, I began to examine my character and conduct as a natural woman and, similarly, I considered other women whose company I frequently kept, princesses, great ladies, women of the middle and lower classes, who had graciously told me of their most private and intimate thoughts, hoping that I could judge impartially and in good conscience whether the testimony of so many notable men could be true. To the best of my knowledge, no matter how long I confronted or dissected the problem, I could not see or realize how their claims could be true when compared to the natural behavior and character of women. (4)

What is perhaps most noteworthy about this passage (besides, that is, its rejection of misogynist beliefs) is that Christine does not simply hold up her own subjective experiences as proof against misogynist claims; rather she calls on the collective experiences of diverse women. Among themselves, it seems, women are much less inclined to accept and internalize the judgement that the female sex is the 'abode of every evil and vice'. Christine characterizes herself as a member of a discursive community of women who share their resistance to misogyny. These other women 'had graciously told me of their most private and intimate thoughts'. Those private thoughts – the hidden transcript of women's resistance to misogyny – are to be set against the public 'testimony' of the powerful in what amounts to a public trial, with Christine as an impartial judge. What gives this passage its emotional power is the collective rebellion Christine describes, and not simply her own individual refusal to accept misogynistic invective as truth. The collective force of this refusal is gathered up in the words of Lady Reason who, in the next chapter, simply demolishes the arguments of those 'authorities' and thereby begins to 'clear the ground' to construct the 'city of ladies'.

My example is meant to suggest that if we approach medieval texts with a very different set of questions, we may bring to light very different representations of medieval women. To do so, however, we must call into question our most basic assumptions about literary inquiry, subjecting them to a methodological redefinition that may significantly alter the terms of literary study as it has been conceived. I have found that my investigations of medieval women writers have led me to a critique of the very terms of my inquiry. The next two chapters will explore that critique even as they attempt to describe the interaction between public and hidden transcript discourses about women. The first chapter will describe how women were officially described in the public transcript. It will explore how these institutional discourses affected their public and private lives and the means by which women resisted those representations. Since the term 'transcript' suggests some kind of written documentation, Chapter 2 will examine the role of writing in medieval culture, the mechanisms by which texts were given cultural authority, and women's access both to the means of writing and authorizing texts.

This study has benefited from the advice and support of many individuals and, as is customary, I would like to thank them here. Though we have never met, my greatest debt is owed to Alexandra Barratt, whose 1992 book, *Women's Writing in Middle English*, provided a road map without which this study would have taken many more years to complete than it did. This book is also a record of my dialogues with many individuals whose words have become inextricably linked with mine; I especially thank Anne Clark Bartlett, Jean Blacker, Joan Cadden, Jane Chance, Marilynn Desmond, Eve Moore, Ronald Schleifer, Marty Shichtman, Mary Suydam, Jane Tylus and Bonnie Wheeler for stimulating and challenging discussions about the subjects of this book. Paul Remley's bibliographic assistance on Anglo-Saxon women was invaluable. Stephanie Maier helped with the preparation of the chronology and spent many hours discussing medieval women with me in an independent study. I also thank the various audiences who listened to and commented on chapters of this study; this includes members of the Kenyon Seminar and of Jane Chance's 1997 NEH Institute on the *Literary Traditions of Medieval Women*, as well as audiences at Otterbein College, Southern Methodist University and the University of Wisconsin where I presented lectures based on this study. An NEH Summer Stipend and Faculty Development Grants from Kenyon College supported trips to British libraries and a sabbatical leave from Kenyon College enabled me to complete the manuscript. Jami Peelle, Kenyon College archivist and librarian, was tireless in tracking down books, addresses, manuscripts and other material. Gary Kelly read the entire manuscript carefully and offered much good advice. As always my children, Stephen and Hannah, and my husband Bob have offered unflagging support, companionship, solace, distraction and the occasional inspirational remark.

NOTES

1. For an insightful discussion of the role of female city builders in *The City of Ladies*, see Quilligan 69–85.
2. My use of 'dialogic' here and throughout the text is indebted to the work of the Russian critic, M.M. Bakhtin, who describes the dialogic as 'the intense interaction and struggle between one's own word and another's word' (*Dialogic Imagination* 354).
3. Joan Ferrante's recent book, *To the Glory of Her Sex*, makes an argument similar to mine that, despite the persistent institutionalized misogyny of the Middle Ages, women were not completely powerless. They were able to participate in medieval culture and even to influence its direction (see especially 3–9).

4. The powerful are also required to enact performances, displays of power, in the public transcript and they, too, may behave quite differently when not in the public eye. For instance, in the public transcript, powerful men were likely to legitimate their control of women through fictions of protection and chivalry. The hidden transcript of such displays included behaviours like wife-beating and rape that contradicted these performances.

5. For a more detailed discussion of Christine's life and works see Chapter 4 below. While *The City of Ladies* is not the work of an English writer, Christine's work circulated widely among powerful members of the English aristocracy during the fifteenth century. Since the English aristocracy would be literate in French, it seems plausible to suppose that *The City of Ladies* was read in fifteenth-century England even if it was not translated into English until the sixteenth century. All citations from *City of Ladies* are taken from the translation by Richards (1982).

6. On the effect standards of 'propriety' had on women writers see Poovey, *The Proper Lady* and Cotton, *Women Playwrights*.

CHAPTER ONE

Women in the Middle Ages

THE MIDDLE AGES

If restoring women's cultural contributions to our histories requires a re-thinking of our most basic assumptions, that rethinking must begin by unpacking the unstated assumptions about the past and its relation to present concerns which dominate the English literary canon. I have been using the term 'Middle Ages' (and its Latin cognate 'medieval') to designate ten centuries of English history as if they were a single, coherent, unified entity. But the term is not a neutral one, though we usually take its meaning for granted. We need to inquire into the set of assumptions this term activates. What, we might well ask, is the Middle Ages in the middle of? To ask this simple question is to expose the nearly invisible model of periodization that structures the English literary canon. It makes visible a system that is not simply a value-free set of ideas. The practice of dividing English literature into Medieval, Renaissance, Enlightenment, Romantic, Victorian and modern periods tells a very particular story about who 'we' are and how 'we' got here. ('We' are always Europeans; everyone else is, in the words of Eric Wolf's excellent 1982 study, 'the people without history'.) The narrative implied by this periodization goes something like this (I invoke the version I learned as a schoolgirl because it reveals the agenda so baldly and suggests how deeply it is embedded into our cultural consciousness): We (Europeans, Americans) identify our origins in the classical period, in ancient Greece where democracy was born and learning flourished. Rome inherited the mantle from Greece. When Rome fell the 'dark ages' all but wiped out that culture and learning. Fortunately it was rediscovered in the Renaissance, which represents the 'rebirth' of classical learning and a return to the glories of ancient Greece and Rome. The Enlightenment follows which represents the endpoint that enshrined humanist ideals – reason, 'man' (not woman) – as the ends toward which culture and civilization had strived. During that time science rose, the middle classes rose, capitalism and industrialism rose. With only one small detour – the 'dark ages' which is usually conveniently glossed over as a historical cul de sac – European progress has been relentlessly teleological, culminating in modern techno-scientific 'man'.

This story is built right into the very names we have selected to designate these periods. Consider briefly the terms Middle Ages and Renaissance. We can imagine people during the sixteenth century thinking of themselves as living in a renaissance, during a time of rebirth and discovery. But what could people in the Middle Ages imagine themselves living in the middle of? Such a term could only have been invented retrospectively and we can glimpse such retrospection in Renaissance writers' self-fashioning, a public relations venture which our literary histories have pretty much accepted at face value. The term 'renaissance' promotes a myth of a return to a pristine origin, a nostalgia for an idealized and distant past. It celebrates the 'rebirth' of the knowledge of the ancients at the same time it promotes a fiction of a break with the ignorance and superstition of the medieval past.[1] In *The Advancement of Learning* (1604), Francis Bacon opposes the knowledge of the classics to 'the bishop of Rome and the degenerate traditions of the Catholic church'. He describes the need to 'awake all Antiquity and to make a party against the present time' with the result that 'ancient Authors . . . which had long time slept in our libraries, began generally to be read' (Spingarn, *Critical Essays* 1).

In the Renaissance, our cultural narrative tells us, western civilization awoke as if from a dream. That dream was the Middle Ages, as Umberto Eco argues in his essay 'Dreaming the Middle Age' (Eco, *Travels* 61–72). Our image of western civilization is dependent on the repression of the nearly ten centuries we call the Middle Ages. Because the Middle Ages does not lend itself particularly well to the narratives about progress and enlightenment that have been major themes in European historiography, it becomes that part of our history we have repressed. And yet the repressed always returns. Many of the institutions by which western culture defines itself were, in fact, created during the period we call the Middle Ages and, although they represented a break with the classical past, these institutions have continued to shape the lives of most of the people living on this planet, whether they are European or not. The list, which is partly mine and partly Eco's, includes the university, legal codes, the book, romantic love, burial practices of inhumation, modern European languages, the political boundaries of contemporary Europe, as well as the nation-state, nationalism, merchant cities, banks, cheques, prime rates, horseshoes, stirrups, gunpowder, modern methods of computing, double-entry bookkeeping, the compass

11

and eyeglasses.[2] As Eco argues, we no longer live in the Parthenon, but we still pray in medieval cathedrals. We admire the classical period, but we inhabit the Middle Ages (Eco, *Travels* 64).

IMAGINING WOMAN

Our stereotypical view of the Middle Ages as a monolithic and backward 'dark age' makes it all too easy to believe that medieval attitudes toward women were static, unchanging and invariably negative. The opening of Christine de Pizan's *City of Ladies* suggests that the major obstacle faced by a woman who wanted to write was the largely negative images of women perpetuated by male authorities who wrote about them. She notes that 'judging from the treatises of all philosophers and poets and from all the orators . . . it seems . . . They all concur in one conclusion: that the behavior of women is inclined to and full of every vice' (4). Who were all of these philosophers, poets and orators and what were they say-ing about women that could so paralyse Christine? Our analysis of the heretofore hidden transcripts of women's cultural production must begin with an examination of the ways in which the public transcript – the religious, legal, medical and cultural discourses monopolized by men and the clergy – attempted to regulate and constrain women's participation in cultural life.

Medieval anti-feminism does not really have a history; it sounds much the same in the fourteenth century as it does in the fourth.[3] It is citational in nature, relying on the incessant repetition of the same passages from a few standard authors: Theophrastus, St Jerome, Ovid, Juvenal and such books of the Bible as Proverbs, Ecclesiastes, the creation account in Genesis and the Epistles of St Paul. All of these texts were of course already cen-turies old by the beginning of the Middle Ages. Despite the limited sources, however, misogynistic commonplaces were pervasive in the writing of the period, occurring in virtually all male writers and in a wide variety of texts designed for very different audiences: sermons, conduct books, theological works, maxims, proverbs, textbooks, encyclopedias, medical texts, ethics manuals, devotional treatises, hagiographies, romances, lyric poetry and histories. The characterization of woman as imperfection is not the sole province of either the theologians or the poets. In medieval scientific writing woman is both weaker than and inferior to man. In the medical tradition deriving from Aristotle and Galen, woman is a defective man.[4]

Aristotle writes that 'we should look upon the female state as being as it were a deformity, though one which occurs in the ordinary course of nature' (737a, 775a), while Galen argues that 'you ought not to think that our Creator would purposely make half the whole race imperfect and, as it were, mutilated, unless there was to be some great advantage in such a mutilation' (2. 299).

Anti-feminist writing endlessly repeats the same message – that woman is 'a fragile thing, steadfast in nothing but crime and always harmful. Woman is a voracious flame, the utmost folly, man's intimate enemy, who learns and teaches every possible way of doing harm. Woman is a vile forum, a public thing, born to deceive, for whom success is the ability to commit crime. All consuming in vice, she is consumed by all' (Dalarun 22). I chose this passage, from the twelfth-century bishop of Le Mans, Hildebert of Lavardin, at random, to illustrate the rhetorical structures of medieval anti-feminism. Notice how the writer repeats the grammatical phrase 'woman is', using it to structure the series of often unrelated charges. Indeed, Howard Bloch defines misogyny as 'a speech act in which woman is the subject of the sentence and the predicate a more general term', the reduction of Woman to a category (*Medieval Misogyny* 5). For Bloch, misogyny encompasses any essentialist definition of Woman, 'whether negative or positive, whether made by a man or a woman' (6). We must continually bear in mind that medieval writing about women deals not with individual *women*, but with *Woman* as an image, as a imaginary concept.

Though anti-feminist works do not have much form beyond a series of unconnected and disjointed charges, the series of predicates attributed to Woman are fairly predictable and fall into three main categories. Women are more closely associated with the material (as opposed to the spiritual) world. They are more bestial (they are often compared to animals, serpents and insects), more fleshly than men, and hence more lustful, as this proverb suggests: 'One cockerel suffices fifteen hens, but fifteen men don't suffice one woman' (Blamires, *Woman Defamed* 8). This passage from Odo of Cluny (d. 942) is also representative: 'Physical beauty is only skin deep. If *men* could see beneath the skin, the sight of *women* would make them nauseous. . . . Since we are loath to touch spittle or dung even with our fingertips, how can we desire to embrace such a sack of dung?' (Dalarun, 'Clerical Gaze' 20). A second charge is that women abuse language; they lie, chatter, gossip and nag. *The Lamentations of Matheolus*, to which Christine refers in the opening of the *City of Ladies*, claims that 'The tongue of a quarrelsome wife never tires of chiming in. She even drowns out the sound of the church bell. A nagging wife couldn't care less whether her words are wise or foolish, provided that the sound of her own voice can be heard' (Blamires, *Woman Defamed* 178). Finally, women are excessively fond of ornamentation.

13

Again, from *The Lamentations of Matheolus*, 'she often transforms and changes her appearance, adopting different hairstyles. She paints her face, rearranges her hair, wears make-up, adorns herself' (Blamires, *Woman Defamed* 187).

Bloch has argued that the association of women with ornamentation and the abuses of language was another manifestation of the medieval condemnation of simulation and representations, of 'all that is plastered on', to quote Tertullian (*Medieval Misogyny* 9). Because she was associated with material embodiment, Woman provided a convenient scapegoat for those aspects of symbolic activity – like rhetoric – that the Middle Ages found distasteful and deceptive.

Chaucer's portrait of the Wife of Bath in *The Canterbury Tales* is perhaps the best known compendium of these anti-feminist commonplaces strung together from several texts. Dame Alice of Bath reminds us that this essentializing genre represents a very particular perspective and not an unbiased one: 'As the lion asked the fellow who showed him a picture of a man killing a lion, "Who was the the painter? Tell me who!" By God if women had written as many histories as these cloistered scholars, they'd have recorded more wickedness on the part of men than all the sons of Adam could ever put right' (185).[5] The anti-feminist tradition represented only one view of women – men's, and not all men at that. In fact, as Ferrante suggests, it may not even have been an attitude consistently held by a single individual. It was very much a performance in the public transcript (*Glory of Her Sex* 6). Much of this writing was produced by celibate clerics living in all-male communities whose experience of women was extremely limited. 'For, make no mistake,' the Wife says, 'it's an impossibility that any [cleric] should speak good of women, except in the case of the lives of female saints; certainly not any other sort of woman' (185). This writing was often directed less toward disciplining and reforming women than toward enforcing clerical celibacy by making women seem less attractive, less a temptation. However, even when the writer was not a cleric, men writing about women tended to rely less on their experience of living women, than on the received authorities – the philosophers, poets and orators that Christine cites – and these authorities wrote only about Woman as an essential category.

This often tedious recital of woman's natural imperfections did have its mirror image in idealizations of women, which become more prominent after the twelfth century. Medieval idealizations of woman may be a more complex and multi-faceted subject than the denunciations, more susceptible to change and history and perhaps even more sensitive to the actual conditions of women's lives. The twelfth century in particular seems to mark a watershed for idealized imagery associated with women in both religious and secular discourse.

The most obvious example of the religious ideal of woman is, of course, the Virgin Mary, whose worship reached its peak in twelfth-century Mariolatry. Two of the four major doctrines concerning Mary were already well established in the early years of Christianity – the doctrine of the mother of God and the Virgin Birth were proclaimed by the Council of Ephesus in 431 and reaffirmed in 451 by the Council of Chalcedonia.[6] The fervour of the late medieval worship of the Virgin is suggested by this fourteenth-century Middle English translation of the Latin hymn 'Ave Maris Stella':

> Hail! Star on the sea so bright,
> To God's holy mother appointed
> Ever maiden made of might,
> that blessed gate of heaven is bright.

The poem celebrates both aspects of Mary's persona, the maternal –

> Show thyself the mother you are
> Take our prayer through thy bliss;
> To Him who for us and our sins
> became thy son, and thou his mother –

and the virginal –

> Only maiden and no more
> Among us all so meekly going,
> Release us of guilt and woe
> Make us both meek and chaste.
>
> Grant us a clean life (58)[7]

The Virgin Mary represented all that a perfect woman was supposed to be – chaste, pure, meek and maternally solicitous. Worship of Mary, however, does not seem to be associated particularly with women; in fact, before the twelfth century it is rare to find a women's prayer addressed to Mary. Many twelfth-century churchmen, however, like Anselm of Canterbury (d. 1109), imagined Mary as a sign of hope for women, a corrective to the imperfections inherent in the daughters of Eve: 'So that women need not despair of attaining the state of the blessed, given that a woman was the cause of so great an evil, it was necessary, in order to restore their hope, that a woman be the cause of so great a good' (Dalarun, 'Clerical Gaze' 24). Praise for Mary did not necessarily translate into praise for women; in fact quite the opposite. Mary is 'alone without parallel, virgin and mother'; she is hardly a model that actual women could hope to emulate successfully. If anything, her perfection stood in sharp contrast to the imperfections of all other women; she is the exception that proves the rule.

As a figure of worship, the Virgin Mary focused the painful contradictions in the struggle, waged throughout the Middle Ages, to control female sexuality. Medieval churchmen divided women into a tripartite hierarchy; at the top were virgins, then widows, and last – and least – wives: in heaven, 'virgins would be rewarded a hundred times their deserts; widows, sixty times; wives, thirty times' (Dalarun, 'Clerical Gaze' 29), that is, of course, assuming there could be such a thing as a good wife, which might have been an oxymoron for most medieval writers. Most could do little more than argue for the necessity of wives; they did not seem able to praise their perfections, or even their virtues.[8] A woman should desire virginity; she settled for being a wife. The Church's celebration of virginity was completely at odds with secular emphasis on the centrality of marriage. Throughout the Middle Ages, marriage was used to cement political alliances between families and even between kingdoms; women – married women – were important to families' political and economic strategies, both as objects of exchange between families and as producers of children – heirs who could continue aristocratic lineages. By contrast, the Church demanded that for women to seek perfection, they would have to renounce their sexuality, surrender their femininity and remain virgins. Of course, if they did so, they could never be mothers. But the Virgin Mary had done both; in a sense she resolved the conflict between the roles of mother and virgin. She is the only woman ever to have done so.

This struggle between the Church's celebration of virginity and the aristocracy's pragmatic stance toward marriage was played out on the bodies of women, especially holy women. Imagine what it must have been like for a woman who had dedicated her virginity to Christ to be told by her father that she must marry and engage in the very sexual intercourse she had disavowed as loathsome. Perhaps the most common narrative feature of women's hagiographies (saints' lives), from the time of the Roman persecution on, involves a daughter trying to escape the marriage arranged for her by her father. There are examples of saints who mutilated themselves to avoid this fate. St Ode cut off her nose to evade marriage (L'Hermite-Leclercq, 'Feudal Order' 217). Aelfric in his *Lives of the Saints* tells of St Euphrosyne who became a transvestite – donning the habit of a monk – to preserve her virginity. She lived successfully as a monk for thirty-eight years. Only on her deathbed did she reveal her true identity to her father. The life of the English saint, Christina Markyate (c. 1096–1155), written by an anonymous monk of St Albans, offers perhaps the most detailed account of a saint's struggle to resist parental pressure to marry. After making a vow to devote her life to Christ, Christina is nearly raped by a Norman bishop and when she eludes him, he persuades her parents to arrange a marriage for her. When she resists the marriage she is kept in 'a close and rigid custody' (*Christina Markyate* 45) until she agrees to marry, but refuses to 'submit to the physical embraces of any man' (47). Three times her parents attempt to arrange her deflowering. Their attempts to debauch their daughter suggest their hostility to the ideals of virginity; at one point her mother swears 'that she would not care who deflowered their daughter, provided that some way of deflowering her could be found' (73). Her father complains: 'Why must she depart from tradition? Why should she bring this dishonour on her father? Her life of poverty will bring the whole of the nobility into disrepute' (59). Eventually she escapes from her family and, to evade them, lives for years as a recluse in a cell so small she can barely move. Representing the parents' secular perspective, the author writes, 'if she had given her mind to worldly pursuits she could have enriched and ennobled not only herself and her family but also all her relatives' (67). As Christina's story suggests, the consequences for women of the cultural ideal of virgin mother could be painful indeed.

If medieval religious writers could rarely find anything good to say about wives, the same could not be said for mothers. From the twelfth century on, in fact, there is a noticeable increase in imagery drawn from uniquely female experiences like childbearing and nursing. Maternity is idealized in the high Middle Ages in the less well-known image of Jesus as Mother. Caroline Walker Bynum documents several twelfth-century religious figures who develop a complex of images that represent Christ and other male figures – Moses, St Peter, St Paul, prelates and abbots – as mothers. In the following passage from Anselm of Canterbury, both Christ and St Paul are envisioned as mothers:

> Paul, mother . . . lay then your dead son [the sinful soul] at the feet of Christ, your mother, for he is her son. Or rather throw him into the bosom of Christ's love, for Christ is even more his mother. Pray that he may revive this dead son, not so much yours as his. Do, mother of my soul, what the mother of my flesh would do. (Bynum, *Jesus as Mother* 114)

Bernard of Clairvaux is particularly drawn toward images of breastfeeding to describe his pastoral duties to instruct. In one of his letters he writes: 'I begot you in religion by word and by example. I nourished you with milk when, while yet a child, it was all you could take. . . . But alas! how soon and how early you were weaned. . . . Sadly I weep, not for my lost labor but for the unhappy state of my lost child' (*Jesus as Mother* 117). Undoubtedly, as Bynum suggests, the prominence of maternal imagery in twelfth-century writers (including also William of Thierry and Aelred of Rievaulx) suggests a new trend toward affective spirituality, as well as a means of mitigating the distant and forbidding paternal images of authority in monastic life, making them more accessible (*Jesus as Mother* 113). The almost sentimental focus on the intimate relationship between mother and infant in this writing suggests that maternity must have held some value for these men – at least in the abstract. At the same time, the gender reversal appropriated what was of value in maternity for men, providing especially those living in monastic communities with alternative views of authority and dependence. It was men – not women – who mothered.[9]

Both the cult of Mary and the Jesus as Mother image participated in a 'feminization of culture' that seemed to sweep across Europe in the twelfth century (Bogin, *Women Troubadours* 44–5, Kelly, *Women* 22–30, Bynum, *Jesus as Mother* 135–46). In the religious sphere that meant an increasing emphasis on female experiences (like childbirth), on gender reversals in which male figures were described in terms of female characteristics, and in the greater prominence of female figures. Not only did the Virgin Mary become a popular devotional figure, but so did many female saints (Bynum, *Jesus as Mother* 137). Mary Magdalene becomes especially popular as a figure of the penitent sinner (Dalarun, 'Clerical Gaze' 31–3). The canonization of female saints increased markedly after the twelfth century and in allegories female figures increasingly came to personify concepts like the soul (Anima) or wisdom (Sophia).[10] Female figures often serve in allegories as guides for the hero's spiritual journey; Dante's Beatrice is perhaps the best known example of a tradition that goes back at least to the portrait of Lady Philosophy in Boethius' *Consolation of Philosophy*.

This feminization of culture was felt in the secular world as well. One secular space that emerged for the worship of women was the development in twelfth-century Provence of a set of attitudes about love and women known as *fin' amor* or courtly love. 'Farai chansoneta nueva,' 'I shall write a new song,' wrote the first troubadour, Guillaume, ninth duke of Aquitaine, at the beginning of the twelfth century. In the poetry of the troubadours who followed Guillaume, and later in that of the trouvères of France, the poets of the *dolce stil nuovo* of Italy, and the minnesinger of Germany, the aristocratic woman becomes the object of the poet's adoration; the noblewoman, or 'lady', becomes the recipient of the poet's homage and obedience. *Fin' amor* spread widely throughout Europe in the late twelfth and early thirteenth centuries, largely through the auspices of powerful women patrons like Guillaume's granddaughter, Eleanor of Aquitaine, and her daughters (McCash 6–8; see below 77), reaching northern France, Spain, Portugal, Italy, England and even Germany. *Fin' amor* celebrates women extravagantly, as in this example by Guillaume.

My lady is trying me, putting me to the test
to find out how I love her.
Well now, no matter what quarrel she moves for that reason
She shall not loose me from her bond.

Instead, I become her man, deliver myself up to her,
And she can write my name down in her charter . . .

I worship no other woman. (Goldin 40–3)

The songs through which these ideals spread (at least in Provence) have
as their principle subject the *dompna* (the term of address directed toward
a married noblewoman in Provençal). She is the most virtuous ('bona') and
beautiful woman in the world. The lover serves and worships her, while
she tests him ('prueva'). His joy and pain both proceed from her. When
she is kind, he is joyful; 'My heart is so full of joy / it changes every nature'
writes Bernart de Ventadorn, another troubadour (Goldin, *Lyrics* 128–9).
When she is cold, he suffers, even to the point of death, as Guillaume's
song suggests. But his love for her is ennobling, making him a better man.
Arnaut Daniel writes, 'Each day I am a better man and purer, / for I serve
and celebrate the noblest lady' (Goldin, *Lyrics* 216–17). As the ideals of
courtly love spread throughout Europe, they found their way into almost
every literary genre including lyric poetry, the chivalric romance (think, for
instance, of the interactions between Gawain and Bercilak's wife in *Sir
Gawain and the Green Knight*), and allegory (*The Romance of the Rose*). Even
religious writers picked up courtly love imagery and applied it to the
relationship between Christ and the soul.[11] Chaucer's *Knight's Tale* uses the
conventions of courtly love to describe the unrequited love of Palamon
and Arcite for Emily, who is, interestingly, another example of a woman
who chooses virginity (she dedicates herself to the pagan Goddess Diana),
but is forced to accept an arranged marriage.

The lady of *fin' amor* embodies a stereotype as impossible for real women
to attain as that of the virgin mother. She must be always sexually available
and, at the same time, always chaste. The non-attainment of sexual consummation is as important to the courtly love tradition as sexual display. In
the case of adulterous relationships (of which there are many), the lady
must be faithful to her lover at the same time she is being faithless to her
husband (the triangles formed around Arthur, Guenevere and Lancelot in
Arthurian romances, or Tristan, Isolde and King Mark are good examples;
see Bloch, *Medieval Misogyny* 143–56).

This exploration of the ways in which official medieval culture imagined
women have led us to a paradox. How do we reconcile the vogue for both
the courtly and religious worship of women and the constant denuncia-
tion of women as the devil's gateway (Remley) so conspicuous in the
Middle Ages and especially after the twelfth century? We cannot simply
argue that denunciations of women correspond to periods when women
were completely oppressed and idealizations correspond to periods in which
women's material condition was improving. The anti-feminist diatribe

exists side-by-side with the ideal images throughout the Middle Ages. Indeed, the ease with which writers can slide from the one register to the other suggests that idealization and invective may simply be two sides of the same coin, two versions of the same essentialized representation of woman. This is the paradox of perfection (Bloch, *Medieval Misogyny* 143): the woman worshipped in medieval idealizations is an abstraction, a hypostasization of desire (both religious and sexual). Actual women are kept at a distance. When real women fail to live up to the ideal, when that desire remains unfulfilled (as indeed it must), then anti-feminist invective takes up where it left off to create an equally fictitious view of woman as monster. Medieval misogyny and idealization are not opposing discourses, but 'intermingling zones of a common conceptualization of gender' (Bloch, *Medieval Misogyny* 160).

Indeed, the extent to which the twelfth century experienced this feminization of culture has been the subject of recent debate. Some scholars argue that developments like Mariolatry and *fin' amor* expressed 'a deep psychological need left unmet by the unrelenting masculinity of feudal culture' (Bogin 44–5, Kelly 22–30). Others contend that these idealizations of femininity have nothing to do with women and everything to do with women's subjugation (Lacan 141; Bloch, *Medieval Misogyny*; Finke, *Feminist Theory* 29–48). Both discourses about women, however, may have served other purposes besides the subordination of women. They may, for instance, have been instrumental in enforcing clerical celibacy and Church discipline. Anti-feminist writings enabled male monastic communities to rid themselves of any vestiges of femininity, any threat from the temptations of the flesh. But the repressed always returns and the idealizations of maternity prominent in twelfth-century monastic writing may have allowed femininity into the cloister in a form abstracted from actual women. In the secular realm, courtly love may have provided a vehicle for articulating the relationships between aristocratic men under feudalism. The affective nature of the feudal relationship – the 'love' between seigneur and vassal – required feminine mediation to transform a relationship between two men into a narrative about heterosexual love. Whatever varied purposes these images may have served, however, they almost certainly had an effect on women's lives. They policed women's behaviour by encouraging them to strive for ideals that, if successfully achieved, would keep them docile and submissive – silent, obedient, patient and uncomplaining in tribulation – while the invectives painted unflattering portraits of what happened to those women who failed to live up to those standards or – worse yet – rebelled against them, a strategy not unlike the often unflattering cartoon images of feminists in the popular media today.

HISTORICIZING WOMEN

At the same time, we must ask whether women simply adopted these images as their own or whether they were able to shape them to suit their own ends? Only a fuller exploration of the historical conditions of women's lives in medieval England can answer that question. It is quite easy to fall into the belief that the attitudes toward women outlined above – especially the Church's attitudes – could only oppress women. Such beliefs enable us to forget that the message of Christianity in its earliest forms presented radical opportunities to women which they readily embraced. Christian women of the first, second and third centuries were able to participate in a radical redefinition of women's social roles. No longer were they to be confined to the roles of dutiful wife and mother. Militant celibacy offered them a freedom that was unknown in the ancient world (Pagels, *Adam* 16–31). The third-century martyr Perpetua Vibia, for instance, does not simply suffer her martyrdom passively. She stages it as a drama, assuming for herself the power to define the meaning of her suffering. In one vision of her martyrdom, which she wills for herself, she sees herself in the amphitheatre, awaiting her execution.

> And there came an Egyptian, foul of look, with his attendants to fight against me. And to me also there came goodly young men to be my attendants and supporters. And I was stripped and was changed to a man. And my supporters began to rub me down with oil, as they are wont to do before a combat. (Petroff, *Visionary Literature* 73)

Perpetua defeats the Egyptian in battle and receives from the trainer a green branch with golden apples. During her actual execution, theatrical details abound as well. After being attacked by a mad heifer in the arena, Perpetua adjusts her robe to cover her thighs and requests pins to fasten her disordered hair. Since torn clothes and dishevelled hair were for Romans a sign of grief, she did not want to seem 'to mourn in the hour of her glory' (76). Similarly the fourth-century St Macrina, sister of Gregory of Nyssa, assumed for herself the power to redefine the roles allotted to her. To preserve her virginity, after her father had betrothed her and her fiancé had died, she called herself a widow: 'she called her father's decision a marriage on the grounds that what had been decided had actually taken place and she determined to spend the rest of her life by herself' (Petroff, *Visionary Literature* 78). Women throughout the Middle Ages would show a similar determination to use official discourses about them for their own purposes.

We must bear in mind that, despite blanket statements about 'women's nature' made by churchmen throughout the Middle Ages, despite the misogyny that marked clerical writing about women, the course of women's lives was largely determined by the specific historical conditions under which they lived. Misogyny has a tendency to de-historicize women and restoring that history will put the misogyny in its place as a performance in the public transcript, while perhaps illuminating the hidden transcript. One cannot assume, however, that women's condition in the Middle Ages was homogeneous over the nearly ten centuries (from roughly the fall of Rome and the abandonment of Britain by the Romans in the fifth century until the advent of printing in the late fifteenth century) we designate by the term 'Middle Ages'. Nor were women's experiences homogeneous across class lines. It made a difference whether a woman was a member of the aristocracy, the artisanal class, the urban 'patriciate' or the peasantry; whether she lived in a convent, a castle or a hovel.

The last two decades of research on medieval women has documented extensively women's participation in a broad range of social, cultural and political activities throughout the Middle Age; they were poets and patrons, saints and heretics, theologians and preachers, rulers and entrepreneurs, abbesses and manuscript illuminators. They went on Crusades, argued with popes and bishops, ruled territories and fought wars, just as they gave birth, managed households from enormous castles to small hovels, and served as inspiration for generations of poets and artists. As a means of conveying at least some sense of the heterogeneity of medieval women's lives within the confines of a brief survey, I will discuss women's status across class lines for both religious and laywomen during each of three periods:

- the Anglo-Saxon period;
- during and after the Norman Conquest;
- during the fourteenth and fifteenth centuries.

I have chosen these periods as representative of major changes in women's status in England throughout the period. I will focus on class differences among women, on the status of married women, and on the special status of religious women, as well as on the differences between court, urban and rural life.

ANGLO-SAXON WOMEN

In the period from roughly the end of the sixth century until the end of the eleventh century English political and cultural life was dominated by the descendants of Germanic invaders who had pushed the previous British inhabitants to the margins of the island, north to Scotland and westward to Cornwall and Wales, even across the Channel to Brittany. Except for a period of Viking invasions from the eighth century on and a brief Danish monarchy, Anglo-Saxon culture was the dominant culture. Of course, at this time, Britain could hardly be thought of as a single, unified nation as it is today, nor was it ruled by anything like a centralized monarchy. Rather England consisted of a number of small kingdoms, each ruled by an elected king. At different periods in its history, different kingdoms would be in ascendancy – Northumbria and Kent in the seventh century, Wessex in the tenth. For this reason, we cannot assume homogeneity during this period. What few records survive from this period survive haphazardly from different regions of Anglo-Saxon England and different times. We cannot assume that what was true of Northumbria in the seventh century will necessarily be true for Kent in the ninth.

Nor can we assume a progressive model of history. We are used to imagining that women's position has steadily improved over the course of history, that our ancestors held women in a state of dependence that was near slavery from which they emerged slowly and progressively over the centuries. Only in the twentieth century were women able to achieve financial independence and public prominence on anything like a par with men. The historical record, however, is more complex. If we use financial independence, self-determination, and public visibility as criteria, the evidence suggests that women's position has improved and deteriorated in fits and starts, unevenly in different times and places. The student of Anglo-Saxon culture will be surprised to find that what fragmentary evidence remains suggests that women in England between the sixth and eleventh centuries may have enjoyed more economic independence from men, more power to determine their own futures, and more public visibility than at any other time in the Middle Ages (Leyser, *Medieval Women* 3–52). Of course, to the extent that women's expectations in life were entirely dependent on the class they were born into, we must bear in mind that the records are fuller for aristocratic women than for women of the lower classes (*ceorl*) or slave women.

As in all periods of the Middle Ages, marriage was a woman's chief occupation and the nature of the marriage contract would largely determine her condition in life. A cursory glance at the evidence might lead us to believe that Anglo-Saxon women were treated as commodities, callously bought and sold by their fathers and husbands. Two kinds of evidence in particular might suggest such an interpretation. In heroic poetry, like the epic *Beowulf*, aristocratic women are most frequently represented as 'peace-weavers', given in marriage to enemy warriors to forge alliances and temporary truces between warring kingdoms. In *Beowulf*, Hrothgar's queen is named Wealtheow, which in Anglo-Saxon means 'foreign slave' (Fell, *Women* 66). These political marriages are often depicted as tragic, suspending the woman between her loyalty to the family into which she was born and that into which she married. *Beowulf*, for instance, tells the story of Hildeburh, the Danish princess who was married to the King of the Jutes to cement peace between them. During a visit from her brother, Hnaef, a fight breaks out between the Danes and Jutes in which Hildeburh's brother and son are both killed. The second piece of evidence comes from the Anglo-Saxon lexicon. The verbs *bicgan* and *agan* are used in a variety of contexts, both legal and literary, to describe the terms of the marriage contract. Generally these words are translated into the Modern English 'buy' and 'own' – a man 'buys' a wife and henceforth 'owns' her – suggesting that women were considered little more than property. But, as Christine Fell suggests, we cannot assume that the semantic range of these words would be identical for both Anglo-Saxon and Modern English simply because they are cognates. The cultural contexts in which the words were deployed would vary enormously. The word *agan* could be understood to refer to the responsibilities of any person – man or woman – in charge of a community. In Anglo-Saxon culture, relationships of authority were determined interpersonally rather than contractually and the person who took responsibility for the action of dependents – the authority – was referred to as the *agend* (badly translated as 'owner').[12] That person might be a husband, but could also be the owner of an estate, an abbot or even an abbess. The term designated the person legally responsible for a group of dependents. The verb *bicgan* used in a marriage contract must be understood within the framework of Anglo-Saxon law in which monetary payments (*wergild*) defined social relationships. It referred not to payments made by the husband to the wife's kin in exchange for a bride, but payments made directly to the woman herself which would ensure her financial security (Fell, *Women* 16–17).

Marriage in Anglo-Saxon England was primarily a financial arrangement rather than a union for mutual affection and love. But there is evidence in both law and charters that the bride's welfare in marriage was protected through the custom of the *morgengifu* (literally 'morning gift'). In order to secure a marriage contract, the husband had to pay to his wife (and not to her family) a substantial amount of wealth. This gift, which was designed to ensure her financial security within the marriage, was called the *morgengifu*. The *morgengifu* was the bride's personal property to be used, given away, sold or bequeathed as she saw fit (Fell, *Women* 56–7). Fell quotes two examples from eleventh-century marriage contracts to illustrate provisions for the *morgengifu*. The first describes a sizable gift, which marks this as a union at the highest levels of Anglo-Saxon society:

> Here in this document is stated the agreement which Wulfric and the archbishop made when he obtained the archbishop's sister as his wife, namely he promised her the estates at Orleton and Ribbesford for her lifetime, and promised her that he would obtain the estate at Knightwick for her for three lives from the community at Winchcombe, and gave her the estate at Aton to grant and bestow upon whomsoever she pleased during her lifetime and at her death, as she preferred, and promised her 50 mancuses of gold and 30 men and 30 horses. (Fell, *Women* 58)

The second describes a more modest, though still generous, gift:

> Here is declared in this document the agreement which Godwine made with Brihtric when he wooed his daughter. In the first place he gave her a pound's weight of gold, to induce her to accept his suit, and he granted her the estate at Street with all that belongs to it, and 150 acres at Burmarsh and in addition 30 oxen and 20 cows and 10 horses and 10 slaves.

Although the agreement is made between two men, it is the woman who receives the gifts ('he gave her'). Fell argues that the woman accepted the suit and not her parents (Fell, *Women* 58). The marriage contract strove to protect the interests of both husband and wife. The marriage must be 'agreeable to her'. The husband must make direct payment to her for her acceptance. There should be a contractual agreement on what the husband will leave the wife in the event he dies before her, and if she is to be taken far away from her family, they still retain the right to act on her behalf if necessary. It is clear that her property is not held under her husband's control. On his part, the husband is protected from deceit. If he finds that she has deceived him, if she is carrying another man's child, the bride goes back to her kin and she must return any money he has paid her. 'From the beginning to the end of the period the laws recognize an element of financial independence and responsibility in the wife's status' (Fell, *Women* 58–9).

These protections extended to widows as well who were protected, at least in law, from forced remarriage. Nor could they be forced into nunneries when their husbands died. A woman's inheritance, including any property from her husband, was protected, even if she did not remarry within a year of her spouse's death (Fell, *Women* 61). While we know little about Anglo-Saxon women as mothers, the laws do not favour either the father or mother in matters concerning the custody of children. If a woman left her husband and took her children, she was entitled to half of the property. If she left her children, she would receive less. If the husband died, her children could not be taken away from her prematurely, though the husband's kin could be given control of their property while they were minors (Fell, *Women* 80). If a woman died before her husband and she was childless, her property, including the *morgengifu*, reverted to her kin (Fell, *Women* 74). Because inheritance law was not based on primogeniture, Anglo-Saxon wills did not favour male heirs over female heirs (Fell, *Women* 75).

It is important to remember that while the laws give us a general sense of women's status in Anglo-Saxon culture, suggesting that their interests, if not their rights, were protected and that, in the upper classes, at least, women were potentially quite powerful, the conditions under which individual women lived would be determined by a rigid and hierarchical class system. Women were classified (for purposes of determining *wergild*) not only by economic class – free or slave – but also by marital status – virgin, wife, widow. Offences were regarded with varying degrees of severity (indicated by the amount of compensation or *wergild*) depending upon the class of the victim. A brief example suggests how a woman's rank determined her independence, financial security and visibility. If a man has sex with the *byrele* (cup-bearer or serving-maid) of an *eorl* (the highest rank of free-man) against her will, he must pay twenty shillings; if a man has sex with the *byrele* of a *ceorl*, he pays only six shillings. The compensation is even less if the woman is a slave. While it is not clear to whom the compensation is paid, Fell argues that it is possible that, when the woman was the injured party, the compensation was paid to her, unless she was a slave (62).

The exploits of Anglo-Saxon queens like Aethelflaed, daughter of Alfred the Great, who ruled Mercia in the early years of the tenth century, or Cynethryth, another Mercian queen who was the only queen to have coins struck in her name (Fell, *Women* 90–1) suggest something of the power an aristocratic woman might wield. But perhaps the most vivid examples we have of Anglo-Saxon women exercising power in the public realm are the great abbesses of the period. Aristocratic religious women in the period just following the Anglo-Saxon conversion to Christianity enjoyed more institutional power, better education, and were more likely to assume duties and privileges that after the twelfth century would be reserved solely for men. Charles Talbot writes that 'never, perhaps, has there been an age in which religious women exercised such great power' (*Missionaries* xiii). The seventh century, following the conversion of the Anglo-Saxons to Christianity, was a great period for the founding of monastic institutions in England. The daughters of aristocratic families founded some of the most well-known Anglo-Saxon monasteries, including Whitby, Ely, Barking and Wimborne. These women were often raised to the status of saint; indeed the Anglo-Saxons produced a remarkable number of women saints during this period. Anglo-Saxon women presided over double monasteries (institutions housing both men and women), as Hild, the founder and abbess of Whitby, did. Apparently such arrangements did not threaten the masculinity of the

English monks who served under these powerful abbesses. Leyser has suggested that this may be because the scholastic discipline and egalitarian living required by the monastic life may have been too incompatible with aristocratic notions of masculinity so that the ranks of the clergy may have been populated with men of a lower class than these royal abbesses (26–7).

Among the correspondence of the English saint Boniface is a letter to the Abbess Cuniburg from three of Boniface's monks – Denehard, Lullus and Burchard – who write, 'We also wish it known to your care and your wisdom that if any one of us should happen to visit Britain we should not prefer the obedience and government of any man to subjection under your good will' (Boniface 77–8).

The range of learning of Anglo-Saxon double monasteries was remarkable, including Latin, the classics, scriptures, the Church fathers and canon law. In these monasteries, women were often instructed not by men, but by other women. St Leoba, an eighth-century English nun who participated in the reconversion of the Germans and presided over a convent at Bischofsheim, studied under Wimborne's erudite abbess, Tetta, and learned how to write poetry from her *magistra* Eadburg (Petroff, *Visionary Literature* 84; Boniface 60).

Perhaps the best view of monastic life for women during the Anglo-Saxon period can be seen in Bede's portrait in *The History of the English Church and People* of Hild, founder and abbess of the monastery at Whitby. Hild was one of the great patrons of the Northumbrian renaissance of the seventh and eighth centuries, a period of unprecedented achievement in art, architecture, poetry and manuscript illumination, following the conversion of King Edwin to Christianity. Hild, the fourteen-year-old daughter of Edwin's nephew Hereric, was among the members of Edwin's household baptized on Easter of 627. Bede tells us that she 'spent thirty-three years most nobly in secular occupations, and dedicated the ensuing thirty-three years even more nobly to our Lord in the monastic life' (Bede, *History* 246). At a time when early marriage was the rule for women, it is noteworthy that Hild managed to remain single for thirty-three years without entering a convent. Bishop Aidan persuaded Hild, who was in Anglia with her sister waiting to cross over to France to take up residence in a monastery there, to return to Northumbria and found a house on the river Wear. In 647 she became abbess of Hartlepool. A few years later she founded a monastery at Streanaeschalch, better known as Whitby. There, Bede writes,

> She established the same regular life as in her former monastery, and taught the observance of righteousness, mercy, purity, and other virtues, but especially of peace and charity. After the example of the primitive Church, no one there was rich, no one was needy, for everything was held in

common and nothing was considered to be anyone's personal property. So great was her prudence that not only ordinary folk, but kings and princes used to come and ask her advice in their difficulties and take it. Those under her direction [presumably both men and women] were required to make a thorough study of the Scriptures and occupy themselves in good works, to such good effect that many were found fitted for Holy Orders and the service of God's altar. (247)

The abbey thrived. Five men who studied at Whitby later became bishops. Perhaps the most famous event in English Christianity – the Synod of Whitby – was hosted by Hild in 663, though she would not have been allowed to take an active role in debating the conflicts between Roman and Celtic Christianity being decided there. Bede writes: 'So when discussion arose there on the questions of Easter, the tonsure, and various other church matters, it was decided to hold a synod to put an end to this dispute at the monastery of Streanaeshalch [Whitby], which means The Bay of the Beacon, then ruled by the Abbess Hilda, a woman devoted to God' (187). Hild's crowning achievement, however, was persuading the poet Caedmon, the greatest Northumbrian poet, to join her community at Whitby. 'So skilful was he in composing religious and devotional songs that, when any passage of Scripture was explained to him by interpreters, he could quickly turn it into delightful and moving poetry in his own English tongue' (250).

Caedmon's song, which Bede quotes in Anglo-Saxon, is the only example of his poetry that survives and the only poem in the entire Anglo-Saxon corpus which can can be attributed with confidence to a particular poet.

> Praise we the Fashioner now of Heaven's fabric,
> The majesty of his might and his mind's wisdom,
> Work of the world-warden, worker of all wonders,
> How he the Lord of Glory everlasting,
> Wrought first the race of men Heaven as rooftree,
> Then made the Middle Earth to be their mansion. (251)

Bede tells us that when Hild heard about the remarkable gifts that had appeared in such an unlikely individual she 'advised him to abandon secular life and adopt the monastic state'. And when she had admitted him into the community as a member, she 'ordered him to be instructed in the events of sacred history' (252). Hild appears to have been patron, mentor and perhaps even teacher to the first English poet, creator of the oldest scrap of Anglo-Saxon poetry that survives.

Of course not all the monasteries of eighth-century England were as wealthy or powerful as Whitby and, whether the foundation was wealthy or poor, the duties of an abbess could be crushing. In a letter to St Boniface, the Abbess Eangyth complains about the difficulties of her position: 'We are further oppressed by poverty and lack of temporal goods, by the meagerness of the produce of our fields and the exactions of the king based upon the accusations of those who envy us. . . . So also our obligations to the king and queen, to the bishop, the prefect, the barons and counts' (Boniface 37).

Eangyth's complaint reminds us that abbesses lived very much in the secular world; they had to promote the economic viability of their houses, as well as the spiritual life. They had to protect their endowments from the encroachments of secular authorities. It is little wonder that so many desired, like Eangyth, to retire to the life of contemplation and seclusion promised by a pilgrimage to Rome (the purpose of her letter is to ask permission to undertake this journey).

It seems clear from letters written by English abbesses that survive in the correspondence of St Boniface that the Anglo-Saxon Church's attitude toward nuns leaving their cloisters differed markedly from the post-Conquest attitude toward monastic enclosure. Among the surviving letters is one from Aelflaed, Abbess of Whitby, to the Abbess Adolana of Pfalzel, near Trier, commending to her care a young abbess on her way to Rome (Eckenstein, *Women Under Monasticism* 124). Eangyth and her daughter Bugga write to Boniface to ask his advice about the propriety of pilgrimages: 'we have long wished to go to Rome, once mistress of the world, as many of our friends . . . have done. We would there seek pardon for our sins as many others have done and are still doing' (Boniface 39). They are well aware that Church councils forbade such travel, prescribing that 'everyone shall remain where he has been placed; and where he has taken his vows, there he shall fulfill them before God' (Boniface 39). Boniface's letter of 738 (16 years after the letter of Eangyth and Bugga) to the Abbess Bugga (presumably by this time the mother has died and been succeeded by her daughter) neither forbids nor encourages pilgrimages. A pilgrimage, he agrees, would offer 'the freedom of contemplation' and escape from the 'labor and wearing anxiety to the words and wishes of men of this world' which Eangyth and Bugga had complained about in the earlier letter (56). He shows more practicality in his concern for the abbess's physical safety than concern for the vows she has taken: 'you would do better to wait until the rebellious assaults and threats of the Saracens who have recently appeared about Rome should have subsided' (56).

Yet in a letter to Archbishop Cuthbert of Canterbury reporting on the Frankish synods he clearly shows his awareness of the Church's moral opposition to nuns' undertaking pilgrimages:

> It would be well and favorable for the honor and purity of your church, and to provide a certain shield against vice, if your synod and your princes would forbid matrons and veiled women to make these frequent journeys back and forth to Rome. A great part of them perish and few keep their virtue. There are very few towns in Lombardy or Frankland or Gaul where

there is not a courtesan or a harlot of English stock. It is a scandal and a disgrace to your whole church. (140)

The Council of Verneuil in 755 decreed that abbesses and nuns could not leave the community unless summoned by the king, while the Council of Friuli, held in 796 or 797, forbade them to leave for any reason (Wemple 191). The pilgrimages contemplated by the Abbesses Eangyth and Bugga at the beginning of the eighth century would have been extremely unlikely for nuns who, after the twelfth century, would have been strictly enclosed.[13]

Standards of dress for Anglo-Saxon nuns may have differed somewhat from later standards as well, as Aldhelm's *In Praise of Virginity*, written for the nuns at Barking, suggests. In it he complains about the inappropriate extravagance of nuns' clothing:

> . . . a vest of fine linen of a violet colour is worn, above it a scarlet tunic with a hood, sleeves striped with silk and trimmed with red fur; the locks on the forehead and the temples are curled with a crisping iron, the dark head-veil is given up for white and coloured head-dresses, which, with bows of ribbon sewn on, reach down to the ground; the nails, like those of a falcon or sparrow hawk, are pared to resemble talons. (Eckenstein, *Women Under Monasticism* 115)

This description hardly fits our stereotypic image of a nun. While it is difficult to tell whether Aldhelm is accurately describing the habits of eighth-century nuns or reproducing a standard trope of an already old anti-feminist tradition (which certainly would not be unexpected in a treatise on virginity), the same charge is repeated by Bede in his description of the convent of Coldingham (256). St Edith of Wilton, who was known to dress more extravagantly than was common to nuns or abbesses, when rebuked for her dress by Bishop Aethelwold and told that Christ takes no delight in external appearances, replied enigmatically, 'Quite so, Father, and I have given my heart' (Fell, *Women* 126).

Edith was a part of the tenth-century monastic revival, which created foundations of vastly different character than those founded during the Northumbrian renaissance of the seventh and eighth centuries. During this later period, no double houses were founded; instead we see monasteries for men and convents for women. Neither monasteries nor nunneries of this period became the centres of learning that the great monasteries of the eighth century had been. Whether this was the result of invasions and destruction by pagan Vikings or general deterioration is unclear. However, Fell's remark sums up the situation on the eve of the Norman invasion: 'The equality of the sexes which flourished in the eighth century in learning and in literacy, was replaced in the tenth century by equality in ignorance' (Fell, *Women* 120).

WOMEN AFTER THE NORMAN CONQUEST

On Christmas day 1066 Duke William of Normandy, after a brief but successful campaign in which he defeated both an English and a Swedish rival, was crowned King of England in Westminster Abbey. His reign spelled the end of the Anglo-Saxon hegemony in England, introducing a new language, laws, customs and social organizations. The Anglo-Saxon aristocracy was replaced by a Norman one. For two centuries England would be, at least among its upper strata, a French-speaking country. A class divide would separate those who spoke French from those who spoke English. Traces of the Norman occupation still survive in the English language today: 60 per cent of the modern English vocabulary derives from Romance languages; 40 per cent from Anglo-Saxon. French feudal institutions were imposed upon existing Anglo-Saxon political institutions (though William was shrewd enough to retain those Anglo-Saxon institutions that served his purposes). The social and cultural changes wrought by succeeding generations of Norman rule would have profound effects on women's lives as well.

The effects on aristocratic women of the transition between Anglo-Saxon and Norman rule might best be illustrated by a brief look at the life of Queen Matilda, the wife of Henry I, the third Norman king. Matilda's father was King Malcolm of Scotland; her mother the granddaughter of Edmund Ironside. Her mother, Margaret, had wanted to become a nun, but was either persuaded or forced to marry the king of Scotland. Margaret's sister, Christina, however, did take the veil and Matilda and her sister were raised in a convent. When Matilda was thirteen, her father was killed fighting William Rufus and her mother died shortly after. From that time until 1100, Matilda and her sister lived at the convent at Romsey in the south of England, where she seemed to have received a fairly extensive education. She may have been content to pass the rest of her life there, perhaps eventually becoming its abbess. In that year, however, Henry I succeeded his elder brother, William Rufus, as king of England. One means by which the Normans could consolidate their rule would be through marriage to an Anglo-Saxon princess and Matilda was a good candidate, a descendent of the kings of Wessex (Huneycutt, 'Literary and Artistic Network' 156). There was only one impediment to the marriage. Matilda may have already taken her vows as a nun. Henry's determination to marry Matilda despite this objection was not unopposed, as William of Malmesbury relates: 'when the king was about to advance her to his bed, [the marriage] became a matter of controversy; nor could the archbishop be induced to consent to her marriage, but by the production of lawful witnesses, who swore that she had worn the veil on account of her suitors, but had never made her vow' (*Chronicle* 453). The record, as related by various Norman historians, is not entirely clear about whether Matilda had professed herself a nun or was simply hiding in a convent to avoid rape at the hands of the invaders. William of Malmesbury tells us that she 'wore the garb indicative of the holy profession'. Several historians portray her as unwilling to give up her monastic life. According to Eadmer, however, who was close to Anselm, archbishop of Canterbury at the time, Matilda wanted to leave the convent; she argued her case before Anselm. Eadmer reports her argument (bear in mind that medieval historians' accounts of actual speeches will be somewhat embellished):

> I do not deny having worn the veil. When I was a child my aunt Christina, whom you know to be a determined woman, in order to protect me against the violence of the Normans, put a piece of black cloth on my head, and when I removed it gave me blows and bad language. So I trembling and indignant wore the veil in her presence. But as soon as I could get out of her sight I snatched it off and trampled it underfoot. (Eckenstein, *Women Under Monasticism* 208–9)

Whatever her true feelings, Matilda was finally married to Henry I. During her married life, she continued the scholarly life she had learned in the convent. Her Latin correspondence with Anselm demonstrates the extent of her convent education, while William of Malmesbury praises her patronage of scholars of all sorts.[14] Matilda's sister also left the convent to marry Eustace, the Count of Boulogne. That the sanctity of the nun's profession often took a back seat to political expediency is also illustrated by King Stephen's treatment of his daughter, Mary of Blois. Mary came to England from the convent of St Sulpice in France and was eventually made Abbess of Romsey sometime before 1159. When Stephen's sole surviving heir died, Mary was brought out of the convent and married to Matthew, son of the count of Flanders, over the protests of the then chancellor, Thomas Becket (Eckenstein, *Women Under Monasticism* 212).

These accounts illustrate the political pressures that shaped aristocratic women's lives after the Conquest (I focus on aristocratic women because their lives are better documented in this period than those of lower-class women). The first thing to notice is that families felt free to use their daughters, even against their wishes, to further their dynastic ambitions. The second is the escalating conflict between the Church and the aristocracy over the nature and character of marriage and the rules that would regulate it.

To be sure, the use of marriage as a political strategy is not a development new to the twelfth century. However, between the eleventh and thirteenth centuries, France and England experienced a transformation within the kinship structures of the aristocracy that fundamentally altered the nature of marriage and the family. This transformation was the result of the aristocracy's changing relation to its primary source of wealth – the land. The noble family of the ninth and tenth century had no fixed residence, no specific piece of land regarded as family 'possession', and no family name. It was, in Howard Bloch's words, 'a loosely defined grouping of relatives and retainers "friends" and neighbors [who] gravitated around the residence of a lord who was, above all, a patron, a distributor of gifts and lands, the spoils of war or exchange' (Bloch, *Etymologies* 65). Kinship was calculated horizontally; little distinction was made between the lineage of the husband and that of the wife, or between relatives linked by blood or marriage. When property was passed on, inheritance practices varied widely; often, however, daughters and younger sons shared in the family wealth (Charlemagne, for instance, divided the Holy Roman Empire between his three sons). But from the second half of the eleventh century on, the aristocratic family began to receive its fortune by inheritance rather than gift. This shift from a system of horizontal exchanges to one based on lineal or vertical exchange in which a piece of land was regarded as a family 'estate', required a 'patrilocal sense of the kin group bound [geographically] by reference to a common residence, a castle' (Bloch, *Etymologies* 67–8). Once such practices became common, the aristocratic family began to calculate its lineage vertically based on descent from a single male founder, to practice strict primogeniture (only the eldest son inherited family estates), and to privilege blood ties over marital ties. The family estate was to be passed on intact from eldest son to eldest son to limit both the growth of the aristocracy and the dilution of feudal holdings through partition among multiple heirs. The policy of the Norman kings from William on was to concentrate their power by holding their feudal prerogatives closely, avoiding the fragmentation and decentralization that plagued the monarchy in France. The reorganization of kinship described above was an important mechanism for accomplishing those dynastic ends.

The transformation of a relatively open class system into a closed and patrilinear caste required a marital discipline based on monogamy, exogamy (that is, marriage outside of the social group), and the repression of pleasure. To maintain the family estate intact and to increase its influence, all daughters had to be married out of the family, but only one son could be married to produce a single, legitimate male heir. Such marital practices were not without their complications. They tended to produced a surplus of marriageable women (the average age of first marriages for women in the twelfth century was around sixteen and often took place as early as twelve; betrothals might occur in infancy) and a shortage of eligible bachelors, as well as a large number of unattached and disinherited males with few future prospects for marriage or independent wealth (see the discussion of Marie de France's *lais* below, 155–65). Georges Duby has argued that courtly love represented one response to this demographic situation. It functioned as a kind of socially sanctioned abduction which occupied unattached males who otherwise might (and sometimes did) resort to more barbaric forms of abduction and rape to improve their fortunes at the expense of legitimate heirs (Duby, *Knight*). The politics of marriage clearly did not work to women's advantage. Women – like Matilda and her sister – were pawns in the patrilinear culture of Anglo-Norman England, sacrificed to the need to assure legitimate succession through a male line (female monogamy) and to achieve the widest possible dispersion of family influence (exogamy). Marriage was an affair between families, arranged by male heads. Women's desires were rarely consulted. As Duby notes, eight Latin words sum up womanly perfection for the aristocratic class of the twelfth century: *pia filia, morigera conjux, domina clemens, utilis mater.*

> Until she married she was a dutiful daughter [*pia filia*]; she accepted the husband chosen for her. Her destiny being that of a wife, she then becomes what all wives should be: meek, obedient, *morigera.* But she was also a *domina*, a mistress of a household, endowed with considerable power. . . . Did motherhood, then, give her some authority at last? No, as a mother she had to be *utilis.* 'Useful' to whom? To other men, to her own sons. (Duby, *Knight* 234)

At the same time, the Church was also trying to extend its authority and consolidate its position. During the eleventh and twelfth centuries the interests of the Church in regulating marriage and aristocratic marital politics frequently came into conflict. Church and nobility were frequently at odds over the definition of marriage. The two major issues of contention concerned the indissolubility of marriage and the question of what constituted valid marriage – sexual consummation or the consent of the parties concerned. The Church had both religious and political reasons for insisting on the indissolubility of validly contracted marriage. Marriage was a sacrament ordained by God and 'what God has joined together let no man put asunder'. The Church was also anxious to extend its control over aristocratic families and their marriages. The aristocratic family was, however, primarily driven by the need to produce heirs to ensure the continuation of its lineage. Often this meant engaging in 'serial polygamy' in which politically expedient marriages were made and unmade when they no longer served the family's political ends.[15] In an effort to limits the grounds for repudiating a wife, the Church in the twelfth century reduced the forbidden degrees of consanguinity from seven to four, hoping to diminish the practice of divorce on the grounds of consanguinity (Duby, *Knight*). While the Church's insistence on the indissolubility of marriage limited the number of heirs aristocratic men could produce, its insistence that a valid marriage required the consent of both partners threatened to alter both the relationships between vassals and their overlords and between children and their parents.

Matilda did manage to produce a male heir for Henry I; however, he did not survive to succeed his father and Henry died leaving no male heir. As a result, England was plunged into forty years of civil warfare and anarchy as his daughter Matilda and his nephew, Stephen of Blois, fought over the inheritance. The conflict was resolved only when Stephen agreed to name Matilda's eldest son, Henry, as his heir. The conflict between Stephen and Matilda raises the interesting question of what happened in those cases in which the only available heirs to an estate were female. How did feudal law and customs handle such an eventuality, which must have happened with some frequency? In the case of Matilda, who sought to rule as a queen, the system broke down when the Norman barons refused to pay homage to a woman and the continuity of the lineage was at least temporarily broken.

An anecdote recounted in Adam of Eynsham's life of St Hugh of Lincoln may illuminate the situation of non-royal heiresses. It relates a notorious scandal involving Thomas of Saleby, a knight of Lincoln, and his wife Agnes. The childless Agnes, fearing that her elderly husband would die without heir, that his estates would pass to her hated brother-in-law, and that she would become his ward, concocted a scheme in which she feigned pregnancy by stuffing a cushion under her gown. 'Eventually, moaning as if in the throes of labour, Agnes took to her bed and feigned giving birth to a daughter' (L'Hermite-Leclercq, 'Feudal Order' 204). At the critical moment she produced a baby girl who had fortuitously been delivered by a peasant in a nearby village and who was subsequently hired as a wet nurse. The girl was named Grace and recognized as Thomas's heir. When Thomas's brother complained about the ruse, the case came before the bishop and Hugh excommunicated the couple after the husband admitted that it was unlikely he was the father. Thomas died in his sleep the next night. Though the family and the Church (in the person of the bishop) sued to recover the property, the king (King John, Henry II's youngest son) married Grace off, at the age of four, to Adam of Neville, the brother of the royal forester, who gained control of the heiress's property. Of course since the girl was only four, Adam could only serve as her guardian. Anxious for an early marriage so he could secure his right to her property, he coerced a priest against the bishop's orders to perform the ceremony. Eventually Alice confessed to her deception but when the family tried to sue to recover their estates, Adam argued in court that under English law a child recognized by the mother's husband is considered legitimate. When Adam died soon after, she was passed on to one of the king's chamberlains. He too died and at age 11 she was married for a third time. Finally Grace herself died, childless to the end, and the estate reverted to Thomas's brother, the 'rightful' heir.

In Grace's marriages and remarriages we can read the whole sexual economy of exchange in which women functioned almost like money to facilitate the circulation of wealth. Agnes's story testifies to the pressures on women to produce any kind of heir at any cost, but it also highlights the special problems posed when that heir was female. Heiresses are striking exceptions to the system of patrilineage that ordered feudal inheritance law, but they are exceptions implicit in – and indeed required by – the very system that excludes them. The death of a landholder who leaves behind only female heirs presents certain legal challenges to the system of primogeniture that dominated feudal inheritance law in both England and France in the twelfth century. The primary argument against female inheritance was that women were ill-equipped to meet the military demands and obligations of land ownership. At the same time heiresses provided a king or lord with a ward whose marriage he could exploit for profit. King John extracted enormous sums of money from Grace's three husbands (L'Hermite-Leclercq, 'Feudal Order' 209).

Unlike the system of primogeniture that organized male inheritance, female inheritance in the twelfth century was structured around a system of *parage* in which all daughters inherit equally as *parceners*; the law shows no preference for the first born. Despite differences between the predominantly Norman laws of England and those of France, both countries' laws show striking accord on this question. According to Philippe de Beaumanoir, for instance, in *Coutumes de Beauvaisis*: 'When realty [*eritage*] passes by descent to sisters, among all the fiefs the oldest takes the principal dwelling and the rest is divided equally between them' (*Coutumes* 100). Though the division was strictly equal, the eldest daughter or her husband would usually act as representative for the whole inheritance for most feudal purposes. The younger sisters would hold their portions from the eldest: 'The younger sisters do homage to the oldest sister for the share that they take; and the oldest sister does homage to the lord for the share she receives in the realty [*eritage*], and for the homage of her sisters' (100). This arrangement would hold for three generations, after which the heirs of all sisters would be required to do homage for their own portions. For the feudal overlord this arrangement had both advantages and disadvantages. On the one hand, the overlord need look to only one person for the whole service due from the inheritance. On the other, he (usually) cannot claim any wardships or marriages from the heirs of the younger sisters. By the thirteenth century, control of marriages and wardships became much more profitable than feudal services (Pollock and Maitland, *History of English Law* 276–7). Control of heiresses provided a ready source of income, patronage for loyal vassals;

they were a target of opportunity for families, and especially for younger sons, looking to expand their influence and holdings. William Marshal, for example, who eventually rose to become the marshal of England under Henry II, was born the fourth son of a minor Norman nobleman. In a world governed by the principles of primogeniture and non-partition, he was a man of few prospects; as a younger son he could not expect to marry or own land. Yet as a reward for his services, the king bestowed on him an heiress and, with her, the lands that would make him Earl of Pembroke. Of course it would be a mistake to assume that all heiresses were docile pawns like poor little Grace. The systems of inheritance for women described by Pollock and Maitland for England and by Philippe for Beauvaisis in France are, after all, only theoretical. In practice things could become rather messier, especially if the heiress had a mind of her own. In the fifteenth century, Elizabeth Berkeley (d. 1422), countess of Warwick, and sole heir of Thomas Lord Berkeley, was, on her father's death, challenged by her cousin James, the eldest male in a collateral line, who claimed his estates by entail. The ensuing legal struggle would long outlive her, lasting nearly two centuries (Jambeck, 'Women's Literary Patronage' 234).

It is perhaps difficult for the late twentieth-century reader to appreciate the appeal that the cloistered religious life may have had for medieval women or why a woman might prefer it to married life. The idea of women being immured in convents, doomed to live their lives as dried-up virgins, isolated from the rest of the world is, to some, downright repellent. The following poem, by three unknown Provençal women, may perhaps shed some light on the motives (beyond piety) that propelled so many women into the religious life. Lady Alais and Lady Iselda ask Lady Carenza whether or not they should marry. While they seem not averse to the sexual side of marriage, they can see benefits in avoiding marriage:

> Lady Carenza, I'd like to have a husband,
> but making babies I think is a huge penitence:
> your breasts hang way down
> and it's too anguishing to be a wife. (Bogin, *Women Troubadours* 145)

Marriage, according to Alais and Iselda, offers women few advantages and many tribulations. Besides the problem of overbearing husbands, there are the difficulties of childbearing, which joking aside, could be terrifying and downright dangerous. The solution Carenza offers is to marry Christ, that is, to become a nun, the only real alternative to marriage:

> I therefore advise you, if you want to plant good seed,
> to take as a husband Coronat de Scienza
> from whom you shall bear as fruit glorious sons:
> saved is the chastity of her who marries him. (145)

The name Carenza chooses to describe Christ as spouse literally means 'Crowned with Knowledge'. Carenza suggests that not only does the religious life free a woman from subjugation to a husband, but the woman who takes Coronat de Scienza as a spouse has some small chance of realizing the ideal held up for women by the Virgin Mary: she produces sons (knowledge) while still maintaining her chastity.

Women's professed religious life, however, reached a low point during the years of transition from Anglo-Saxon to Norman rule. The turmoil created by centuries of intermittent Viking invasions and the Norman conquest took their toll on the great convents of Anglo-Saxon England. Many women's houses that had been abandoned or laid waste by invasion were either left in ruins or restored as men's houses. The great houses that had been founded and ruled by women – Ely, Whitby, Wimborne – passed into the hands of men. Only in Wessex did women's houses emerge at the end of the eleventh century with anything like the wealth and importance they had during the height of the Anglo-Saxon period and these convents were not the double houses of men and women that characterized Northumbrian foundations, but nunneries exclusively for women (Gilchrist, *Gender* 32). When religious life for women began to flourish once again during the twelfth century, it would take on a form much changed both by the Norman preference for more centralized administration and by the reform movements that were revolutionizing monastic life. After the Conquest, nunneries tended to be fewer in number (male houses outnumbered female houses six to one) and poorer than male houses. Most Anglo-Norman nunneries were founded at a later date than male houses and many of the smaller institutions may have had founders who came from a different social class – perhaps the gentry rather than the aristocracy – than the founders of male communities (Gilchrist, *Gender* 42–4, 61).

The Normans were not the only ones who saw the benefits of more centralized forms of government. By the twelfth century the Catholic Church was also concerned with consolidating its authority and centralizing the control of the papacy. Indeed the series of conflicts known as the Investiture Controversy involved a struggle between the king and the pope over the right to appoint bishops and invest them with the symbols of their office. The quarrel between Thomas Becket and Henry II was essentially a continuation of this ongoing power struggle. One means by which the Church sought to consolidate its authority was by stressing the special power of the priesthood. This jealous guarding of its prerogatives can be seen not only in the Investiture Controversy, but also in the many calls to pastoral care, a renewed emphasis on the sacraments, where the priest most directly exercised his authority, and in conflicts between proponents of a monastic life of contemplation and advocates of an active life of pastoral care.

The growing distance between the clergy and the laity meant that the Church in general, and the Norman brand of monasticism in particular, had little use for women in official positions of either temporal or spiritual power. One sign of the deterioration of women's position in monastic life during the Norman period is the change in status of the woman who presided over the convent. All the nunneries founded during the Anglo-Saxon period were presided over by an abbess. Even during the Norman period, abbesses, where they retained their positions, could be extremely powerful, with extensive rights and responsibilities. Control of the material and spiritual possessions of a wealthy foundation like, say, Godestow Abbey conferred considerable authority on a woman like Edith, the widow of a knight from Winchester, who was the founder and first abbess of that convent in the early twelfth century. She could hire and dismiss her own chaplains; they were responsible to her and not to the archdeacon or other minister. She could also appoint chaplains to the churches that belonged to Godestow. Besides six or more churches, the abbey's possessions included several mills, a manor, rents, dwellings, a shop in London, numerous plots of land and a salt pit (Elkins, *Holy Women* 64–5). The abbess controlled all of these sources of income.

Of the sixty-four Benedictine convents founded after the Conquest, only three were abbacies. The remainder were priories, daughter houses of larger monasteries, ruled by a prioress who was appointed by and subject to the authority of an abbot or abbess who resided in the parent house, which might not even be English; it might be located on the Continent. All of the Cistercian convents founded after the Conquest were priories. Even houses that during the Anglo-Saxon period had been abbacies – like Sheppey, which had been deserted during the Viking invasions – were restored under the Normans as priories (Eckenstein, *Women Under Monasticism* 204–5). While her authority would vary depending on the nature of her appointment, the prioress could never wield the same authority as an abbess. Since the same policy was not carried out in convents founded on the Continent, it seems reasonable to conclude that English religious institutions were no more anxious to promote the independence of women from men than were the Norman rulers.

Some convents were even downgraded from abbacies to priories to limit their autonomy. The situation of Amesbury Abbey is instructive. In 1177 Henry II dispersed the Benedictine nuns living there and introduced twenty-four nuns from Fontevrault in France, restoring Amesbury as a priory dependent on the abbess of Fontevrault. According to one chronicle this drastic measure was necessary because of the scandalous behavior of the nuns there. Purportedly the abbess, after becoming a nun, had given birth to three babies. Elkins argues, however, that the charge is anomalous enough to be suspicious, especially since the king retired the abbess on a pension of ten marks of silver a year, hardly the sort of punishment one would expect of a nun who had so flagrantly flouted her vow of chastity (Elkins, *Holy Women* 146). Other evidence suggests that the transfer of Amesbury from a Benedictine abbacy to a priory of Fontevrault may have had more to do with economics than sexual scandal. The abbess of Amesbury had fiercely defended abbey property and feudal rights against encroachments by the crown. If the abbess were unfairly dispossessed, the generous pension makes much more sense. The new prioress of Amesbury would not be nearly as independent and troublesome as its abbess had been (Elkins, *Holy Women* 147).

The twelfth-century monastic revival was characterized by a reforming spirit resulting in the emergence of several new orders that offered more diverse ways for women to serve God. During the Anglo-Saxon period, convents had been primarily a retreat for aristocratic women. At least some of the new orders that appeared in the twelfth century expanded opportunities for women of non-aristocratic classes to participate in religious life. One such reformer was Robert of Arbrissel, who founded the order of Fontevrault as a means of ministering to the lower classes: 'men of all conditions came, women arrived, such as were poor as well as those of gentle birth' (Eckenstein, *Women Under Monasticism* 193). The Premonstrant Order which was founded at Prémontré by Norbert also attracted women of different classes. Both of these orders founded priories for women in England. The English order of St Gilbert of Sempringham, founded at the beginning of the twelfth century, also afforded girls and women of the lower classes the opportunity to become nuns (Eckenstein, *Women Under Monasticism* 193–5, 213–21). In these combined communities of canons and nuns, the emphasis was less on intellectual and scholarly pursuits than on labour. Gilbertine houses required the strictest asceticism from their inhabitants, especially from their poorer inhabitants: 'Gilbert ruled that the lay sisters were permitted no more than a pound of coarse bread and two vegetables each day; water was to be their only drink. The lay sisters were to wear contemptible clothing and spend most of their time watching and laboring, with only the rarest moments of quiet' (Elkins, *Holy Women* 80).

The convent, though the most common, was not the only means by which women could devote their lives to God. From the earliest days of Christianity, a few men and women chose to live the life of a hermit or recluse, perhaps the strictest of all medieval ascetic practices. The reclusive life was slightly more popular among women than men in the twelfth century; in the following two centuries it became more so (Warren, *Anchorites* 20). The Anglo-Saxon version of the rule of St Benedict (tenth or eleventh century) makes the following distinction between the monastic life and the life of a recluse:

The first kind are those in monasteries, *mynstermonna*, who live under a rule or an abbot. The second kind are the hermits, *ancrena*, that is settlers in the wild (*westensitlena*), who, not in the first fervor of religious life, but after probation in the monastery, have learned by the help and experience of others to fight against the devil, and going forth well armed from the ranks of their brethren to the single-handed combat of the wildernness are able without the support of others to fight by the strength of their own arms and the help of God against the vices of the flesh and their evil thoughts. (Eckenstein, *Women Under Monasticism* 312)

That the distinction between monks and hermits applied to women as well is evident from the repetition of this distinction in thirteenth- and fifteenth-century English translations of the Rule written for nuns (Eckenstein, *Women Under Monasticism* 313). Anchoresses were women who, after being trained in a convent for a prescribed period of time and with the permission of their family and the bishop, left the convent and took a vow to live a solitary life sealed in a small enclosure that, by the late twelfth century, was usually connected to a church or convent. Her religious practices would include periodic silence, fasting, poverty, celibacy and obedience to religious superiors (Bartlett, *Male Authors* 42; Warren, *Anchorites*). The Rule's unequivocal condemnation of men and women who take up such practices on their own, without prior monastic training, suggests the extent to which the Church feared unregulated religious fervour. Before the twelfth century, the lives of recluses varied enormously. During the twelfth and thirteenth centuries, perhaps as a response to the increased popularity of this way of life, rules designed to impose structure on the lives of recluses began to appear. Aelred of Rievaulx wrote a Latin rule for his sister, *De institutione inclusarium* (*A Rule of Life for Recluses*), which appeared around 1160 and contained advice both for outward behaviour (such things as food and clothing) as well as inward behaviour (virginity, the dangers of temptation). The thirteenth century *Ancrene Riwle*, written at the request of three sisters who, 'in the flower of your youth gave up all the joys of the world and became recluses', followed Aelred's general layout and amplified it.

The twelfth-century *Life of Christina Markyate*, while in many ways atypical, offers some insight into the asceticism of the anchoritic life; it describes the cell that the English saint Christina shared with Roger the hermit:

Near the chapel of the old man and joined to his cell was a room which made an angle where it joined. This had a plank of wood placed before it and was so concealed that to anyone looking from outside it would seem that no one was present within, since the space was not bigger than a span and a half. In this prison, therefore, Roger placed his happy companion. In front of the door he rolled a heavy log of wood, the weight of which was actually so great that it could not be put in its place or taken away by the recluse. And so, thus confined, the handmaid of Christ sat on a hard stone

until Roger's death, that is, four years and more, concealed even from
those who dwelt together with Roger. O what trials she had to bear of
cold and heat, hunger and thirst, daily fasting! The confined space would
not allow her to wear even the necessary clothing when she was cold. The
airless little enclosure became stifling when she was hot. Through long
fasting, her bowels became contracted and dried up. There was a time
when her burning thirst caused little clots of blood to bubble up from her
nostrils. But what was more unbearable than all this was that she could not
go out until the evening to satisfy the demands of nature. Even when she
was in dire need, she could not open the door for herself, and Roger
usually did not come till late. (*Christina Markyate* 105)

Christina's case is unique in that she did not come to this solitary life following a period of training in a convent. Instead she became a recluse as a
means of escaping the marriage her family would have forced upon her. Yet
the description of her cell and the discomfort it causes her suggests something
of the hardships the anchoress would have to endure. Some anchorholds
were larger than others, perhaps including even a walled courtyard (Bartlett,
Male Authors 42), but all were small. The cell usually included two windows.
One faced the altar of the church and allowed the anchoress to receive
communion and be observed by the priest. The other, which faced outside,
was covered by black cloth on which a white cross was inscribed, 'by the
help of which it becomes safe to look abroad' (Bartlett 42; Eckenstein 317).
The anchoress was considered to be dead to the world; the ceremony of
enclosure was modelled on the monastic Office of the Dead and would
include the Last Rites. Anchoresses appear, however, to have been allowed
to have conversation with visitors. Some seem to have kept servants; the
author of the *Ancrene Riwle* suggests two, one to stay at home, the other to
go abroad. Both Aelred and the author of the *Ancrene Riwle* advise against
anchoresses running schools, which suggests this may have sometimes happened. In addition, both men and women may have consulted anchoresses
for spiritual advice. In her fifteenth-century autobiography, Margery Kempe
describes her visit to the anchoress Julian of Norwich (see below 176).

WOMEN AT THE END OF THE MIDDLE AGES

In the early centuries of the Middle Ages, evidence for women's lives and
activities is fragmentary, especially for non-aristocratic women. The later
Middle Ages offers us a much wider range of documentary evidence, both
because more written records were being kept and because those documents

have been better preserved. This plethora of evidence, however, does not necessarily allow us to sketch out medieval women's lives with any greater consistency. Whether we see women in the period as being oppressed by a cultural system that denied them full humanity or as fully participating in cultural life depends on which evidence we turn to and on the class, marital and occupational status of the women that evidence represents. History, however, rarely presents us with such unambiguous alternatives. While women were still considered inferior to men in most religious, legal, scientific and philosophic writing of the day, they did participate in – and even benefit from – the increased possibilities for social mobility, technological improvements in agriculture and trades, and new cultural and spiritual movements.

Women's legal status varied depending on her marital status, class and occupation. In common law, which was an outgrowth of feudal conditions which applied more appropriately to landholders – to the upper classes of society – women were generally treated as wards of men. They were considered legally incompetent and represented by a guardian, usually a father or husband. In the cases of widows and orphans, guardianship passed to the nearest male relative or to a feudal lord. A guardian would have complete control over his female wards; he could dispose of their property or arrange marriages. Married women were *femmes couvertes*, literally 'covered' by their husbands; like underage children, they had no independent legal status (Patterson, 'Marriage' 135). Such practices made more sense for a class whose primary source of wealth was land. Land has certain economic characteristics. It is not portable. Those who possess it and those who work it need to be tied to it and to one another. Furthermore, because it cannot reproduce itself, it is not easily partible. When inheritance law calls for its division each generation will receive an increasingly smaller portion than the last. In England, this problem was solved by the custom of primogeniture, which required a marital strategy that assured the legitimacy of the heir by limiting women's sexual and economic freedom.

But such strategies and the laws that enforced them were not particularly well suited to the class of wealthy traders and merchants who populated medieval English cities. Money, which was the source of their wealth, is a very different economic resource. It is eminently portable, so that it tends to free individuals from the old ties to land and other people. It creates a social mobility that is destructive of feudal relationships. Money is also partible. A monetary inheritance divided up among several heirs does not impoverish them in the same way that the partition of land does because money can breed more money. In such an economy, very different marital strategies are possible. In a money economy, one can hold wealth in one's own right, rather than as the representative of a family. Merchants might place less emphasis on the production of an heir than on the maximization of family labour: a wife and children serve less as conduits of family power than as cheap labour. Because wealth is detached from land and family, heirs might even prove to be a liability in subsequent marriages. In the fifteenth-century letters of the Paston family, Edmund Paston, writing about a rich widow of a wool merchant he is courting, reassures his family that her two children will not be a problem (Davis, no. 398). One of the potential impediments to a proposed marriage between Elizabeth Paston and Stephen Scrope is the question of inheritance. Scrope had a daughter by a previous marriage and the Pastons worry that her claims will take precedence over those of any children of the marriage. Elizabeth Clere reassures John Paston that the daughter will have no more than one mark of Scrope's fortune (Davis, no. 446). She has previously set his worth, with an eye for a good fortune worthy of a Jane Austen, at three hundred and fifty marks.

By the fourteenth century, in the customs of the cities, towns and villages, married women were treated differently from their aristocratic sisters. Customs of the bourgeoisie, which had the effect of law, 'kept women's property free from her husband's control, accord her liberty of contract (which was denied at common law), and even allow her to trade separately upon her own account' (Carruthers 210). Thus, while women's economic and legal status would be primarily determined by her marital status, it was possible for a married women to maintain herself as a *femme sole*, a women whose legal status was independent of her husband. The following borough ordinance from Lincoln is characteristic:

> if any woman that has a husband follow any craft within the city in which her husband is not involved, she shall be charged as a sole woman in respect of such matters as pertain to her craft. And if a plea is made against such a woman she shall answer and plead as a sole woman, and make her law, and take other advantage in court by plea or otherwise for her discharge. And if she be condemned, she shall be committed to prison until she comes to terms with the plaintiff. And no goods or chattels that belong to her husband shall be attached or charged for her.
> (Goldberg 196)

Margery Kempe, for instance, recounts in her autobiography how she began both a milling and a brewing business independent of her husband's business affairs and against his wishes. Kempe provides us with a glimpse of the limits of women's autonomy. Her independence as a businesswoman is attested to by her business dealings and also her ability to pay her husband's debts, which are clearly separable from her own finances. However, that she agrees to pay his debts in exchange for his co-operation in maintaining celibacy suggests the limitations on women's freedom from male control. She needed his permission to travel, to wear white clothes, and to live celibate. She could control her economic affairs, but not her own person.

If a woman's fate was tied to the family into which she was born, it was also clearly tied to the family into which she married. Family dominated women's lives. While the extended family never entirely disappears, the nuclear family gained more importance in the late Middle Ages, especially in cities where households tended to be smaller, often housing only two generations. For this reason, women's position depended more than ever on marital status. By the fourteenth century, the Christian model of marriage as an 'indissoluble union based on mutual affection and the consent of both partners' (Opitz, 'Life' 272) was widely accepted. But the freedom to choose a spouse remained largely theoretical where large fortunes were concerned. Among the aristocracy and the wealthy merchant classes, children – especially daughters – were betrothed and married off early in life, so early that we can speak of consent only as a formality. Twelve was considered the legal age at which girls could marry; they might be betrothed much earlier. Sue Walker suggests that one reason aristocratic families may have been in such haste to marry, or at least betroth, their children was the lucrative market in wardships of minor children. Landed parents may have feared that if the father died before his child was married, the child would become a ward of his feudal lord who could then sell the marriage rights. These lucrative rights could be bought and sold like so much stock (Walker, 'Widow and Ward' 159–67). Chaucer, for instance, was given custody of the heirs of Edmund de Staplegate, a Canterbury merchant. This grant was worth ten pounds, which Sheila Delany estimates would translate to about $25,000 in the late twentieth century (Delany 79). Given such practices, it is hardly surprising that families feared that control of the marriage of a minor might pass outside of family with disastrous results for the family.[16]

Children of the lower classes, however, while never entirely free of the constraints imposed by family and friends, were much more likely than their upper-class counterparts to choose their own spouses in the course of normal social interaction. The reasons for this relative freedom from parental control are many. Especially in the cities, most couples of the non–propertied classes married late, usually after serving as apprentices or servants from their mid-teens to their mid-twenties. The late age of first marriages facilitated this free choice. Women were fully adults by the time they married; they married men who were only two or three years older than them, not men who were their seniors by twenty or thirty years. Finally, their work as servants usually took them away from their families; geographic distance from families meant that, if they desired, they could consult their own wishes rather than those of their parents in contracting a marriage.

However, marriage was never simply an individual choice, nor was it only a transaction between two people; it always involved a network of family, relations, friends and other community members. Parents were consulted for advice and consent; friends, including employers, served as intermediaries in the negotiations, bringing gifts to a potential partner and reporting on how the gift was received. The proposal itself might be conveyed through an intermediary. The wider community could also exert pressure on a young couple through both formal and informal means, encouraging a couple living in sin to marry or bringing a case of bigamy or adultery to the attention of the Church courts (McSheffrey, *Love and Marriage* 18–19).

Depositions from marriage cases brought before fifteenth-century ecclesiastical courts (in this case, the Consistory and Commissary Courts of London) shed light on the marital practices of the unpropertied. Even if large inheritances were not at stake, economic considerations were never far from the forefront, even in lower-class marriage contracts. In one case, John Brocher v. Joan Cardif, John is suing Joan, a widow, claiming she has not fulfilled the contract of marriage she made with him. John Miller, a weaver, testifies that he acted as an intermediary in arranging the marriage contract. He claims that he discussed with Joan 'the substance of John's goods and debts, and [he] told her that John's debts did not exceed 40 s[hillings]' (McSheffrey, *Love and Marriage* 38). The implication is that John's financial situation was such that Joan, whose widowhood conferred on her some financial independence, did not wish to become entangled in his affairs, so she claims that she could not have entered into a contract without her mother's permission. In another case, John Ely denies that he made a marriage contract with Agnes Whitingdon, saying that 'he did not want to contract with Agnes without first knowing how much her friends were willing to give as her dowry' and that 'he would like to have her as his wife if he could have with her five marks' (McSheffrey, *Love and Marriage* 57).

We tend to think of marriage as a one-time event – a wedding – in which two people publicly declare their desire to marry. Before the wedding, the two individuals are 'single'; after, they 'are married'. In the Middle Ages, rather than consisting of a single decisive event, marriage was a 'series of ever widening circles of publicity' (McSheffrey, *Love and Marriage* 10) which might take place in as many as five stages. First a couple exchanged consent without witnesses (although this stage could involve other parties as intermediaries). Second, consent was exchanged in a domestic setting in front of family, friends or employers. In both of these exchanges, the exact words spoken were important to the contract. In the latter event, an older man – a senior member of the family or a friend – would act as an intermediary, advising the couple on the correct wording. In the case of Brocher v. Cardif, for instance, which I cited above, the deposition directly quotes the following exchange, made while the the couple join their right hands: 'I, John, take the, Johan, for my weddid wif, by my feith and trouth.' Since the depositions usually record conversation as indirect discourse, we must assume that the direct quotation signals the use of an appropriate formula that would be legally binding on the couple. Joan's response suggests that individuals were often knowledgeable and careful about the meaning of the words they uttered at this stage: 'I wil have you to my weddid husbond by my feith, but I will not pli3t you feith and trouth till after Ester, that I cover [it] before my mother' (McSheffrey, *Love and Marriage* 38). The significance of the proper words in these exchanges which seem so informal to modern ears is also apparent in Margaret Paston's account of the bishop's examination of her daughter, Margery, about her clandestine marriage to Richard Calle. The bishop says that he 'would understand the words that she had said to him, whether it made matrimony or not' (Davis, vol. 1, 342; see below p. 193). In the third stage, word of the marriage was spread through 'public voice and fame', a phrase used repeatedly in the depositions. Fourth, banns (announcements of impending solemnization) were issued in the parish churches of the couple, allowing anyone who knew of an impediment (such as prior marriage) to come forward. Finally, almost as an afterthought, the marriage would be solemnized by a priest in a church (McSheffrey, *Love and Marriage* 10). Not all marriages followed every one of these steps, nor were they required to do so. Frequently, as the court depositions make clear, it is not easy to tell when or if a marriage has taken place, especially since marriages were not officially recorded in England until the sixteenth century.

Once recognized, however, a marriage could not be ended except by the death of one of the spouses. Canon law (church laws which governed marriage after the twelfth century) recognized only two forms of divorce, neither of which is equivalent to the modern use of the word. A divorce *a mensa et thoro* (literally 'from table and bed') was the equivalent of a separation. The marriage still existed, neither party could remarry, but the couple were no longer required to live and sleep together. Divorce *a vinculo* ('from the bond') is equivalent to an annulment. This was granted in cases in which the marriage contract was invalid from the beginning so that the contract never really existed. The most common cause for a divorce *a vinculo* was bigamy; coercion was another potential cause. Though consanguinity has often been cited as the most common way out of an inconvenient marriage, there is evidence for few such cases in the late medieval Church. Most marriages of the period, however, probably did not last any longer than marriages today. Early deaths undoubtedly ended many marriages within ten or fifteen years. Childbearing, which was perilous for both mother and child, was a common cause of early death among women (McSheffrey, *Love and Marriage* 6–7).

Evidence from ordinances, court rolls, guild records, tax records and household accounts shows that women participated in a variety of trades and occupations, including cloth-making, brewing and food production, but usually they did so alongside their husbands or as widows. Women's entry into most occupations was limited by training and access to capital. Marriage may have provided the only entry for women into most occupations. While women could inherit wealth, inheritance customs favoured men over women, so that it would be difficult, though never impossible, for a woman to acquire sufficient capital to set up even a modest business (Goldberg, *Women in England* 29). Widowhood probably provided the best opportunity, as this will of Thomas Wod of York, which favours his wife over his son, suggests: 'I leave to Margaret my wife my terms in my fulling mill if she keeps herself sole after my death, if not then I will that my son William shall have them' (Goldberg, *Women in England* 198). Few women served apprenticeships, which was the primary means of entry into the craft guilds (which were more like employer monopolies than trade unions) that controlled most occupations. Borough and guild ordinances determined who could set up shop, hire apprentices, and enjoy the full privileges of burgesses. Such ordinances tended to favour men, sometimes to the complete exclusion of women. A weaver's ordinance from Bristol suggests an attempt to counter the effects of a declining market using strategies designed to force women out of the labour market that sound all too familiar:

> It is agreed . . . that for as much as various persons of the weavers' craft of the said town of Bristol direct, employ and engage their wives, daughters, and maids some to weave on their own looms and some to engage them to work with other persons of the said craft, whereby many and various of the king's subjects, men liable to do the king service in his wars and defence of this his land, and sufficiently skilled in the said craft, go vagrant and unemployed, and may not have work for their livelihood, therefore that no person of the said craft of weavers within the said town of Bristol from this day forward set, put, or engage his wife, daughter, or maid to any such occupation of weaving at the loom with himself or with any other person of the said craft within the said town of Bristol. (Goldberg, *Women in England* 205)

There are, however, examples of women enjoying such privileges, usually as the spouse or widow of a burgess, sometimes as 'sole women', as this fifteenth-century London ordinance suggests: 'married women who follow certain crafts in the city by themselves without their husbands may take women as their apprentices to serve them and to learn their crafts, and these apprentices shall be bound by their indentures of apprenticeship to the husband and his wife to learn the wife's craft' (Goldberg, *Women in England* 197; see also Jambeck, 'Patterns' 244–5).

Convents remained the only acceptable alternative to marriage for women, as well as the primary centre of women's education outside the home. The quality of that education, however, was not as high as it had been during earlier periods. While during the Anglo-Saxon period it would be possible to compare the education of an aristocratic nun with that of a contemporary monk, a convent education in the fourteenth and fifteenth centuries could not even remotely compare with the education being offered in the universities of the day, from which women were rigorously excluded. Devotional interests tended to dominate convent life in the late Middle Ages and stricter enforcement of enclosure kept nuns isolated from secular pursuits. Nuns' usual studies would include liturgies, saints' lives, scriptures and some theology. They learned only enough Latin to allow them to recite their prayers, follow the mass, and perhaps transcribe a devotional text. But the evidence suggests that French and later English were replacing Latin in the convents. The comments of a fifteenth-century translator of the Bene-dictine rule is characteristic of medieval commentary on women's educa-tion: 'Monks and learned men may know the rule in Latin and gather from it how to work serving God and Holy Church; it is for the purpose of making it intelligible to women who learnt no Latin in their youth that it is here set into English that they may easily learn it' (Eckenstein, *Women Under Monasticism* 359). A nun in the late Middle Ages was represented as a person 'careful in her devotion, pious in her intent, of good manners and gentle breeding, but one-sided in the view of life she takes' (Eckenstein, *Women Under Monasticism* 357). Chaucer's portrait of the Prioress in the General Prologue of *The Canterbury Tales* is not, it seems, too far off the mark.

Of course the position of abbess or prioress of a convent would have required both more education, including a fairly good Latin education, than was typical of the average nun and considerable business acumen. Most late medieval convents were ruled by a prioress, but a few were still abbacies. A convent with an abbess at its head would likely be a wealthy foundation with extensive land holdings. An abbess often had to protect the same rights, immunities and privileges as a feudal lord, especially if she ruled over one of the larger and wealthier institutions like Shaftesbury, Barking or Syon. She would have estates to manage and claims to litigate, which she might even do in her own person. An abbess or prioress was much more likely than other nuns to travel outside the convent – and even perhaps, like Chaucer's Prioress, to go on a pilgrimage.

The regulations governing the lives of women living in monastic com-munities in the later Middle Ages can be illustrated by looking at the Bridgettine house of Syon Abbey which, in the fifteenth century, was a centre for the translation of continental women writers like St Bridget, Catherine of Siena and Mechtild of Hackeborn. The last significant monastery founded in medieval England – and the wealthiest convent in late medieval England – was endowed by Henry V in 1415 at Twickenham, though later it was moved to Isleworth near London. It was the only English house to follow the rule handed down by the Swedish saint Bridget who died in 1373 and was canonized in 1391. The link between the Lancastrian kings of England and the Swedish royal house was most likely forged when Henry IV's daughter Philippa was married to Eric XIII of Sweden. By the time of the Dissolution it was among the wealthiest English foundations. Its patrons included members of the Lancastrian, York and Tudor royal families. Syon's regulations survive in four manuscripts and several fragments. My remarks about the arrangements of Syon Abbey are based on two sources: the Middle English translation (most likely prepared for the nuns at Syon) of the Latin *Rule of St Saviour* (CUL MS Ff.6.33), the rule Bridget claims was handed down to her by Christ himself, and the *Orders and Constitutions of the Nuns of Syon*, which contains the regulations for the British foundation (BM MS Arundel 146). The Bridgettine order was established as an order for women. In the *Rule*, Christ says, 'This religion therefore I will set: ordained first & principally by women for the worship of my most dear beloved mother' (CUL MS Ff.6.33, f. 42). However, Bridgettine foundations were to house both men and women in a single institution, which was presided over by an abbess elected only by the sisters, an arrangement dictated by the *Rule*.

The organization of time and space is everywhere evident in the *Rule*, constituting the very life of the abbey. Most monastic institutions, of course, partitioned time into the seven canonical hours: matins, prime, tierce, sext, nones, vespers and compline. The monastery was one of the first places in which the day was temporally regulated in a precise and ordered fashion. Space was also carefully partitioned within the monastery for both symbolic and practical purposes; there is a connection, for instance, between the layout of the monastic church and the body of Christ. However, salvation history suffuses every detail of material life at Syon from its architecture, to the number of inhabitants, to their required clothing. It transcends the limitations of human time and space that are everywhere emphasized in the routinized day-to-day life of the nuns that binds them to human time and space. While human time is understood as irreversible so that no two times can co-exist, the time of salvation history links the here and now with the climactic events of salvation through a complex symbolism. The number of inhabitants in the Bridgettine house was limited by the *Rule* to precisely 85 members. Of those there were to be 60 sisters, 13 priests, 4 deacons and 8 lay brothers. These numbers symbolized the 13 apostles, the 4 Fathers of the Church, and the 72 New Testament disciples, thus linking the bodies of the inhabitants to those who enjoyed the closest proximity with the living

Christ. Similarly, the most fundamental – even obvious – attribute of space is that no two bodies can occupy the same space. Yet the habits required of Bridgettine nuns were designed to mark the symbolic transcendence of that limitation, especially the distinctive crown of the Bridgettine habit:

> Furthermore, upon the veil must be set a crown of white linen cloth, to which must be sown five small pieces of red cloth, resembling five drops [of blood]. The first piece shall be in the forehead, another in back of the head, the third and fourth above the ears, the fifth in middle of the head, in manner of a cross. This crown shall one pin in the middle of the head securely. And this crown shall both widows and virgins wear as a sign of continence and chastity. (CUL MS Ff.6.33f.33; translation mine)

The five pieces of red cloth signify the wounds of Christ, so that the nun wearing it, at least symbolically, merges with the body of Christ.

At Syon men and women were strictly segregated and the nuns strictly enclosed. Even in church the sisters sat on the north side of the chapel while the brothers occupied the southwest with a wall between them. Both could see the high altar and hear the chanting, but they could not see one another. According to the rule, the sisters were to go to confession, receive communion and speak to the brothers only through windows; they could be heard but not seen. Even in death, the separation of the sisters from their male counterparts was maintained through elaborate burial rituals.

If the differences between the sexes was defined by this strict segregation, gender was accentuated by social status, which for the nuns was produced by their physical separation from the rest of the world, as well as by internal partitioning that defined social hierarchies – in the church, the chapter, the refectory, even the dormitory. The disciplinary power that regulated monastic life demonstrated a persistent concern with temporal and spatial distribution. As the sociologist Anthony Giddens notes, the exercise of disciplinary power requires closure, 'a sphere of operations closed off and closed in on itself' (Giddens, *Constitution* 145). The nuns' physical separation from the rest of the world was complete; no one was allowed to enter the monastery of the sisters. Communication with the outside world was strictly regulated. The *Rule* dictates the circumstances under which any nun may 'speak at the grate':

> Only at specified times may nuns speak with seculars, but they must always be accompanied by another & speak by leave of the abbess. . . . They may not go out, but must sit at designated windows. After her entrance, no one may go out of the cloisters of the monastery. . . . If any should desire to be seen by her father or mother, or dear and honest friends, she may open the window with permission of the abbess at designated times during the year, but if she does not open the window, the reward promised her will be so much more plentiful in the time to come in the advent of Our Lord. (CUL MS Ff.6.33, f. 40)

The rewards are greatest for those sisters who refused to allow themselves ever to be seen by an outsider. Listed as a 'grievous fault' in the *Orders and Constitution of the Nuns of Syon* are 'speaking with any brother, or with any secular person, man or woman' and revealing 'the secrets of the religion to an outsider' (BM MS Arundel 146, f. 4v). The monastery is a container; the nuns' lives are sealed off from potentially intrusive encounters from outside. The elaborate procedures for enclosing a new nun, because of their liminal status in bringing the secular and religious worlds together for a brief time, suggest the power of this temporal and spatial separation of the nuns from the rest of the world.

But separation from the outside world is not itself enough to ensure the formation of appropriately religious identities. This was achieved through internal regional division or partitioning (Giddens, *Constitution* 143). Within the cloistered community, each individual was assigned her 'proper place' at any particular time of the day. Upon entry into the community, a new sister was assigned by the abbess places in 'the church, chapter, fraitour, dortour, and all other places' and those assigned places regulated movements and interactions among the inhabitants. According to Michel Foucault in *Discipline and Punish*, such internal regionalization serves several disciplinary functions:

> In organizing 'cells,' 'places,' and 'ranks,' the disciplines create complex spaces that are at once architectural, functional and hierarchical. It is spaces that provide fixed positions and permit circulation; they carve out individual segments and establish operational links; they mark places and indicate values; they guarantee the obedience of individuals, but also a better economy of time and gesture. (Foucault, *Discipline and Punish* 148)

In other words, internal regionalization partitions space (fixed positions, individual segments) and time (circulation, operational links which can only unfold in time) in routinized activity, activity which strips individuals of their secular identity and produces a specific religious identity.

As with all disciplinary organizations, the economy of time and gesture in the convent allowed for a very precise regulation of bodies. Fasting, silence, prayer, singing, confession, discipline, reading, eating, sleeping and labour all had their assigned times and places ('due time and place' is the formulistic phrase repeated again and again in the *Rule*). For instance, the *Rule* requires that silence be observed at particular times:

> From earliest morning until after the Mass sung for the Blessed Virgin, no one may speak at all, except in case of necessity and with the permission of the abbess. When that Mass is ended, in the proper places, until it is time for the blessing of the table to be read ... license for speaking is granted. ... Furthermore after grace is read in the church, the sisters may speak among themselves until they begin evensong. And then also silence

is to be held until they have read grace after supper in the church. In that little interval that is between grace and collation license for speaking is granted. Once collation has begun, silence must be observed. (CUL MS Ff.6.33, f. 45v)

The most severe forms of spacing allowed for a meticulous specification of bodily positioning, movement and gesture as in this rule governing bodily discipline:

When the fault of any sister is such that . . . she deserves discipline, the sister commanded to make herself ready shall stand up in the same place where she knelt before the abbess, taking off her mantle & letting it fall down behind her. And then under her cowl she shall take the ends & lay all honestly around her neck, drawing her arms out of her sleeves to the elbows & bearing the shoulders of her back, exposing the bare skin. Then she should kneel again in the same place & inclining with meekness shall take her discipline, which she or they whom the abbess biddeth shall administer. However, none of them who proclaimed against her should give it, but another sister or sisters. (BM MS Arundel 3–3v)

The other sisters are not to watch but must 'cast down their head & sight toward the earth'. Such bodily discipline is recommended not only for those who have committed some offence; rather every Friday 'the dortour bell shall be tolled & the sisters shall take bodily discipline in due time and place', using the same form outlined above (BM MS Arundel f. 60). The sisters, then, did not simply engage in regularized bodily penance, they did so through an elaborately and precisely choreographed ritual that spelled out the smallest movements.

This analysis of the regimentation of convent life illuminates the complex mechanisms by which gendered religious identities were produced and regulated by the end of the Middle Ages. Since cloistered nuns (however constrained their daily lives were) enjoyed more freedom from domestic duties and leisure for contemplation and other intellectual pursuits than their secular sisters, it is not at all surprising that the majority of women's religious writing, and even some secular writing, was produced in this environment. Syon Abbey is an strategic site for the recovery of women's intellectual and cultural activity during the Middle Ages. Its royal patronage and wealth made it not only a centre for the production of women's writing, but for its circulation and consumption as well.[17]

I have been able in this chapter to sketch only briefly something of the conditions of women's lives in the Middle Ages. But even in such a brief profile what emerges most strikingly is the heterogeneity of women's experiences, the many different paths they pursued despite the limited options of marriage or religious seclusion available to them. This variety is largely obscured by the stark oppositions of misogynist discourse, both medieval and modern. The extreme examples of Virgin Mary and Eve, the views that women are either virginal saints or unregenerate whores, are too simple to comprehend the diversity of women's experiences. My analyses may have emphasized medieval women's abilities and accomplishments at the expense of documenting their oppression. This is not to deny that medieval women were oppressed. They were sometimes not considered fully human, certainly they were not considered fully citizens. They suffered at the hands of despotic husbands, tyrannical fathers and authoritarian clerics.

However, I find that my students (and sometimes my colleagues) simply assume that medieval misogyny and anti-feminism are justifiable because 'everybody felt that way'. To criticize it would be anachronistic. Medieval women internalized these beliefs; it would not be possible to think otherwise, so there is little point in condemning it. It is, of course, easy to come away from studying the Middle Ages believing this is true, because the history of the Middle Ages we have chosen to preserve records a public transcript that consists primarily of men's actions, beliefs and perceptions. This chapter revises that history by restoring women to visibility, by looking at the period from the perspective of women, and by recounting what they accomplished, despite their subjugation. Before we can turn to an examination of medieval women's writing, however, we need to investigate the conditions under which writing was both produced and consumed in the Middle Ages. That is the subject of the next chapter.

NOTES

1. In common parlance the term 'medieval' has come to be synonymous with barbarism, superstition, ignorance and benighted prejudice.
2. Many of the above were, ironically, borrowed from a vastly superior Muslim culture that we now devalue as inferior to European culture; see Abu-Lughod, *Before European Hegemony* 3–24.
3. For a fuller treatment of medieval misogyny than can be given here see Blamires, *Women Defamed*, Bloch, *Medieval Misogyny* and Dalarun, 'Clerical Gaze' 13–15.
4. For a discussion of medieval medical beliefs about sex difference see Cadden, *Sex Difference*, Thomasset, 'Nature of Women'.
5. All quotations from *The Canterbury Tales* will be taken from the translation by David Wright.
6. The other two – the Immaculate Conception and the Assumption – did not become doctrine until 1854 and 1950, though they were debated throughout the Middle Ages; see Dalarun, 'Clerical Gaze' 25.

7. The translation from the Middle English is mine. See Brown, *Religious Lyrics* 58.

8. Medieval holy women who had been married were acutely aware of their imperfections; see the discussion of Margery Kempe below, 186.

9. The most extended exploration of the image of God as mother by a woman writer occurs in the *Showings* of the English anchoress Julian of Norwich; see below 171–3.

10. See Bynum, *Jesus as Mother* 135–46 and Ferrante, *Woman as Image*.

11. See the discussion of Marguerite Porete's *Mirror of Simple Souls*, below 135–8.

12. On the interpersonal nature of patronage relationships such as these see Eisenstadt and Koniger, *Patrons*, esp. pp. 178–84.

13. Such pilgrimages would not have been impossible, however, since Chaucer imagines a Prioress among the group of pilgrims who make the Canterbury pilgrimage.

14. For a more detailed description of Matilda's cultural patronage see Huneycutt, 'Literary and Artistic Network'.

15. The term 'serial polygamy' is used by Kinoshita 'Courtly Love' to describe twelfth-century marital politics.

16. For a description of the kinds of conflicts that developed between parents and children, especially daughters, over marriages see the discussion of the Paston letters 190–4.

17. See below pp. 128–9, 132, 138–42, and 146–7 for a more detailed discussion of literary activity at Syon.

CHAPTER TWO
Women and Regimes of Writing in the Middle Ages

The Longman's History of Women's Writing in English locataes women's writing within the project of nationalistic literature that has dominated the study of English departments during this century. A major assumption that we bring to this study is that the activity we call literature has taken place primarily in English as an expression of some kind of national spirit (Eagleton, *Literary Theory* 11). Our language defines us as a nation because that shared language facilitates the kind of horizontal bonding required of the 'imagined community' that Benedict Anderson argues constitutes nationalism (*Imagined Communities* 5–6). As we attempt to construct the history of women's writing, it seems only natural that we should try to fit the newly recovered woman writer within this structure, if only to enable us to carry on with the teaching of English literature without too much disruption or rewriting of syllabi and anthologies. However, if we simply append women writers to the canon of English literature without challenging its premises, if we simply 'add women and stir', then we run the very real risk of obscuring or missing altogether women's contributions to culture; we risk missing altogether the most revolutionary aspect of women's writing: its ability to make us look at our culture in new and different ways which may be more empowering than the old. To understand women's relation to the modes of production, dissemination and consumption of texts during the Middle Ages we must interrogate and perhaps even dismantle the very terms of our inquiry. In other words, the study of the woman writer in England during the Middle Ages requires a questioning of the terms 'woman', 'writing', 'English' and 'Middle Ages' and I hope in this chapter to continue interrogating these terms, illustrating the ways in which the questions they raise have guided this inquiry.

In the area of cultural production, the Middle Ages saw two major shifts – revolutions even – in the practices that governed textual production.

Both of these shifts not only defined the ways in which medieval readers consumed texts, but continue to shape our own understanding of literature as well. The first was the emergence in the eleventh century of written culture. Before this period, Brian Stock argues, while writing existed, large areas of cultural life could still be produced and disseminated orally. By the millennium, written texts were coming to dominate cultural life – not just religion, but law, politics, finance, administration and literature – even where literacy was not widespread. Writing did not simply replace the spoken word, Stock argues; rather oral discourse, even among the non-literate, began to function within the structuring constraints of written texts (Stock, *Implications of Literacy* 3–11). Even when they could not themselves read or write, people's lives were shaped in very real ways by texts. The second major shift occurred at the end of the Middle Ages with the introduction of the printing press into England. The press that William Caxton set up in Westminster did more than just make books more widely available at less cost. It would fundamentally alter the ways in which people related to the written word.

For these reasons, despite daunting gaps in the records, the Middle Ages is a particularly good place to begin the recovery of a tradition of women writers. The period's 'otherness' encourages us to recognize that the information we retrieve might challenge those narratives we have been telling about the tradition of male writing into which women only rarely and only after the eighteenth century gained entry. The first challenge we must consider is to the dominance of English as the language of *English* literature and the language which most uniquely defines something like an English national spirit. The English language is the single concept that binds the books in this series together. But what is lost if we limit our study of women writers only to women who wrote in the English language?

THE LANGUAGES OF LITERARY PRODUCTION

To many of us the idea of English is so obvious as to require no explanation. English is the language we speak – our mother tongue – and so it is only 'natural' that our literature should be written primarily, even exclusively, in that language. Rarely do we pause to reflect on how that language achieved its priority. When and how did it emerge as our national language? Was it inevitable that it did? Most English literary histories project the dominance of the English language backward onto times when the idea of English as a literary language was perhaps even laughable (see Salter, *English and International* 4–28). The Middle Ages was such a period. When we study English literature, however, we act as if the 'tradition' of early English literature from *Beowulf* to Chaucer to Shakespeare were sufficient to explain literary activity in the British Isles.

Yet we might reasonably argue that the percentage of literary writing in English that survives from the Middle Ages is about as meagre as the percentage of women's writing that survives. English was not in the Middle Ages the only, or even the dominant, literary language and our construction of an artificial tradition of medieval writing in English obscures much of what we might call the 'multiculturalism' of medieval England. Medieval England was, of necessity, heteroglossic,[1] to borrow a term from Bakhtin; it was a culture in which several languages coexisted and mingled in more or less conflicted ways. The hegemony of English as a cultural marker of Englishness was by no means assured during the Middle Ages. At any given time English would jostle with the Celtic languages spoken in outlying areas in Scotland, Ireland, Wales and Cornwall (outlying precisely because the Celts had been pushed into these remote areas by invading Anglo-Saxons), with the Scandinavian languages brought by Viking raiders, the Norman French spoken by eleventh-century invaders, and later the Parisian French spoken by the fashionable court, as well as with the Latin spoken and written by the literate clerical elite throughout the period. The cultural dominance of a particular language at a particular moment in time would depend on either military or political power (or both). What we would think of as nationalism, the horizontal and imaginative ties that bind large numbers of people, giving them a national identity, were unknown and, many would argue, unthinkable at this time, or only beginning to emerge at the very end of the period (Anderson, *Imagined Communities* 9–22, 33–6) Class, as I suggested in the previous chapter, was a far more salient marker of cultural identity and identification than nationality. An Englishwoman of the aristocracy in, say, the twelfth century would have far more in common – including language – with a French woman of the aristocracy than she would with an English peasant woman. An Anglo-Saxon nun might be as fluent in Latin as her male monastic contemporary, much more so than her fifteenth-century sister. Only by restoring this heteroglossia to English culture can the extent of women's contributions to 'English' literature become fully visible. The literary canon's erasure of this multiculturalism ensured the hegemony of the 'English' tradition at the cost of obscuring much of the literary activity, and in particular literary activity by women, that went on during this period. This literary activity becomes the province of specialists in other fields: historians, Latinists, Celtic scholars, scholars of French literature.

Recognizing the heteroglossia of medieval England leads to several questions that must guide this study. Who can speak or read in which languages? What languages are being used to produce literary works during any given time? What genres get written in what languages? What texts get translated into which languages? Under what circumstances and by whom? For the purposes of this study must we consider only women who originally wrote in English or do we need to consider that, in a culture in which many languages compete for hegemony, English was only one language, and perhaps not the most prestigious, in which a woman might choose to write.

In the Middle Ages, as Malcolm Parkes has argued, the ability to read and write Latin defined the *literatus* (or literate man, note the masculine noun ending). As I shall argue in subsequent chapters, many works by and for women written in English (or translated into it) were done so precisely because women were not considered literate enough to read the texts in Latin. This is the reason the fourteenth-century translator of the Benedictine Rule gives for his translation; he expects it will be used by nuns whose Latin is not advanced enough to read the original. The anonymous author of the thirteenth-century *Ancrene Riwle* wrote in English because the women for whom he wrote it could not read Latin; whenever he uses Latin in the text, he is careful to translate it. Finally a fifteenth-century translator of the medical texts of the eleventh-century Italian physician Trotula 'drew' the 'diverse causes of women's maladies' out of Latin into English 'because women of our tongue better understand and read this language than any other' (BM Sloane MS 421a f. 2ᵛ; translation mine).

Women's access to Latin literacy obviously varied by class and social status throughout the Middle Ages. Aristocratic women were more likely than most women to have some exposure to Latin literacy, aristocratic nuns even more so. But access to Latin learning also varied over time. The evidence suggests that at least some Anglo-Saxon nuns were fluent readers and writers of Latin. Aldhelm addressed the nuns of Barking in *De Virginitate* in a Latin that is notoriously difficult and complex; yet this text was used as a regular textbook for both men and women in religious institutions. The nuns were apparently able to follow Aldhelm's convoluted syntax and obscure vocabulary with only minimal difficulty, as suggested by early manuscripts containing not only the Latin text but also translations of difficult words into Anglo-Saxon or more accessible Latin (Fell, *Women* 109–10). Both men and women in monasteries wrote Latin letters to one another that were influenced by Aldhelm's style and vocabulary. During his missionary work among the Germans, for example, St Boniface carried on a lively correspondence in Latin with several English abbesses, among them St Leoba, who later joined him in his missionary work in Germany. The nuns sometimes derogate their efforts to write Latin prose. In one letter to

Boniface, an abbess and her daughter refer to 'our rude and unpolished speech' (Boniface 39), while Leoba begs Boniface 'to correct the unskilled style of this letter' (60). It is likely, however, that such requests were largely formulaic, a gesture of deference to a superior. When three of Boniface's monks write to the abbess Cuniburg they make the same request, using much the same language: 'We also beg you to correct this unlearned letter' (78). Despite their claims to the contrary, these letters are not simply formulaic business letters, but elaborate rhetorical performances that display a range of complex emotions and ideas – joy, grief, loneliness, longing – using metaphor, simile and other rhetorical devices, quoting scriptures and other texts, demonstrating an impressive mastery of the syntax of learned medieval Latin (see below pp. 113–14).

By the eleventh century, women's learning in Latin is perhaps not as impressive as that of these eighth-century nuns, but there are signs that it had not died out completely. Matilda, the Scottish wife of Henry I, who had been educated by nuns at Romsey, carried on a Latin correspondence with Anselm, the Archbishop of Canterbury, which shows something of her ease with Latin and the extent of her convent education (Eckenstein, *Women Under Monasticism* 209–10). Agnes de Harcourt notes in her biography how St Louis's sister Isabelle corrected the Latin of her chaplains (Thompson, *Literacy* 146). However, other evidence suggests the decline in women's Latin literacy. One French cleric, Adam of Perseigne, writing to a noble woman around 1200 suggests her confessor might help her with any difficulties she had understanding the Latin. When Blanche of Navarre, wife of Thibaut III of Champagne, requested of him a collection of sermons, he expressed doubt that she would be able to understand it (Thompson, *Literacy* 145). By the twelfth century, Aelred of Rievaulx can still write in Latin a handbook for anchoresses addressed to his sister, but the Latin is much simpler than that of his other works. The thirteenth-century rule for anchoresses, *Ancrene Riwle*, is written entirely in English, its Latin quotations always translated. Even though it was written for three high-born and influential ladies, it is clear that they were not expected to master Latin.

If Latin was falling into disuse among cultivated women readers, there were still other barriers to the emergence of English as a literary language. One of the most significant outcomes of the Norman invasion of England was that Anglo-Norman became for two centuries the dominant language of the island and hence the most significant language for vernacular literary production. For two centuries members of the largely Norman aristocracy continued to use their native French. Anyone hoping to advance within the Norman ruling class, whatever their ethnicity (this included English wives of Norman magnates) would speak French, so that its use became a sign of social distinction, as the following passage from the chronicle of Robert of Gloucester (c. 1300) suggests:

Thus, lo! England came in to Normandy's hand.
And the Normans knew how to speak then only their own speech
And spoke French as they did at home, and taught it to their children;
So that high men of this land that come of their blood
Hold all that same speech that they took from them.
For unless a man knows French, men count of him little.
But low men hold to English and to their own speech yet
(Baugh and Cable, *History* 114; translation mine)

The reasons for the continued dominance of French among the ruling classes are doubtless many. Both the Norman kings and their barons maintained large land holdings in France so that they were required to maintain close ties with their homeland. With the exception of Stephen who was fighting a civil war during most of his reign (1135–54), the Norman kings of England spent more time in France than they did in England. Henry I was the only English king until the late fifteenth century who took an English wife. The Norman aristocracy may have known some English – Duke William apparently attempted to learn the language with little success, and Henry I knew some; however, before the loss of Normandy at the beginning of the thirteenth century, there appeared to be no real impetus to cultivate English as a language of social distinction and erudition. The relative status of French and English during this period has left its mark on the English language even today in the large percentage of modern English words borrowed from the Romance languages, especially French. The survival of French and Anglo-Saxon words reflects social distinctions. For instance, our words for meat on the hoof – pig, cow, lamb, deer – are Anglo-Saxon in origin, while our words for meat on the table – beef, pork, mutton, venison – are French, reflecting the distinctions between those who would be tending the animals and those who would be eating the meat. This is a distinction unique to English, a sedimentation of past usage.

Because literature is primarily produced and consumed by those with leisure, education and wealth and because the literature produced by the dominant classes is most likely to be preserved for posterity, it is not surprising that there is virtually no English literature of note produced during the period of Norman hegemony from 1066 until the beginning of the thirteenth century. There is, however, a considerable body of Anglo-Norman literature produced during this time written in French, but addressed to English patrons. The exclusion of this literature from English literary history (it tends to be the province of French scholars) promotes the fiction of an unbroken line of English poets from the Beowulf-poet to Chaucer, while completely obscuring a period of 'English literature' significant for the development of literary genre and technique in the vernacular. During the Anglo-Norman period the genre of romance appears both in England and on the Continent, and reaches perhaps its highest development. The writing of vernacular history becomes prominent at this time. And it is difficult, if not impossible, to understand the development of English prosody (the metrical techniques of verse) from alliterative long lines to rhymed verse without understanding the dominance of the French language and culture (and hence French metrical forms) during this period. To fill, at least partially, this gap in English literary history, this volume will examine texts produced by English women writing in Anglo-Norman. To leave out these documents would, I believe, fundamentally obscure the history of women's writing in England.

During the later Middle Ages, the monopoly over education enjoyed by the universities, from which women were entirely excluded, meant the continuing deterioration of women's Latinity. As teachers of Latin migrated from convent schools to the universities, Latin became more and more the province of a specialized cadre of clerics and administrators, an exclusively male domain (Krueger, *Women Readers* 22). Even the education of nuns in Latin was becoming rudimentary. Many were proficient enough only to understand the liturgy and the most common prayers. As a result, despite evidence of growing numbers of cultivated female readers of vernacular literature, women were systematically excluded from the most important activities of political and intellectual life not only because men actively excluded them, but also because they could not read or write the language that was its entrance requirement.

During the fourteenth and fifteenth century, English comes into its own as a literary language, producing English writers like Chaucer, the Gawain-poet, Langland, Gower, Hoccleve and Malory, but it would be a mistake to conclude from this activity the triumph of the English language. While it is easy with the benefit of hindsight to see as inevitable the emergence of English as the literary language of Britain, to the fifteenth-century writers promoting the adulation of Chaucer, that outcome was anything but certain. Even though after the thirteenth century the English kings and nobility spoke English as a native tongue, the style of the court continued to be international and fluency in French continued to be a mark of social standing. It was no longer Norman French but the fashionable Parisian dialect of the French and Burgundian courts that set the tone in the courts of fourteenth- and fifteenth-century kings from Edward III to Edward IV. Ironically the Hundred Years War with France encouraged a continued French cultural presence despite the hostilities. French aristocrats being held for ransom in England would have mingled with their English coun-terparts at court. The English court patronized French intellectuals like

Froissart and Machaut, contemporaries of Chaucer. Christine de Pizan enjoyed a steady popularity among the English nobility throughout the fifteenth century (see below pp. 201–12). During the successful early years of the war, English magnates plundered French libraries, bringing back to England scores of French manuscripts as spoils of war. Many of those manuscripts are still in English libraries today. The spectacularly illuminated manuscript of her works that Christine de Pizan had made for the French queen Isabeau of Bavaria (BL MS Harley 4431) was acquired by the Duke of Bedford from the royal library in the Louvre when he was regent of France (1422–35). His second wife's name (Jacquette of Luxembourg) appears on the fly-leaf of the manuscript, along with that of her son by a subsequent marriage, Anthony Woodville.

Neither the prominence of languages such as French and Italian in the international style of the English court, nor the persistence of Celtic languages on the geographical fringes[2] was by itself enough to account for the heteroglossia of the late Middle Ages. Regional dialects also hindered the development of English as a standardized literary language. In his preface to the *Eneydos* (1490), William Caxton, England's first printer, complains of the lack of just such a standard for English, suggesting that at times regional dialects were mutually incomprehensible:

> And certainly our language now used varyeth far from that which was used and spoken when I was born, for we Englishmen been born under the domination of the moon, which is never steadfast but ever wavering, waxing one season and waneth and decreaseth another season. And that common English that is spoken in one shire varyeth from another. Insomuch that in my days happened that certain merchants were in a ship in Thames for to have sailed over the sea into Zeeland. And for lack of wind they tarried at Foreland and went to land for to refresh them, and one of them named Sheffelde a mercer came into an house and asked for meat and specially he asked after eggs. And the good wife answered that she could speak no French, and the merchant was angry for he also could speak no French, but would have had eggs, and she understood him not. And then at last another said that he would have eyren; then the good wife said that she understood him well. Lo, what should a man in these days now write, eggs or eyren? Certainly it is hard to please every man by cause of diversity and change of language. (Caxton, *Prologues and Epilogues* 108)

A people who cannot even understand one another's simplest communication cannot imagine the kind of communal bond necessary to identify themselves as members of a nation or take collective pride in a national literature.

Throughout the Middle Ages there is no standard for the English language. Rather it exists as a series of regional dialects that differed almost from county to county. While these dialects may have been mutually incomprehensible to one another only at the extremes, as Caxton and others suggest,[3] there were considerable differences in vocabulary, pronunciation and grammar among them to make it unlikely that medieval writers – male or female – would have thought of themselves as part of a tradition of 'English' writers. Caxton's concern for the lack of an agreed-upon standard for the language is not, in this regard, surprising. As England's first printer, he introduced the technology that would enable a standard English that could serve as the language of a national literature because it could serve as a sign of 'Englishness': native speakers of the language could be imaginatively connected across time and space as part of the imagined community of the nation (Anderson, *Imagined Community* 5–7).

WOMEN AND LITERACY

The next issue we must consider is what we mean by writing. We assume that a literary document will be a written text designed to be read, silently, usually by a single and isolated reader. This is, of course, the way we read and we find it difficult to imagine literature produced any other way. But in fact the situation is rather more complex in the Middle Ages. A literary 'artifact' might be written to be read by a single reader. However, it might also be written to be read to a large or small audience, by one individual to another, to be performed, or it might not be written at all. It might be orally composed. In defining reading and writing in the Middle Ages, we must consider all these possibilities.

In addition we must consider what we mean by literacy and illiteracy and the role writing plays in the transmission of culture. In our culture, literacy is the standard and measure of education and cultural authority, while illiteracy is equated with lack of intelligence, certainly with a lack of education. But it is possible to have a highly developed culture, including a high level of education, in the absence of any written documents. Indeed in the *Phaedrus*, Plato considered writing to be a dangerous threat to the morality and truth that are the central mission of education because it detaches speech from its 'authentic living presence'. According to Plato, the threat writing poses to culture lies not only in the deterioration of memory, but also in the divorce of knowledge from authority. Of the mythical god Thoth, said to have invented writing, Plato says, 'Thanks to you and your invention [writing], your pupils will be widely read without benefit of a teacher's instruction' (Derrida, *Dissemination* 102; Norris, *Derrida* 30–1). For Plato, writing breaks the personal ties among individuals (usually men) that ensure the passage of truth from one generation to the next.

There is little evidence in the Middle Ages for the kind of exclusively oral culture that Plato describes, pure verbal discourse uninfluenced by any kind of written text. Reconstructed visions of the Anglo-Saxon *scop* or the Celtic bard weaving history, law, genealogy and poetry with only words and formulae is a tantalizing, if somewhat romantic, image requiring the suppression of a great deal of inconvenient manuscript evidence. Texts that survive do provide some indirect evidence that pure oral cultures may have predated the introduction of Christianity but our knowledge of such pre-literate cultures is always filtered through *written* texts. Someone, most likely several individuals in monasteries, wrote down Anglo-Saxon poems, Old Irish laws, or Welsh tales that they had heard. In so doing, however much indirect evidence they were preserving of these texts' oral transmission, the texts would invariably be inflected by the literate culture that dominated monastic life from the seventh century on. Indeed this is the kind of orality for which the Middle Ages provides the best evidence – orality that exists in interdependence with written texts. For the period of English history that is the subject of this book – beginning with the Christianization of the English in the seventh century – oral discourse functioned within a framework of legal and institutional textuality (Stock, *Implications of Literacy* 7–8). For most of the period, literacy was the jealously guarded prerogative of a privileged few, clerics primarily and later administrators and professionals. The vast majority of people remained illiterate – or non-literate. All forms of literacy – law, politics, literature, science, religion – needed to take account of the needs of both the literate and illiterate.

To understand the nature of women's writing in medieval England we must understand how the functional interdependence of oral and written modes of communication affected the production and consumption of texts of all kinds. By way of an example of this interdependence, we might return to the legal mechanisms for assessing the legality of marriage contracts discussed in Chapter 1. The legality of modern marriages is generally assured by a written document – the marriage licence.[4] In the Middle Ages, however, the situation is, as we have seen, rather more complicated. There is no marriage licence or even a legal record of a new marriage. Instead jurists looked to three things to assess the validity of the contract: (1) the declaration by the couple in front of witnesses of their intent to marry, often using specific formulaic words; (2) the existence of a 'public voice and fame' of the marriage in the community; (3) publication of banns announcing the marriage in the parish church. Any one of these could be definitive in establishing the validity of a contract; none required any writing whatsoever. These oral rituals would be the most effective way of ensuring widespread knowledge of a new marriage within communities many of whose members would be unable to read or write. In the event of disputes, verbal depositions would be taken in a special church court and written down by a scribe and this record would be the first *written* evidence of this marriage (McSheffrey, *Love and Marriage* 1–2).

Estimates of the extent of literacy at any time during the Middle Ages vary enormously among medieval historians. Stock's assessment represents the pessimistic end of the spectrum. While insisting on the importance of written texts in the lives of all medieval people, literate or not, he argues that:

> Medieval and early modern society hovered between the extremes: there was a tiny minority who were truly literate and a much larger majority for whom communication could take place only by word of mouth. Down to the age of print and in many regions long afterwards, literacy remained the exception rather than the rule. Despite primary schools, cheap paper, spectacles, and the growing body of legal and administrative material, the masses of both town and countryside as late as the Reformation remained relatively indifferent to writing. For this vast group, marginal to literacy, the graphic world represented only a complex set of signs, frequently tied to authority. . . . Although scribal pressures rose from many directions and gathered momentum as the age of print neared, many peasants, burghers, and even aristocrats remained essentially within oral-aural culture. (Stock, *Implications of Literacy* 13–14)

Other scholars, however, are more optimistic about the spread of literacy, especially in the late Middle Ages. Michael Van Cleve Alexander estimates the proportion of English adults who could read at 25 to 30 per cent by the eve of the Reformation (*English Education* 36), while Sylvia Thrupp speculates that 40 per cent of English tradesmen could read Latin and 50 per cent English. Even many women of the artisan and merchant class were finding ways to learn how to read and write at least English (*Merchant Class* 158).

We might expect that literacy would be highest among the clerical classes, followed by the aristocracy, while the lowest literacy rates would naturally be found among the lower classes. But as we begin to examine the evidence, exceptions are many and often surprising, once again demonstrating the unevenness of historical 'progress'. The tenth-century Wessex king Alfred argued, at least theoretically, for extensive literacy among his free subjects; in a letter addressed to his bishops that accompanied his translation of *Cura Pastoralis* he wrote, 'all the young people who are now in England, free-born, who have the aptitude to apply themselves, should be set to learning . . . until they can fully understand how to read English writing' (Fell, *Women* 10). The term Alfred uses, *geoguth*, is usually translated as 'young men', but Christine Fell argues that it might just as reasonably be translated 'young people' and applied to both boys and girls. In the twelfth century, William Marshal, marshal of England under Henry II and one of the most powerful men in England, was illiterate all of his life, while his contemporary Walter Map complained about the spread of literacy among the 'base-born', suggesting that literacy had not yet become a mark of social distinction (though undoubtedly Map thought that it should):

> the high-born of our country disdain letters or delay to apply their children to them, although to their children only is it rightly permitted to study the arts. . . . Slaves on the other hand (the which we call peasants), are eager to nourish their base-born and degenerate children in the arts unfitted to their station, not that they may rise from their rudeness, but that they may level in their richness. (Parkes, 'Literacy' 560)

Late fifteenth-century depositions from the Consistory and Commissary Courts of London provide support for Thrupp's contentions about the extent of literacy among late-medieval citizens of London. The depositions for men usually report whether or not the deponent was literate (no information about literacy is given for female deponents). Of 25 depositions taken from men of various ranks that Shannon McSheffrey includes in her collection of documents relating to late medieval marriage, 14 indicate that the deponents were literate, 11 that they were illiterate. The range of occupations is illustrative of the spread of literacy by the end of the Middle Ages. Among the literate are included not only the lord of a manor, a gentleman, and a servant of the Duchess of York, but also a tallow-chandler, a pewterer, a grocer, a cheesemonger, a linen draper, a tailor and a tailor's apprentice (*Love and Marriage*).

If, however, during the late Middle Ages, many members of the merchant and artisan classes were achieving some level of literacy, at no time would the literacy of a tailor be the same as the literacy of a bishop or lord. While literacy is notoriously difficult to define, especially during this period, it is necessary to make some distinctions among different kinds of readers who would use written texts for very different purposes. Parkes suggests three general types. Professional readers were clerics, scholars, lawyers and administrators whose reading was done primarily in Latin. Cultivated readers were interested in reading as recreation and were more often literate only in their vernacular. Finally, pragmatic readers used texts primarily for the transaction of business rather than scholarship or recreation (Parkes, 'Literacy' 555). Before the twelfth century literacy was the domain of the professional and clerical scholar. The first indications of a cultivated literacy appear among the Anglo-Norman aristocracy and are accompanied by a steady increase in the number of surviving vernacular manuscripts (Parkes, 'Literacy' 556). The growth of pragmatic literacy among the middle classes also begins around this time as written texts become increasingly important to business, law, property transactions and politics. By the end of the Middle Ages the distinction between pragmatic and recreational readers was beginning to collapse as pragmatic readers of the middle classes began to extend their interests into recreational and instructional reading. As one of the editors of the Paston Letters notes, 'No person of any rank or station above mere labouring men seems to have been wholly illiterate. All could write letters: most persons could express themselves in writing with ease and fluency' (cited in Kingsford, *Stonor Letters* xlvi). Kingsford, in his introduction to the collection of letters by the Stonor family writes that 'Generally the country squires of Oxfordshire and their women folk, and the better class merchants of London could write with ease' (*Stonor Letters* xlvi).

What does the evidence reveal about literacy among women? Anne Bartlett suggests that there is extensive evidence for women's literacy which has been ignored by scholars claiming women's nearly complete illiteracy (*Male Authors* 5–15). The belief that medieval women were mostly illiterate may be fuelled by the disapproval of women's education increasingly evident in the writing of medieval churchmen after the twelfth century. Philippe de Novare in *Les Quatres Ages de l'homme* (*The Four Ages of Man*) writes, 'One ought not to teach a woman reading or writing, unless it is specifically so that she may be a nun; because women's reading and writing have caused much harm' (Krueger, *Women Readers* 23). The fifteenth-century cleric Jean Gerson (d. 1429) suggests the harm that women's literacy might cause:

> the female sex is forbidden on apostolic authority [1 Tim. 2:12] to teach in public, that is either by word or by writing. . . . All women's teaching, particularly formal teaching by word and by writing, is to be held suspect unless it has been diligently examined, and much more fully than men's. The reason is clear: common law – and not any kind of common law, but that which comes from on high – forbids them. And why? Because they are easily seduced and determined seducers; and because it is not proved that they are witnesses to divine grace. (Bynum, *Jesus as Mother* 136)

Not only might women themselves be seduced by false teachings, but they would seduce others as surely as Eve seduced Adam. Gerson's scepticism that women could be 'witnesses to divine grace' is particularly striking.

Of course the existence of a book on women writers in the Middle Ages suggests that at least some women in the Middle Ages must have been literate. Bartlett points to the existence of female scribes in the sixth, eighth, ninth and eleventh centuries as evidence of women's facility with the technologies of writing (*Male Authors* 5). And there is evidence to suggest that Christine de Pizan oversaw the production of at least two manuscripts of her works (Harley 4431 and BN MS fr. 606), making her a publisher of sorts. But I believe it is possible to demonstrate that these women are not simply the occasional exceptions to the rule of women's ignorance. Medieval women belonged to communities of readers and their membership in these reading communities enabled at least some women to become writers.

I would like to explore briefly, in this section and the next, the nature of those communities.

During the Anglo–Saxon period, many aristocratic nuns, as we have seen, were professionally literate. They were members of sophisticated reading communities that included both men and women. The Boniface correspondence suggests that nuns were as active in book production as monks. In one letter the abbess Bugga apologizes for being unable to send Boniface the copy of *Sufferings of the Martyrs* that she has promised him (40). In another letter, Boniface requests of the abbess Eadburga a copy of the Epistles of St Paul in letters of gold, an expensive and lavish book for which Boniface sends her materials 'so that here also your works may shine forth in golden letters for the glory of our heavenly Father' (64).

At the close of the seventh century Aldhelm attributes a wide range of learning to the sisters at the convent of Barking, describing them as 'gymno-sophists . . . scholars and fighters in the arena of disciplines' (Eckenstein, *Women Under Monasticism* 113). They are like bees, 'roaming widely through the flowering fields of Scripture . . . now exploring wisely the fourfold texts [of the Gospels] . . . now duly rummaging through the old stories of the historians and the entries of chroniclers . . . now sagaciously inquiring into the rules of the grammarians and the teachers and experts on . . . the rules of metrics' (Fell, *Women* 110–11). Aldhelm describes a serious programme of education not much different in range, weight or depth from the education of male monastics. A ninth-century monk of Fulda describes St Leoba's education in terms very similar to those Aldhelm uses:

> For, since she had been trained from infancy in the rudiments of grammar and the study of the other liberal arts, she tried by constant reflection to attain a perfect knowledge of divine things so that through the combination of her reading with her quick intelligence, by natural gifts and hard work, she became extremely learned. She read with attention all the books of the Old and New Testament and learned by heart all the commandments of God. To these she added by way of completion the writings of the church Fathers, the decrees of the Councils and the whole of ecclesiastical law.
> (Petroff, *Visionary Literature* 110)

This description of a nun's education does not differ significantly from the description written by the abbess Hugeberc of St Willibald's education (Petroff, *Visionary Literature* 93), nor do the writers express any surprise that these women should be so learned.

If, as Parkes has suggested, the Anglo-Norman nobility provide the earliest evidence of an extensive cultivated lay literacy, that is of communities of non-clerical readers interested primarily in books that offered edification and pleasure, women are from the beginning active participants in these communities. The best evidence we have of Anglo-Norman women's participation in these reading communities is through their direct patronage of literary texts, a subject I will explore more fully in the following section. Women figure prominently among the dedicatees of Anglo-Norman texts and in accounts of literary patronage.

There is also evidence that Anglo-Norman aristocrats were not simply patronizing writers, but actively reading them as well. The flurry of translations of Geoffrey of Monmouth's *History of the Kings of Britain*, first into Anglo-Norman (Wace) and then English (Layamon) at the end of the twelfth and beginning of the thirteenth centuries suggests that members of the aristocracy desired not merely to possess histories of England's ancient past, but to be able to read them in their own vernacular as well. The epilogue to Gaimar's *Estoire des Engleis* (*History of the English*) relates how, some time between 1135 and 1139, Walter Espec of Helmsley lent a copy of Geoffrey of Monmouth's *History of the Kings of Britain* to Ralph Fitz-Gilbert. He passed it along to his wife, Constance, who gave it to Gaimar, presumably to translate it (Parkes, 'Literacy' 556).

The fourteenth and fifteenth centuries saw a substantial increase and diversification in book ownership among women. The reading practices of nuns are especially well documented, showing that convent libraries, depending on how well endowed they were (and convents were always less well-funded than monastic institutions for men), would include liturgical, devotional and theological texts in Latin, French, and Middle English (Bartlett, *Male Authors* 7–8). Laywomen could and did receive training in both reading and writing and the libraries of laywomen also expanded dramatically during the later Middle Ages. The evidence from manuscript inscriptions and wills indicates that women had networks for acquiring books, that they passed them on to one another, and read them to each other, often within households (Riddy, 'Women Talking' 107; Meale, 'Laywomen' 138–9). Devotional and didactic reading seems to constitute the largest part of laywomen's reading. Indeed, Felicity Riddy has argued that the literary culture of devout laywomen was virtually indistinguishable from that of nuns. Cecily of York, for instance, modelled on monastic practice her custom of having a 'lecture' read to her during her meals (Riddy, 'Women Talking' 110–11).

Yet records also reveal women's eclectic tastes for books. Alice Chaucer, to cite just one example, seems to have had access to a wide variety of different kinds of books – several service books, a book of pricksong (written vocal music), didactic works in Latin, French and English, a copy of Christine de Pizan's *Livre de la Cité des Dames*, and the French romance of the 'quaterfitz Emond' (Meale, 'Laywomen' 134). The Vernon Manuscript (Oxford Bodleian Eng.poet. ms a.1), a book compiled at about the same time as Chaucer's *Canterbury Tales*, provides material evidence for female reading practices. It contains several devotional and didactic treatises, several miracles of the Virgin, and some poetry. It is written mostly in English with a little Latin and French. It is believed to have been written either for a community of nuns or a household of devout women (Riddy, 'Women Talking' 106).

What enables scholars to characterize women of the later Middle Ages as the 'first generation' of English female readers (Bartlett, *Male Authors* 7), however, is that literacy was no longer the sole preserve of the aristocratic class. Women of the middle as well as the upper classes could benefit from book ownership. Wills reveal a number of non-aristocratic women who bequeathed books (Bartlett, *Male Authors* 12–13). Claire Cross has documented extensive involvement with books among Lollard women of the artisanal class.[5] In the fifteenth century, Lollard women in several English cities took part in organizing book distribution. They taught Lollard doctrines, acquired Lollard books, and memorized Lollard tracts. One London Lollard woman was accused of being 'a great doctress'; another husband and wife of the same parish were called 'great reasoners in scripture' (Cross 377–8). These were not compliments but dangerous accusations of heresy directed at women whose gender and class affiliations afforded them little protection from powerful churchmen (see below, pp. 181–4).

Evidence of women's literacy from the fourteenth and fifteenth centuries suggests that reading was much more likely to be organized as a communal activity than as a private and individual experience. Even women who owned books but could not actually read them could have those books read aloud to a group of women. The Vernon Manuscript, a large book designed for public display, seems ideal for just such communal reading. The practice of collective reading has important implications for how we understand literacy; it may require a radical shift in what we mean by 'reading' and 'writing'. Communal reading, as Riddy argues, constitutes a 'textuality of the spoken as well as the written word' ('Women Talking' 111), in which literacy relies less on technical mastery of letters than on memory and learning, spreads less through individual acts of reading on the part of single women than by word of mouth among groups of women who may be connected by family ties, by residing in the same convent, or by geographical ties. To understand women's literary activity, then, we must understand more fully their family and social networks and relationships.[6] Whatever writing medieval women produced must have grown out of the kinds of reading communities to which they belonged. The existence of these reading communities also raises the intriguing question, explored in the next two sections, of whether we can designate as writers women who could not read or write in the way we technically understand these skills but who participated in a communal life structured by books. Before we can understand the role of the writer in the Middle Ages, however, we must understand the role of the patron.

AUTHORSHIP AND PATRONAGE

Our understanding of literary production is still very much governed by an author-centred paradigm that has dominated European literary criticism since the end of the eighteenth century. This paradigm assumes that the author is the sole creator and genius of his (or her) text. Feminist literary criticism, with its promotion of 'gynocriticism', has inherited the unstated assumptions that accompany this paradigm.[7] Even after the challenges posed by poststructuralist theory and the new historicism, literary criticism in the late twentieth century still very much revolves around the trinity of text/author/reader, often excluding other considerations as extraneous 'noise' or relegating them to mere 'background'. Only the text (enshrined by the New Criticism as a 'verbal icon') and its author matter; they can, and often are, examined in complete isolation from the cultures that produced them. More sophisticated criticism recognized the extent to which the text and author are realized only through the work of readers, which led to the articulation of reader-response criticism in the 1970s. But this 'reader' is always an abstracted and idealized reader, the reader the text calls forth; it is never the actual flesh and blood historical readers of the text, who are usually viewed as potential sources of textual contamination.

Roland Barthes challenged this set of assumptions in his 1971 essay 'From Work to Text', recognizing the extent to which such a view of authorship resulted from the specific material conditions of book production. In literary criticism, he argued, 'the author is regarded as the father and the owner of his work; literary research therefore learns to respect the manuscript and the author's declared intentions, while society posits the legal nature of the author's relationship with his work (these are the "author's rights" which are actually quite recent)' (78). Barthes argues for the need to replace this view of authorship, contingently produced by the exigencies of mass book production and copyright law, with a paradigm in which the text is constructed collaboratively with the reader: 'It is not that the author cannot "come back" into the Text, into his text; however, he can only do so as a "guest," so to speak' (78). How might Barthes's repudiation of the author's centrality help us to rethink authorship in the Middle Ages in ways that make women's contributions to literary culture more visible?

The common-sense view of authorship challenged by Barthes is the result of the mass production of books. The relative ease with which a printing press can produce an almost endless number of identical copies of a text encourages us to vest the author with sole power to determine the text's significance because, in order to produce identical copies, there needs to be some standard for identity, some original. In literary production after the invention of the printing press, the author became this standard. The physical presence of a writer, or, where impossible, a holograph manuscript, stands behind and guarantees the authenticity of any copy.[8] Any other contributions to a book's production – by editors and copy-editors, typesetters, layout artists or cover designers – are relegated to a secondary status. They can help to realize the author's intentions, but they cannot supplant them. Furthermore, the production of so many identical copies means that the author cannot possibly know all of the readers of her text personally, so that while the author is assumed to be an actual historical figure, 'the reader' comes to be idealized as an abstraction, a fiction.

This 'auteur' theory of literary production seems even less convincing for a period like the Middle Ages in which book production was so manifestly different. In a manuscript culture, book production is a much more obviously collaborative art, the physical book itself much more a work of art. According to Stephen Nichols:

> Book production involved such varied craftsman as those who made the vellum (or paper), the scribes who did the actual writing, the artists responsible for the miniatures, the decorated or historiated initials, and the rubrications that served both as legends for the miniature paintings and as an ordering structure in the visible text to help readers find their way through the finished book. (McCash, *Cultural Patronage* xii)

Any of these artisans may have had their own intentions, artistic or otherwise, which may or may not have coincided with those of the writer. The writer may have had little or no direct control over the work of these artisans. This is the frustration Chaucer expresses toward his scribe Adam when he wishes scabs upon him unless 'after my makyng thow wryte more trewe' (*Riverside Chaucer* 650). Literary criticism has conditioned us to think of scribes as desecrators of medieval texts, as sources of error and inauthenticity. A more Barthesian criticism would encourage us to think of them, along with the other artisans responsible for the production of books, as collaborators in the artistic process.

Because each copy of a text had to be laboriously written out by hand, far fewer copies of any work are likely to exist and they would find their way to many fewer readers. Because it is impossible to write out a copy of a book that is identical to the original, each copy will be not a copy, but a unique event. Our belief that a medieval text, like say Chaucer's *Canterbury*

Tales, is a single work is entirely the result of a fiction produced by the mass production of *editions* of that text which are made to seem identical by the suppression of manuscript variations in favour of what the editor thinks the author is most likely to have written (those editorial decisions are underwritten by the *auteur* theory of literary production I described above). In all likelihood, the conditions under which a medieval audience read (or heard read) such texts were quite different. There are at least fifty surviving manuscripts of *The Canterbury Tales*, each unique, each with its own networks of readers who could have read only the manuscript that came into their possession. Each manuscript has had its own history of circulation and use. In fact, this is the anxiety Chaucer expresses at the end of *Troilus and Criseyde*:

> And because there is such a great diversity
> In English and in the writing of our tongue
> So I pray to God that none miswrite thee
> Nor mismeter thee for default of tongue
> And wherever thou are read, or else sung
> That thow be understood, God I beseech!
> (*Riverside Chaucer* ll. 1793–9; translation mine)

These are the words of an author who knows that once he sends his writing forth – 'Go, litel bok, go, litel myn tragedye' (1786) – he thenceforth may visit it only as a guest, if at all. Chaucer is anxious about those readers he can never know, not because he expected to reach a mass audience as a modern author would, but because he cannot predict the path of his work's circulation; he can not know who will pass it on, who will copy it, which parts of it will be copied and how completely. Twentieth-century readers have simply chosen to ignore the implications of manuscript variation, reducing the complexities posed by several different versions of the same text, with many different 'authors', in favour of a fiction of standardization that fits better with our own aesthetics of authorship.

Because the production of books was so labour-intensive, however, requiring the orchestration of so many artisans and involving great expense, their production required some kind of co-ordination. It is unlikely that either authors or scribes would often produce books on speculation, in the hopes that some as yet unidentified person would pay for them. The whole system of reward for literary labour must have been very different than our own. Today authors maintain an illusion of independence through a capitalist system of rewards that pays authors royalties for their published work. This system tends to create distinct boundaries between the production of literary texts and their consumption. Writers at least appear free from the need to ingratiate themselves with any particular readers and their work appears to compete for rewards more or less equally within a marketplace of ideas. Writing can be conceived of as a job (and hence a social identity) for which one can be remunerated.

In the Middle Ages the labour of writing out a book – whether an original or a copy – was usually undertaken either at the direction of a patron or in the hopes of being rewarded by a potential patron, that is, it might be either the product of a patronage relationship or the means of initiating one. The task of co-ordinating book production and underwriting its expense was often assumed by the patron who commissioned the work, and who might supply materials (as for instance Boniface supplied Eadburga with the gold leaf to make him a copy of the epistles of St Paul), oversee, co-ordinate and reward the various artisans involved in its production. Nichols even suggests that the patron might be seen as a collaborator in the artistic process: 'The patron who commissioned a work and the author who wrote . . . were linked in a common effort to demonstrate divine purpose and thus human deviation from or adherence to that plan' (McCash, *Cultural Patronage* xiii). To be sure, the role of the patron would vary enormously from book to book. Cultural patronage, McCash argues, could take many forms: 'the support or backing of a prosperous or powerful benefactor for an artist, an artifact, or an institution in the form of gifts, money (sometimes in the form of a household position for an artist), political influence, personal encouragement, or assistance in helping to gain currency for a particular work, idea or project' (4). The term 'patronage' covers a wide range of practices and customs in which the relationship between the benefactor and artist – the patron and client – is often deliberately left ambiguous. Perhaps the Anglo-Norman writer Wace put it most succinctly when he wrote that writing is for those who can pay for it, those 'who have the incomes and the cash, because for them books are made' (Parkes, 'Literacy' 557).

Most scholars who study the role of patronage in the arts tend to isolate cultural patronage from the larger system of patron–client relations that organized social, political and economic relations at every level of society. However, we cannot fully understand the effects patronage had on the production of literary texts if we ignore the larger cultural work patronage performed. Patronage is an informal means of structuring social relations. Patron–client relations, according to S. N. Eisenstadt and Luis Roniger (*Patrons* 178–84), are particularistic and diffuse, rather than legal or contractual. Because they are personal relationships, they are entered into voluntarily and, as a result, are highly unstable; they can be terminated voluntarily by either party at any time. They differ from other forms of exchange in that they are not one-time exchanges, but involve long-term obligation and credit. And unlike forms of exchange that are impersonal and alienate individuals from one another, patronage draws individuals together, establishing personal bonds between them. Yet, despite this affective dimension, patron–client relations are marked by extreme inequality.

Because patronage relationships are unequal, patronage almost always involves the exchange of different kinds of resources. These resources might be material and economic (such as money, property or material wealth) or political and military (support, loyalty); often, however, they were intangible, but no less vital resources such as power, influence and status. Pierre Bourdieu uses the term 'symbolic capital' to describe the means by which the wealthy convert some of their disproportionate wealth into forms of prestige, status and social control through what are understood as voluntary acts of generosity or charity (like bestowing a gift on a courtier who wrote a history of one's family line). This symbolic capital could later be converted into labour and services, which, in turn, would generate more material wealth. Bourdieu argues that all precapitalist economies must 'extend economic calculation to *all* the goods, material and symbolic, without distinction, that present themselves as rare and worthy of being sought after in a particular social formation' (*Outline* 178). In such an economy it is not clear that artistic products are treated any differently from other sorts of economic and material wealth. Nor is it clear that, within such a system, the occupation of writer or author existed as a distinct social identity separable from other services a client might be called upon to perform. Status was not a function of one's occupation or role, but of one's proximity to powerful patrons.

Because women were rarely allowed to hold official positions of power in the Middle Ages, patronage relations of all types offered women an ideal informal mechanism through which they might exercise some effective personal power outside of the official institutions of medieval government. There is evidence that throughout the Middle Ages women were significant sources of political, economic and cultural patronage. This patronage is an important index of their status in the medieval world because one could not be in a position to be a patron unless one wielded some kind of power or influence worth gaining access to. Patronage networks, therefore, provide a means by which we can better understand women's informal exercise of power in medieval society, as well as their contributions to medieval culture. We have already seen the abbess Hild's sponsorship of the Anglo-Saxon poet Caedmon. The twelfth-century historian William of Malmesbury praised the patronage of Matilda, the first wife of Henry I: 'Her generosity becoming universally known, crowds of scholars, equally famed for verse and for singing, came over; and happy did he account himself who could soothe the ears of the queen by the novelty of his song' (*History* 453). Philippe de Thaon wrote a bestiary for Adeliza of Louvain, Henry's second wife (Parkes, 'Literacy' 556). Hugh of Fleury preferred to dedicate his *Historia ecclesiastica* to Adela, the daughter of William the Conqueror, rather than to 'illiterate princes who scorn the art of literature' (Krueger, *Female Readers* 268; Ferrante, *Glory of Her Sex* 97).

Eleanor of Aquitaine, wife of Henry II, was one of the greatest patrons of twelfth-century Europe; the network of patronage relations that Eleanor and her daughters established might be credited with virtually single-handedly spreading the ideology of courtly love, or *fin' amor*, throughout Europe. Eleanor was the granddaughter of Guillaume IX of Aquitaine, the first troubadour poet and the first to articulate the tenets of *fin' amor* (see above p. 18). Marie, Eleanor's eldest daughter by her first marriage to the French king, Louis VII, married the Count of Champagne and became patron to Chrétien de Troyes, author of several Arthurian romances, and Andreas Capellanus, whose *Art of Courtly Love* is an attempt to codify the practice (or fantasy) of courtly love. Her half-sister Matilda of Saxony is credited with introducing courtly love into her husband's German lands, while Leonor of England, another of Eleanor's daughters, made her husband's land in Castile a haven for troubadours (McCash, *Cultural Patronage* 15). The geographic dispersal of Eleanor and her daughters through marriage suggests something of the role women's cultural patronage played in international diplomacy. Many aristocratic and royal women were married off in alien lands where they neither spoke the language nor understood the local culture. As the cultural traditions and languages these women brought with them mingled with those of their new home, new styles and genres emerged. The spread of an indigenous legend like, say, that of King Arthur, from a marginal northern outpost like England to nearly all of Europe can perhaps only be explained by the patronage of foreign brides (Salter, *English and International* 19). These peripatetic brides were at least partly responsible for much of the international flavour of medieval culture, the heteroglossia of its languages and uniformity of its high culture.[9]

Patron–client relations are highly interpersonal relationships established between individuals or networks of individuals rather than between organized corporate groups. In the late Middle Ages it is possible to trace networks of patronage among aristocratic women that link generations of patrons along matrilineal lines. Karen Jambeck examines the intergenerational patronage networks associated with four fifteenth-century families – those of Elizabeth Berkeley, Countess of Warwick; Blanche, Duchess of Lancaster; Joan Fitz-Alan, Countess of Hereford; and Joan Beaufort, Countess of Westmoreland ('Patterns' 233–46). Together these women, their daughters, granddaughters and nieces patronized, among others, medieval poets of such stature as Chaucer, Hoccleve, Lydgate, Froissart and Deschamps. The patronage activities of these aristocratic ladies may also have encouraged the circulation of women's writing during the fifteenth century.

The example of Joan Beaufort (d. 1420) is instructive. Illegitimate daughter of John of Gaunt and Katherine Swynford, Beaufort lived as a wealthy widow for fifteen years after the death of her husband; most of her literary activities date from this period, including Hoccleve's dedication to her of a manuscript of his collected works (Jambeck, 'Patterns' 239). Both of Beaufort's daughters – Anne Neville, Duchess of Buckingham, and Cecily Neville, Duchess of York and mother of Edward IV – were also active literary patrons. Though no specific works have been traced to her patronage, Cecily's literary activities, which followed from her exceptional piety, are perhaps best known from her bequests, which included a significant number of books, including the writings of several religious women. She left a life of St Catherine of Siena and *The Revelations of St Mechtild* to her granddaughter Brigitte. She also left a book of the revelations of St Bridget to her granddaughter Anne de la Pole, who was prioress of Syon Abbey (Jambeck, 'Patterns' 240).

Anne Stafford, the granddaughter of Joan Beaufort, daughter of Anne Neville, and niece of the Duchess of York, also merits attention as a patron of women's writing. Carl Buhler identifies her as the 'high princess' to whom Stephen Scrope dedicated his translation of Christine de Pizan's *Epistle of Othea* (*Epistle* xix-xx). Also among Joan Beaufort's granddaughters was Margaret Beaufort, Countess of Richmond and Derby and mother of Henry VII, the first Tudor king. As befits the daughter of a family of women renowned not only for their wealth and influence, but for their piety and literary interests as well, Margaret is known as the translator of two devotional treatises, *The Imitation of Christ* and the *Mirror of Gold* (see below pp. 148–51).

The network of connections that link members of the Beaufort family to most of the significant literary activity of the fifteenth century suggests something of the way in which patronage shapes reading and writing as cultural activities within a manuscript culture. Unlike the impersonal and corporate relationships between writer and reader that characterize literature in an age of mechanical reproduction, manuscripts circulated within a much narrower field of patronage networks in which writers and readers knew one another, in which works might be commissioned for a single reader, and a book was an art object to be possessed. If a writer like Chaucer can imagine future unknown readers who might misunderstand his work it is only because he can imagine the circulation of his work through ever-widening circles of patronage; these networks proliferate and intersect with one another in the process, reshaping and reconfiguring a text that is essentially fluid, not fixed. The spread of books and literacy was always limited by the labour involved in copying a text by hand. Only a major change in the technology of book production itself could alter the relationship between writers and patrons. Because it instigated a major transformation of the relationship between the producers and consumers of literary texts, between writers and readers, the invention of the printing press provides a convenient endpoint for a study of the woman writer in the Middle Ages.

THE PRINTING PRESS

I would reiterate, however, problems I noted earlier associated with our practice of dividing literary study into periods and the unevenness of development that accompanies any epochal change. The book, as Natalie Zemon Davis has pointed out, is not merely a receptacle for ideas; it is also a 'carrier of relationships' (*Society and Culture* 192). The invention of the printing press by Gutenberg around 1440 would eventually transform the social relations of reading and writing, creating new modes of signifying that would distance author, reader and text from each other. But at the end of the fifteenth century the effect of this new technology was far from clear. When William Caxton, an English mercer who had served as governor of the English merchants in Bruges and learned the art of printing in Cologne, set up the first British press in Westminster in 1476 (Painter, *William Caxton* 24, 49–51, 82), his operation did not look all that different from the London bookshops that supplied manuscripts to the literate public. The books he chose to produce had all circulated in manuscript and those first printed books still looked very much like manuscripts.

Most importantly, Caxton was still very much dependent on the patronage system to maintain his livelihood. If Russell Rutter describes Caxton as 'a man of business, a prosperous merchant, a successful administrator, and a sometime diplomat' engaged in the high-risk endeavour of attempting to derive profit from a relatively new technology (Rutter, 'William Caxton' 469–70), he was by no means a full-blown capitalist whose only responsibility was to a mass-market readership. The feudal system of patronage minimized Caxton's financial risks, even if they could not supply all his capital needs. Caxton's patrons provided access to markets and to the foreign labour necessary for printing, as well as protection from enemies and competitors. In many of his prefaces Caxton gratefully acknowledges those supporters who offered him both material and symbolic capital (see Caxton, *Prologues and Epilogues*). For instance, in his 1489 translation of Christine de Pizan's *Fayttes of Armes and of Chivalry* he says that her book, 'was delivered to me, William Caxton, by the most Christian king and redoubtable prince, my natural and sovereign lord King Henry the VII, King of England and of France in his palace of Westminster'. The king 'desired and willed me to translate this said book and reduce it to our English and natural tongue and to print it so that every gentleman born to arms and all manner of men of war . . . should have knowledge of how they ought to behave in the acts of war' (Oxford Bodleian MS Douce 180, H ii^v; translation mine).

Some of Caxton's most influential patrons were women of the royal family. He began his printing career in Bruges in the service of Margaret, the Duchess of Burgundy, Edward IV's sister, for whom he translated the *Recuyell of the Histories of Troy*. Among his British patrons he also counted Edward's queen, Elizabeth Woodville, whose brother, Anthony Woodville, was his principal patron until his execution in 1483. During the reign of Richard III, the dowager queen was housed in the precincts of Westminster Abbey through the offices of its abbot, John Eastney, not far from where Caxton had his press, suggesting that Caxton's ties with the Woodville family did not end with Edward's and Rivers's deaths, though they ceased to be quite as conspicuous. After the Wars of the Roses, when Henry Tudor emerged victorious, Caxton enjoyed the patronage of the new Tudor monarch who married Elizabeth Woodville's daughter, Elizabeth of York.

WOMEN WRITERS?

Given the distinctiveness of practices associated with writing in the Middle Ages outlined above we must finally ask, what, for the purposes of this study, will constitute a woman writer? Like the other terms examined in this chapter – 'English' and 'writing' – the idea of 'woman' seems on its face self-evident. Yet on further inspection, it becomes more slippery. How does gender operate in the signatures of medieval texts? That the most prolific writer in the Middle Ages was anonymous was hardly an insurmountable problem for the study of English literature when we could simply assume that anything unsigned was authored by a man. Once we ask whether any women wrote during the Middle Ages the vast number of anonymous medieval texts begins to raise some daunting questions. How can anyone confirm the sex of a unsigned text's author? Arguments about an author's sex that are based on the text's contents are extremely unreliable. Just because a text deals with a woman's unrequited love or other subjects assumed to be part of some female realm of interest does not mean we can assume the text was written by a woman, any more than we can simply assume that texts about hunting or warfare were authored by men. After all, Juliana Berners seems to have written in graphic detail about how to dress a slain deer and Christine de Pizan wrote a manual on warfare. If they had not signed their work we would never dream of attributing texts about such subjects to women (and even these signatures have not gone unquestioned). The argument that a text was authored by a woman because it expresses 'feminine' sentiments simply will not hold. Literary cross-dressing is too easy.

In looking for women writers, the questions we asked, as evidenced, for instance, by the recent anthology, *Women and Literature in Britain, 1150–1500* (Meale 1993), tend to run: Did she really write it? Did she physically set quill to vellum? How can we be sure it is really hers if we do not have her autograph manuscript? Was she merely translating someone else? Was she translated by a man? Did anyone at the time know this text was written by a woman? The tests of authenticity we impose on women writers of the Middle Ages are far more stringent than any we impose on male writers (and by 'we' I mean feminist literary critics who have set themselves the task of recovering women writers). We would be as horrified to discover a man cross-dressing in a text as we would be to discover him in the women's lavatory.

But even proving a signed text was written by a woman is no easy task. As we have seen, medieval texts circulated in manuscript; the work is created anew each time it is copied. Each recension (the term for a copy of a manuscript) is a unique event. In a manuscript culture, authorship itself – even when the text is signed – is a doubtful concept. A writer cannot so easily 'own' her words and texts can circulate quite fluidly. One author might appropriate whole passages – even whole texts – from another without comment. Chaucer does this frequently. The twelfth-century Anglo-Norman writer Marie de France expresses just this anxiety in the epilogue to her *Fables*. As far as I know, she is the first medieval writer of either sex to express openly anxiety about plagiarism:

> I am from France, my name's Marie.
> And it may hap that many a clerk
> Will claim as his what is my work.
> But such pronouncements I want not.[10]

On the other hand, a scribe might attribute a text to a particular writer which she or he had not written. Christine de Pizan's *Moral Proverbs*, for instance, turn up in Richard Pynson's 1526 edition of Chaucer's poetry and are attributed to him. A significant portion of the texts attributed to the Sicilian physician Trotula – primarily those that deal with cosmetics – were almost certainly not written by her.

How then do we identify the woman writer? Do we require holographic evidence or can we count a woman as a writer if she dictated her words to a male amanuensis? How do we describe critically the relationship between the two? Given the frequency of both translation and appropriation of other writers' texts, can we count a woman translator as a woman writer? Can a book on medieval English women writers include works written by women in other languages and translated into English, perhaps by a man? How does this situation differ from a situation in which a man records the words of a woman who is illiterate? These are questions that will be explored in subsequent chapters which will take the broadest possible view of the woman writer.

NOTES

1. A rough translation of Bakhtin's *raznojazychie* meaning many-tongued (*Dialogic Imagination* 263).
2. Celtic languages like Welsh and Irish continued to be spoken throughout the Middle Ages, but their influence is largely limited to the marginal geographic areas inhabited by speakers of these languages. There was a flourishing tradition of Welsh poetry throughout the Middle Ages, much of it oral; little of it was committed to writing much before the eighteenth century (see Lloyd-Morgan, 'Women and their Poetry in Medieval Wales').
3. The author of the *Cursor Mundi*, a poem written in the northern dialect around 1300, says that he translated it from its original southern dialect because 'northern people . . . can read no other English' (Baugh and Cable, *History* 189).
4. At least the judge who married me assured me that, whatever kind of public ceremony we had, as long as we signed the licence, the marriage was legal.
5. Lollards were a group of fourteenth- and fifteenth-century English heretics, followers of John Wycliffe, who primarily believed that 'priests and bishops had no more authority than another layman that followeth the teaching and good conversation of the apostles' (Cross, 'Great Reasoners' 359). It is not difficult to see the appeal such beliefs might have for women, who were excluded from the ecclesiastical hierarchy, though McSheffrey, *Gender and Heresy*, argues against this thesis.
6. The essay by Karen Jambeck in *The Cultural Patronage of Medieval Women* (McCash 1996) is a model of the kind of scholarship necessary to elucidate these social networks of female readers.
7. Elaine Showalter ('Feminist Criticism' 1981) coined this term to describe the study of literary texts by women.

8. I am self-consciously avoiding using any gendered pronouns in these sentences. While historically the vast majority of writers described by the 'author-function' were men, and while it is quite likely that authorship itself is theoretically construed as a masculine concept, the continued use of the masculine pronoun to describe the author seems to perpetuate women's exclusions from the histories of authorship.

9. John Carmi Parsons describes the patronage activities of two foreign Plantaganet queens of the thirteenth century, Eleanor of Provence and Eleanor of Castille, both of whom were required to adapt to life in an alien land; see 'Of Queens'.

10. All references to Marie's fables are from the translation by Spiegel.

CHAPTER THREE

Genres of Women's Writing in the Middle Ages

A literary history and aesthetics built on the assumption of women's textual silence has serious consequences for any literary criticism. In her 1983 book, *How to Suppress Women's Writing*, Joanna Russ writes that 'A mode of understanding literature which can ignore the private lives of half the human race is not "incomplete"; it is distorted through and through' (11). In the previous chapter I have tried to suggest that the distortions created by such an androcentric literary tradition go beyond the missing lives of half the population of medieval Britain. It also flattens out the linguistic and cultural diversity of medieval England; projects backward in time our own obsessions with nationalism, while obscuring the kinds of imagined communities that were important to medieval people; promotes narrow views of literary genre that perpetuate our own aesthetic tastes at the cost of obscuring medieval aesthetics; and encourages a literary scholarship that privileges the author over the reader as the source of meaning in the text.

In an investigation of the hidden transcript of medieval women's writing, the various excuses that have prevented serious consideration of writing by women and resulted in such distortion will provide some useful guidelines and important caveats. Because a hidden transcript will, by its very nature, be ephemeral, the most serious obstacle to recovering a tradition of women's writing in the Middle Ages is the fragmentary nature of the historical record. Even in the public transcript, for every medieval text that has survived, we have to assume that at least twenty have disappeared without trace. Under the best conditions, working with medieval literature is much like trying to put together a jigsaw puzzle with only about one-fifth of the pieces. Since women's writing is even less likely to have survived than men's, we must always wonder when we find a text by a woman how much like it has simply been lost. We must continually bear in mind how fragmentary, incomplete, and hence tenuous our reconstructions of medieval life and letters must be.

The most frequently encountered and perhaps obvious argument against women's authorship is that women lacked access to both the education and leisure necessary to write. I hope in the last two chapters I have been able to show that at least some women – granted, mostly privileged women – were able to obtain both. Armed with more information about women's lives and educations than we have ever had before, thanks to recent feminist scholarship in medieval history, literary critics are now poised to consider Virginia Woolf's suggestion, made over half a century ago, that 'Anon, who wrote so many poems without signing them, was often a woman' (*Room* 51). At the same time, the burden of proof is on anyone wishing to suggest female authorship for anonymous texts. In following up on Woolf's proposition, we must avoid, on the one hand, the kind of circular logic that argues that women most likely did not write these anonymous works because most of the signed texts are by men and, on the other hand, veering off into wild speculation.

Where texts clearly bear women's signatures there have been attempts to rationalize away women's authorship by arguing that a man might use a woman's name to increase the credibility of his representations of female experience.[1] Another ploy is to dismiss women's texts as second-rate – bad literature, doggerel, hack writing – or to claim that they are not literature at all but unsophisticated theology, naive piety or corporeal rather than transcendental mysticism. Even when a writer like Marie de France is admitted to the literary canon, she is neutralized as anomalous, one of a kind. To do so, her work must be isolated from the historical processes that engendered it, from the alliances, associations, conflicts, struggles and debates with predecessors and contemporaries, as well as the material networks that govern the production and distribution of literary texts. Precisely because the medieval woman writer looks much less like an anomaly when she is immersed in her own historical time, close study of the genres of women's writing is essential. But we must understand genre not as a set of timeless, abstract and universal categories of literature, but as historical processes in their own right, as grids of intelligibility[2] that organize all the activities of the literary and cultural field at any given historical moment.

LYRIC POETRY

The earliest example of a lyric poem written by an English woman is found in the correspondence of St Boniface. In a letter written to her kinsman, St

Boniface, sometime after 732, Leoba, an Anglo-Saxon nun of Wimborne, sends a Latin poem composed 'according to the rules of poetic art, not trusting to my own presumption, but trying only to exercise my little talents and needing your assistance.' She writes:

> The omnipotent Ruler who alone created everything,
> He who shines in splendor forever in His Father's kingdom,
> The perpetual fire by which the glory of Christ reigns,
> May preserve you forever in perennial right. (Boniface 60)

It may be, as the poem's translator suggests, that these are awkward verses written by a beginning student of poetry (60); they suggest, however, that the education of eighth-century Anglo-Saxon nuns included instruction in versification. Most likely Leoba had been studying Aldhelm's treatise on the writing of Latin verse, which, during this period, would have been the standard work on Latin poetry (Leyser, *Medieval Women* 31). She tells Boniface that she has learned the art of poetry under the direction of the abbess Eadburga, which suggests as well that women were teaching other women to write poetry.

The existence of these Latin lines so felicitously preserved in St Boniface's correspondence lends credence to the belief that at least two poems in the corpus of Anglo-Saxon poetry may have been written by women. Two of the elegies of *The Exeter Book*, 'The Wife's Lament' and 'Wulf and Eadwacer', have female narrators, a fact which has led to some speculation that the poets were also women. If women in Anglo-Saxon monasteries were writing complicated Latin epistles, versifying and copying manuscripts, then it is at least feasible that some small portion of the anonymous body of Anglo-Saxon poetry might have been the work of an unrecorded female poet. The prominence of aristocratic women within Anglo-Saxon religious institutions suggests that accomplished women were not unknown in pre-Christian secular courts.

Uncertain authorship, however, is not the only, or even the most pressing problem confronting the reader of these two poems, which are perhaps the most difficult and enigmatic poems in the corpus of Anglo-Saxon poetry. It is not easy to figure out what these poems are even about. Without context, of course, it is impossible to tell whether any text is a poem or a laundry list. Our understanding of how to read a poem in a particular culture is totally dependent on our understanding of that culture and, while we know something about the day-to-day lives of aristocratic men in Anglo-Saxon culture, what we know about women's daily lives outside of monasteries comes at best from the fragmentary evidence of cemeteries and the exceedingly brief glimpses we get of women in poems like *Beowulf* (Leyser, *Medieval Women* 3–18). We know that 'The Wife's Lament' and

'Wulf and Eadwacer'[3] are poems because they appear in a manuscript (*The Exeter Book*) along with other texts we call poems ('The Wanderer' and 'The Seafarer').[4] We infer that the narrators are female because the narrators refer to themselves using feminine adjectives and pronouns. Line 1 of 'The Wife's Lament,' for instance, 'Ich þis giedd wrece bi me ful geomorre / minre sylfe sið' ('I make this song of my deep sadness, of my own lot'), contains two feminine adjectives (*geomorre* and *minre*) and a feminine pronoun (*sylfe*) (Gordon, *Anglo-Saxon Poetry* 87; Desmond, 'Voice of Exile' 583–4). Beyond the basic identification of the narrators, however, it is difficult to tell what is going on in the two poems, though the identification of the speaker's gender will activate particular assumptions about the events the poems are describing.

If we assume that the narrator of 'The Wife's Lament' is a woman, the poem appears to be a lament by a wife who has been separated from her 'lord' (husband), perhaps by the kind of blood feud that is described in *Beowulf*: 'The man's kinsmen began to plot in secret thought to part us, so that we should live most wretchedly, most widely sundered in the world' (Gordon, *Anglo-Saxon Poetry* 87). She describes her persecution at the hands of her husband's enemies and her current exile: 'They bade me dwell in the forest-grove under the oak tree in the earth-cave' (87). The poem ends with her hope that her enemy will know the loneliness of exile and a reminder of the suffering of her 'friend'.

'Wulf and Eadwacer' is, if anything, even more obscure, full of difficult words and phrases and offering few contextual cues to the events being described, though at least one critic notes that 'its articulation of an apparently unadulterated [and adulterous] sexual passion is startlingly vivid, (Bradley, *Anglo-Saxon Poetry* 365). The speaker, once again identified as female by the feminine adjectives *reotugu* (line 10) and *seoce* (line 14, Desmond, 'The Voice of Exile' 584), mentions two men – Wulf and Eadwacer. Eadwacer appears to be her husband; she has perhaps been married against her will to cement a political alliance:

> When the warlike man wound his arms about me,
> It was pleasure to me, yet it was also pain.

Wulf appears to be her lover:

> Wulf is on an island, I on another. . . .
> I waited for my Wulf with far-wandering yearnings,
> When it was rainy weather and I sat weeping. . . .
> Wulf, my Wulf, my yearnings for thee
> Have made me sick, (91)[5]

Much of the poem's power comes from its form, which 'embodies its motifs of like and unlike, common and separate' (Gordon, *Anglo-Saxon*

Poetry 91) through symmetry and parallelism. The poem ends with an inscrutable and chilling statement of melancholy and loss:

> They can easily sunder that which was never joined together,
> The song of us two together. (91)

Do these lines refer to the joining of the two lovers or of husband and wife? This double separation leaves the narrator utterly alone in her misery, like the narrator in 'The Wife's Lament', 'an exile from the center of power and the central sources of identity in her culture' (Desmond, 'Voice of Exile' 585).

Marilynn Desmond has proposed that feminist criticism of these two 'female-voiced' elegies needs to focus less on the gender of the author and more on the gender of the text ('Voice of Exile' 577). This is a solution that is unlikely to satisfy everyone, but it does prompt us to ask what stakes are involved in identifying the voice of the poem as female. Scholars continue to propose textual emendations to the manuscript that write out the female voices altogether. 'The Wife's Lament' has been read as an allegory for the city of Jerusalem (Bradley, *Anglo-Saxon Poetry* 382–3) or, once the text is emended to get rid of feminine adjectives and pronouns, as a complaint by an exiled thane in the vein of 'The Wanderer' (Desmond, 'Voice of Exile' 575). 'Wulf and Eadwacer' has been variously read allegorically, as a riddle, a charm against wens, and the dream of a female dog (Leyser, *Medieval Women* 64). What is it about these two poems that so disturbs scholars that they are willing to resort to 'perverse and willful misreadings' (Desmond, 'Voice of Exile' 575) to eliminate the female voice altogether? Could it be that the connection between the lyric 'I' and the poet is so strong in medieval lyrics that to admit to a female speaker would be tantamount to an admission of female authorship, or at least to female authority? It has been fashionable since the New Criticism to avoid the fallacy of identifying the narrative voice of a poem with the poet, but I wonder if medieval readers and writers were as likely to make such a fine distinction. This is not, of course, any kind of proof of female authorship, but it does raise intriguing questions about what assumptions readers of the *Exeter Book* elegies might make about authorship.

The body of lyric poetry by English women during the Middle Ages is so sparsely scattered throughout the period and so tenuously attributed that it is difficult to make any generalizations about them as a group. For this reason, it will be useful at least to note the lyrics produced by the *trobairitz*, a group of some twenty Provençal noblewomen who wrote between 1150 and 1250. Only in Provence do we have evidence that the lyric forms of courtly love poetry described in Chapter 1 were adapted by women to express their own perspectives. Recent criticism of these lyrics reminds us of certain recurrent stereotypes about women's poetry as therapeutic outburst rather than carefully constructed works of art. Women's poetry focuses on the emotional, subjective – their joy and suffering in love. Meg Bogin, for instance, prefaces her 1976 edition and translation of the *trobairitz* poems by stating that unlike the male troubadours, 'who created a complex poetic vision, the women wrote about their own intimate feelings. . . . This gives the women's poems a sense of urgency that makes them more like journal entries than carefully constructed works of art' (*Women Troubadours* 67–8). This emphasis on emotion miniaturizes women's poetry, perpetuating, even in feminist criticism, a literary double standard by which male poet's works are judged and canonized by so-called objective artistic criteria, while women's poetry is deemed emotional and personal, more like a diary than poetry.

The lyric poetry produced by medieval women ought to be examined both for its formal, artistic features and for the ways in which it participates in the various social institutions that shape gender relations in the medieval world. All courtly poets – whether male or female – shared and contested the same cultural representations, the same language, the same poetic forms. It is the interplay among representation, language and form that creates genres, understood not merely as formal, aesthetic systems of classification but as agents of social and cultural behaviours – producers as well as products of social meanings. Women's poetic self-representations, no less than men's, emerged from within a genre (the lyric) that, in the Middle Ages, promoted a very narrow range of social relations between the sexes. To understand the lyric poetry produced by women within the generic conventions of courtly love, it is not necessary to view women as more emotional and less concerned with artistic convention than their male counterparts. It is only important to understand that aristocratic men and women occupied different ideological positions within an intricate web of social relationships that courtly love attempts to represent. Those different positions will occasion very different rhetorical strategies.[6]

The poetry of *fin' amor* may strike the modern reader as clichéd, repetitive, even hackneyed. *Fin' amor* expresses itself through an elaborate and ritualized literary language which is less the possession of any one poet than of the culture it represents. It was one means by which members of the medieval aristocracy could articulate their relations to one another. Central to the courtly poem's function is its formal construction. The form of the poem itself is a complex system of signs and we cannot claim to have historicized the courtly lyric without understanding the kinds of meanings encoded in their elaborate forms.

The poetic tradition of the troubadours was specific to the south of France and had pretty much died out by the middle of the thirteenth century. But the ideals, themes and vocabulary of *fin' amour* spread throughout Europe, reaching northern France, Spain, Portugal, Italy, Germany and England, due in no small part to the efforts of Eleanor of Aquitaine, granddaughter of the first troubadour, Guillaume IX. As we have seen, Eleanor's journey north traces the movements of courtly love to England. Her daughter from her first marriage to Louis, King of France, was the patron of Chrétien de Troyes, writer of several Arthurian romances, and Andreas Cappellanus, who wrote the Latin treatise *De Amore* (translated as *The Art of Courtly Love*). Subsequently Eleanor became the wife Henry II of England, bringing her artistic tastes to Henry's Anglo-Norman court. As it spread out from Provençal, courtly love became abstracted from the specific set of patronage relationships that engendered it, the triangulated desire that linked poet, lady (*la dompna*) and overlord (often depicted in troubadour poetry as the *jealos*, or jealous husband). It mingled with other new ideas, specifically the Church's insistence after the twelfth century that the basis of marriage was the mutual consent of husband and wife (Duby, *Knight*) which, in literature if not in life, led to a belief that marriage should be companionate, based on mutual affection between husband and wife, rather than on political expediency. This mixture of the idealizations of courtly love and the ideal of the companionate union of mutually consenting lovers characterizes English versions of courtly love.

We know of no other women writers of Middle English lyrics until the fifteenth century, but it is important to remember that all but a very few Middle English lyrics are anonymous, circulating primarily in manuscripts that were intended for an intimate circle of patrons and friends rather than a reading public, and that until the fourteenth century, French, not English, was the primary literary language among cultivated readers (Richard the Lionheart, for instance, wrote several courtly lyrics in French). Several fifteenth- and early sixteenth-century manuscripts contain poems which could be described as 'female-voiced' and which Alexandra Barratt has argued could have been written by women (*Women's Writing* 262–3). Only three of these are attributed to women in the manuscripts themselves. Oxford Bodley Rawlinson MS. C. 86, an early sixteenth-century collection of poetry, much of it by Chaucer and Lydgate, contains a hymn to Venus which ends 'Finis quod Quene Elyzabeth'. Barratt identifies the author with Elizabeth Woodville, wife of Edward IV and sister of Anthony Woodville (*Women's Writing* 275), although it might also be her daughter, Elizabeth of York, who married Henry VII. A manuscript compiled by the fifteenth-century amateur bibliophile John Shirley (Bodley MS Ashmole 59) attributes a hymn to the Virgin to 'an holy Ankaresse of Maunsffeld' (*Women's Writing* 277). Finally, a Book of Hours in the British Library (Arundel 310) contains on its final page a macaronic poem (written in more than one language) which begins: 'the prayer of Eleanor Percy, Duchess of Buckingham'. This translation of the Latin hymn 'Gaude virgo, mater Christi', had been written out by Anne Arundel, Eleanor's sister (*Women's Writing* 279).

The themes of most of the 'female-voiced' lyrics in Barratt's collection are commonplace in fifteenth-century versions of courtly love; many can be seen in Chaucer's lyrics. Stability and instability in love are frequent subjects, as in this charming short poem found in a sixteenth-century collection of poems written in different hands (Bodley Rawlinson C. 813):

> For to one I have my troth plighted
> And another has my heart in hold.
>
> He that hath my troth plight,
> He dwelled with me a while.
> But he that holds my heart,
> I will him never beguile. (*Women's Writing* 264; translation mine)

Others deal with the joys and pains of love, as in this lyric from the Findern manuscript:

> My woeful heart, thus clad in pain
> Does not know what to do or say
> Long absence grieves me so. (270; translation mine)

What, for Barratt, distinguishes these female-voiced lyrics from countless other anonymous lyrics is 'a stoic acceptance of abandonment' that contrasts with the 'unbridled despair' that marks 'women's laments' that, she argues, are more likely to have been authored by men (262).

But what is perhaps more remarkable about these lyrics is their range of experimentation with verse form, which once again calls into question the stereotype that women's poetry issues from some emotional *cri de coeur*. Writing almost a century before the iambic pentameter line would become the standard for English verse, these poets were free to try out a number of different poetic forms. Eleanor Percy's bilingual prayer to the virgin, for instance, uses a four-line stanza.

> Gaud,* Virgin of all humility,   *praise
> Showing to us thy son's humanity
> When he without pain was born of thee
>   *In pudoris lilio.** (280)   *in the lily of chastity

The first three lines of each stanza, written in English, have a single rhyme and vary between four and five stresses per line. The fourth short line is always in Latin and rhymes on *-o*.

Queen Elizabeth's hymn to Venus is another good example of experimentation in verse form. It uses a seven-line rhyme royal stanza (rhyming ababbba) similar to the type Chaucer frequently uses.

Myne herte is set uppon a lusty pynne
I praye to Venus of good continuaunce
ffor I rejoyse the ease that I am in
Delyverd from sorow annexed to plesaunce,
Of all comfort havyng habundaunce.
This joy and I, I trust, shal never twynne.
Myne hert is set uppon a lusty pynne[7]

The first line of the poem is difficult since the meaning of 'set uppon a lusty pynne' is not entirely clear. It is possible the poet is using an image of a musical pitch to convey her merry mood (Barratt, *Woman's Writing* 275). In this unique elaboration of the sestina, not only are the first and last line of each stanza the same, but the second line of the first stanza becomes the first line of the second stanza, the third line of the first stanza becomes the first line of the third stanza, and so on throughout the poem. This form allows the poem to create balance and contrast throughout between two emotional and two temporal states – past pain and present joy; the poet is 'delivered from sorrow' at the same time she is 'annexed to pleasure'. This balanced antithesis between joy and sadness is repeated throughout the poem in phrases like '*Thus departing from* all sorrowful disease / *Now stand* I whole far from all grievance' (l. 223), 'My *gladness* is such there grieveth me no *pain*' (227), and '*My* joys are double where *others* be but thin' (249). The first phrase contrasts past and present states (thus / now), the second different emotional states (gladness / pain), the third, the poet's emotional state with that of unspecified 'others'.

One of the ironies of this poem, which must have been apparent to the poem's original audience, is the play between the poet's exalted status as a queen and the position she assumes as humble supplicant to Venus. Elizabeth picks up on the metaphors of patronage that run through the courtly love tradition; she gives to Venus 'My heartfelt service with my homage' (221), 'And so to serve never shall I cease' (228). Elizabeth, who as Queen of England was patron to all her subjects, represents herself in the more lowly position of client to Venus. She remarks: 'That all my joy I set, as a rightful possession / To please [Venus], in my own simple capacity' (ll. 234–5). In this last phrase, the referent of the phrase 'aught of ryght' is not entirely clear. Does the joy she possesses belong by right to herself or to Venus?

The poem's celebration of joy, ease and pleasure seems somewhat at odds with the more typical medieval discourse about fortune.

ffor I am stabely set in suche a place
Wher beaute cresith* & euer wellyth grace**   *increases   **flows constantly
Whiche is ful famous & borne of nobil kyn
This joy and I I trust shal neuer twyn,

The vocabulary of the final lines can hardly fail to call to mind a whole medieval discourse about the instability of good fortune, the transience of youth, beauty and grace, and the brevity of present joys, yet the poem ends with the hope that the poet will never be separated from her joy.

A survey of lyrics written by medieval Englishwomen would be incomplete without a brief glance at the lyric poetry of the non-English speaking peoples of the British Isles. Throughout the Middle Ages, the Welsh maintained a distinct language and poetic traditions which were quite alien to the invaders — Anglo-Saxons, Vikings and Normans — who would attempt to subdue them. No doubt geographical isolation enabled the Welsh to preserve much of their own language and culture in the face of foreign invasion. Several characteristics of medieval Welsh poetry, however, increase the difficulty of finding any women poets. The difficulty of the Welsh language means that Old Welsh poetry tends to be inaccessible to all but a handful of specialized scholars. Until recently those scholars have not been particularly interested in speculating about female authorship. Because the poetry itself tends to be highly technical verse, written in strict metres with many more formal rules about rhyme, alliteration, and assonance than is usual for even the most formalistic English verse, it seemed reasonable to assume that women would not have had access to formal training in the strict metres (Lloyd-Morgan, 'Women and their Poetry' 188). Finally, for all Welsh poetry there is almost always a gap, sometimes of centuries' duration, between the composition of a poem and the date of the earliest manuscript, a gap which makes dating and attribution of poems somewhat fanciful, reliant on oral tradition rather than scholarly evidence. Perhaps because of its marginal status vis-à-vis English, Welsh poetry came to be committed to writing late, and women's poetry even later than men's. While it is possible, once again, that some portion of the body of anonymous Welsh poetry may have been written by women, Lloyd-Morgan cites only two women who are identified as having written Welsh poetry before 1500. The earliest identified woman poet is Gwenllian ferch Rhirid Flaidd, who probably wrote during the last decades of the twelfth century. Her name and the one poem attributed to her most likely survive because she is the daughter of a male poet, Rhirid Flaidd. Yet even the attribution of the one surviving poem is uncertain because it is not contained in manuscript collections of poetry by her contemporaries and no manuscript copies of it exist before the sixteenth century (Lloyd-Morgan, 'Women and their Poetry' 185). A more promising figure is the late fifteenth-century poet, Gwerful Merchain, to whom at least thirty-eight poems, most likely written between 1462 and 1500, have been attributed. This is a substantial *oeuvre* for a medieval woman poet. Furthermore her poems must have considerable artistic merit since after her death scribes confused them with those of the greatest Welsh poet, the fourteenth-century Dafydd ap Gwilym. Merchain's poetry covers a wide range of subjects, including religion and love. They range from the sublime – her *cywydd* to Jesus – to the ridiculous – an *englyn* to her maid while shitting. Yet, despite her considerable reputation as a poet, to date no published editions or translations of her poems are available.[8]

DREAM VISIONS

The anonymous fifteenth-century dream visions, *Floure and Leafe* and *Assembly of Ladies*, draw upon the conventional form of the allegorical love vision popularized by French poets like Guillaume de Lorris and Jean de Meun (in the *Roman de la Rose*), and later Guillaume Machaut, Jean Froissart and Eustache Deschamps, as well as by Chaucer (in *Parliament of Foules* and *House of Fame*) and Lydgate. The generic features of such poems include a narrator, who is either unhappy or unlucky in love and finds himself (almost always) wandering in a stylized landscape where he encounters allegorical figures who engage in a debate, usually over some issue having to do with love. The aesthetic focus in such poems is on the description of the landscape and its inhabitants and the debate itself.

The Assembly of Ladies is included anonymously in three fifteenth-century manuscripts, but in William Thynne's 1532 edition of Chaucer's works it is attributed to Chaucer. Thomas Speght also attributes both poems to Chaucer in his 1598 edition; because no manuscript copies have survived, Speght's edition of *Floure and Leafe* is the earliest extant version of that poem. The attribution to Chaucer is hardly surprising given the fifteenth century's veneration of that poet. Both poems imitate characteristic Chaucerian genres, themes and metrical features (the rhyme royal stanza for instance). Both contain a large number of Chaucerian echoes. For instance, one need scan only the opening lines of *Floure and Leafe* to recognize the extent of the poet's indebtedness to Chaucer:

> Whan that Phebus his chaire of gold so hie
> Had whirled up the sterry sky aloft,
> And in the Boole★ was entred certainly;   ★Taurus, the Bull
> When shores sweet of raine discended soft. (1–4)[9]

Even readers only cursorily familiar with Chaucer will recognize the echoes of the opening lines of the *Canterbury Tales* from the 'whan that . . .' structure of the opening dependent clause through the references to the Zodiac to the 'sweet showers'

What distinguishes these two poems from others of its kind (including Chaucer's own dream visions) is their use of a female narrator, which has led critics to an impasse over authorship which, as Derek Pearsall has remarked, no amount of ingenuity could solve (3). Walter Skeat was the first to suggest that both poems were written by the same woman, most likely because he believed that there could not have been more than one female author in fifteenth-century England (Skeat 111–12). His argument was criticized by G.L. Marsh a few years later. More recently, Derek Pearsall (31) believes that at least the *Assembly of Ladies* was unlikely to have been written by a woman. Julia Boffrey, disdaining 'the more recent sentimental feminism which [seeks] to identify a woman's mind behind every expression of strong personal feeling' (174), argues that it is more fruitful to think of these texts as pseudo-Chaucerian love visions than to insist on female authorship. Contemporary feminist critics like Alexandra Barratt ('Sexual Difference'; *Women's Writing* 262) and Jane Chance ('Christine de Pizan'), though more cautious than an earlier generation of critics, still think they are the work of women.

Since it seems unlikely that there will ever be sufficient evidence to determine whether the authors of these two female-voiced poems were male or female, perhaps it would be more useful to stop looking *through* the sexual ambiguity in these works – trying to resolve it – and instead look *at* it. Unlike the female-voiced lyrics examined above, we might speak of the authors of *Floure and Leafe* and *Assembly of Ladies* as 'epicene writers', establishing a third term which is not a category or sex in itself, but a space of possibility that puts sexual identity into play.[10] In these poems, the epicene is not simply the result of our own lack of information about the author's identity; rather it constitutes the characteristic poetics of these two texts. These poems present us with a conundrum of textual sexuality.

Floure and Leafe perhaps best illustrates my argument. Its most obviously epicene feature is its narrator, a fact I discovered quite serendipitously. Reading it in the context of arguments over its female authorship, I was struck by how late in the poem it is when we discover the narrator is female, the feature most often cited as the best evidence for the poem's female authorship (Barratt, 'Sexual Difference' 4–5). The textual evidence for the narrator's gender occurs only in line 462 of a 595-line poem, roughly four-fifths of the way into the poem, when one of the ladies in the Leaf retinue addresses the narrator as 'My doughter', an apostrophe rather casually dropped into an explanation of the scene she has just witnessed, but one that is repeated often enough to call the reader's attention to it (four times in the last 100 lines). For most of the poem we do not know that the narrator is female. The poet's withholding of this detail seems a deliberate act of suspension whatever the actual gender of the author may have been. It encourages the reader to imagine the narrator as a man, for the simple reason that virtually all the instances of this genre have male narrators. Since it is the function of genre to create expectations, without strong textual encouragement to see the gender of the narrator differently (such as one gets at the beginning of *Assembly of Ladies* where the narrator identifies her sex in the first stanza), readers will assume, based on past experience with the genre, that the speaker is a man.

The poem invokes all of the generic markers of allegorical dream vision, though it has neither allegory nor dream (evidence that the poem confounds our expectations in other ways). However, it does concern itself primarily with vision, not only with the series of tableaux describing the retinues of the Flower and Leaf that constitutes its visions, but with a way of seeing that in all other poems of its type is strongly associated with the masculine. The poem opens with a conventional *locus amoenus*. The narrator is unable to sleep, takes a walk, and happens upon a 'pleasant arbor'. Much of the poem is taken up with the description of this arbor and its occupants: the company of the Flower representing the transitoriness of love and beauty and that of the Leaf representing perseverance and fidelity in love.[11] The proprietary eye / I (here I invoke the homonym) that arranges and orders the tableaux before us is familiar enough from the work of Guillaume de Lorris, Jean de Meun, Chaucer, Machaut and others. This eye / I – this subjectivity – is always strongly linked to the poet's self-fashioning. The objectifying gaze in this genre is almost always male (the only counter-example I can think of is Christine de Pizan whose visions may have influenced the poem; see Chance, 'Christine de Pizan'). The poem's withholding of any markers identifying the narrator's textual gender creates sexual ambiguity. We will 'read' the details of the tableaux in one way if the poet / narrator is a man, another if it is a woman. The discovery in line 462 that the narrator is female requires a revision of all that has come before it. This reading of the poem is not simply an artifact of the way in which we encounter the poem as belated twentieth-century readers. A fifteenth-century reader reading this poem privately might experience the same shock at line 452. But more likely this poem's original readers would encounter it as members of an audience hearing the poem read aloud, either by the author or someone else. In a culture in which poets were likely to read their works to an audience, the gap between poet and narrator would be harder to maintain. The poet's material body would certainly have influenced the audience's responses to the poem.

The Assembly of Ladies is generally considered to be inferior in quality to *Floure and Leafe*. Pearsall calls it the work of a hack, pointing to the monotonous regularity of its versification and the 'threadbare repetition of tags and conventional phrases'. He concludes from this that 'women had occasion and good reason to write in the fifteenth century, but not like this' (31). However, though it does not play with generic expectations as skilfully as *Floure and Leafe*, the poem has its own epicene features which are not without interest. In the poem, the narrator, one of a company of five 'ladyes' and four 'gentil wymmen' tells a knight about her dream in which she is summoned by a 'gentil womman' named Perseverance, who identifies herself as Usher of the Chamber to Lady Loyalty, to appear together with her company dressed in blue before Lady Loyalty to present their grievances. The poem is taken up with describing the preparations for attending the assembly, the arrangements when they arrive, and the various functionaries of Lady Loyalty's entourage. It climaxes in the presentation of the company's 'bills' or petitions, which seek redress for grievances they have suffered in love. As is the case in many dream visions involving assemblies or debates (Chaucer's *Parlement of Foules* comes to mind), Loyalty's judgement is postponed to some unspecified future date and the narrator wakes up.

The most interesting feature of the poem is its casting of Lady Loyalty's entourage in administrative court positions that are usually occupied by men. As C.S. Lewis wrote in *Allegory of Love*, what the poet seems to want to describe is 'no inner drama with loyalty as its heroine, but the stir and bustle of an actual court' (249). Unlike *Floure and Leafe*, however, which presents the two companies of Flower and Leaf as elaborate court entertainments – as *play* – *The Assembly of Ladies* depicts the presentation of the women's petitions as the *work* of the court, the administration of justice. The positions described in the poem correspond to real household positions in fifteenth-century courts that carried distinctions of rank and privilege that would be carefully observed among the men who held them. Loyalty's entourage includes an Usher of the Chamber, who would look after food and service, a Marshal of the Hall, who would handle the arrangements for ceremonies and banquets, a Secretary who would collect and read the bills presented, a purveyor, a chancellor and a chamberlain. Indeed Pearsall argues that the entire presentation of the 'bills' suggests that the poet is trying to emulate contemporary legal procedures. The bill, according to Pearsall, would be the 'initiatory action of all procedures in equity'. It would consist of a statement of complaint and a petition for redress. The statement would be 'vague in point of fact but vehement in presenting the enormity of the offense' (Pearsall 58). The poet certainly seems to capture the convoluted syntax that marks such petitions:

> Nothing so dear as death will come to me
> As a final end to my sorrows and pain;
> What should I desire more, do you think,
> If you knew it all certainly beforehand
> I believe you would; and to tell you plainly,

Without her help that holds the remedy to all
I can not think it may long endure.

And as for my loyalty, it has been tested well –
To tell the truth, it can be no more –
For a long time and I have suffered everything
In patience and kept it all in silence;
Of her goodness beseeching her therefore
That I might have my thanks in such a way
As I deserve from Justice. (ll. 694–707)

Indeed the loosely strung participles are virtually impossible to translate grammatically and several critics have commented on the difficulty of figuring out the referents of the various pronouns in this passage (Barratt, 'Sexual Difference' 19–20). Pearsall has suggested that stylistically the bills are much like the bills presented to the King's Council (58). *The Assembly of Ladies* casts its female personae in decidedly male occupations.

Even if we can never finally decide whether these two poems were written by women, both poems present in closing a portrait of the woman writer since both poems close with the narrator describing how she put her experiences into a book (Barratt, 'Sexual Difference' 15). *Floure and Leafe*, for instance, ends with the narrator taking leave of the lady of the Leaf retinue and returning home,

And put all that I had seen in writing,
In hopes of support from those who desire to read.
O little book, you are so ignorant,
How dare you put yourself into the throng for fear?
It is a wonder that you don't turn red,
Since you do not know who might behold
Your rude language, set forth boisterously. (589–95)

The author clearly links herself with Chaucer, echoing the closing of his *Troilus* – 'Go little book, go my little tragedy' – perhaps calling attention to her sex by making her book blush at its audacity. This image might merely be a conventional humility topos or it might point to the writer's lack of self-confidence in her work, but it unquestioningly presents a woman as a writer.

ROMANCE

While the romance is the genre of medieval literature most popular among modern readers, no medieval romance can be attributed to any woman writing in English. However, a series of *lais*, or short metrical romances, were composed in Anglo-Norman by the poet who called herself Marie de France. Even though she proclaims herself to be 'from France' and wrote in the Anglo-Norman dialect of French, there are good reasons to claim her as an English writer. In the preface to the *lais* she identifies her principal patron as Henry II, King of England at the end of the twelfth century. Presumably, then, she lived in England and may in fact have been the abbess of the wealthy convent of Shaftesbury (see pp. 155–6 for more details). Reclaiming Marie as an English poet of some stature is crucial to understanding English literary history. Her work reminds us that Anglo-Norman was the literary language in England during the two centuries following the Norman Conquest. After 1066, William the Conqueror all but eliminated the Anglo-Saxon aristocracy and replaced it with a Norman nobility; the distinction between English and French was as much a class division as a national one. Since written literature was the province of the leisured upper classes, and the language of the leisured classes was Norman French, those Anglo-Norman works produced in England between the eleventh and thirteenth centuries fill in the gaps in English literary history between *Beowulf* and Chaucer. It is not that there is no great literature produced in England between 1066 and the beginning of the fourteenth century (the impression one can get from surveys of medieval *English* literature); rather, the great literature was being written in French because that was the language spoken by the English aristocracy. This is the reason the author of the *Life of St Edmund* gives for translating his life from Latin and English into French:

> I have translated it to the end, both from the English and from the Latin, for both the great and least can understand it in French. (Quoted in Legge, *Anglo-Norman* 7)

As Dominica Legge has argued, our view of Middle English literature is much distorted when we neglect its Anglo-Norman antecedents or leave them solely to those who study Old French (2; see also Salter, *English and International*) in order to perpetuate the nineteenth-century belief that national languages and literatures correspond perfectly to national boundaries.

The Breton *lais* as a genre give witness to England's multicultural heritage. They have a Celtic origin, perhaps in Wales or Cornwall, as evidenced by a peculiarly Celtic form of magic that pervades them. From there they may have migrated by oral transmission to Brittany. Marie says very little about her sources in her prologue to the collected *lais*; however, in the opening of 'Laustic' she locates the origin of the tale in Brittany: 'I shall tell you an adventure / about which the Bretons made a *lai*' (155).

The *lai*, as Thomas Garbáty has written, is to the romance what the short story is to the novel. Where romances are diffuse and episodic, lais generally focus on a single episode or plot; the emphasis is on economy and tight plotting (Garbáty, *Medieval English Literature* 6). They are designed to be read or performed in a single sitting. In fact, Marie's *lais* quite effectively bear out Edgar Allen Poe's contention that a short story must aim to achieve a single effect; they are perhaps the most masterful examples of the genre that survive, rivalling the greatest modern short stories. Each of the twelve *lais* is organized around a single symbolic creature or artifact – for instance the nightingale in *Laustic* or the werewolf in *Bisclavret* – 'for maximum intensity and suggestiveness within the least possible duration' (Hanning and Ferrante 2). Because they are so congruent with twentieth-century aesthetics, Marie's *lais* are perhaps, for modern readers, the most readable medieval texts that have survived.

Two of Marie's *lais* were translated into English during the later Middle Ages. An early fourteenth-century translation of *Le Fresne* appears as the *Lay le Freine* in the Auchinleck manuscript (National Library of Scotland Advocate's MS 19.2.1). In addition, there are several Middle English romances that derive from Marie's *Lanval*, including the early fifteenth-century *Sir Launfal* by Thomas Chestre. These translations may suggest an expansion of the audience for tales of this type. Romances could circulate in French as long as the audience for them was exclusively a French-speaking and aristocratic one. But by the fourteenth century there appears to be less fluency in French among the aristocracy and more demand among the professional and mercantile classes for recreational literature of this type. It would be a mistake, however, to assume that the tastes of the aristocracy and those of the wealthy bourgeoisie would have diverged. The development of a distinct middle-class culture was the project of the eighteenth century, not the fourteenth and fifteenth. Several scholars have shown that the division between the aristocracy and the bourgeoisie was not as great as it was on the Continent and that the bourgeoisie was content to emulate aristocratic style.[12]

Chestre's adaptation of *Lanval*, which derives from a shorter and much more faithful Middle English version called *Sir Landevale*, reflects not a shift in the audiences of these tales, but the changing tastes of fifteenth-century audiences both aristocratic and bourgeois. Chestre adapts Marie's octosyllabic couplets to the popular tail-rhyme stanza (the verse form Chaucer parodies in *Sir Thopas*). This stanza consists of four sections of three lines each for a total of 12. Each section consists of a rhymed four-beat couplet and a three-beat line with a different rhyme. This last 'tail' rhyme continues the same rhyme throughout the stanza. In *Sir Launfal* the stanza is divided into two six-line stanzas. Because he incorporates scenes from other romances, Chestre's version seems less compact and more episodic than Marie's. He shifts the focus of the lay, rationalizing Marie's fairy-tale world; it is a more material and practical world than that of the Anglo-Norman *Lanval*. In

Marie's tales all the action results from Arthur's failure to give proper patronage to the deserving Lanval; Chestre shifts the focus to the Queen's infidelity and her bad faith. Early on Guenivere's behaviour is described as less than queenly:

> For the lady had a reputation
> For having many lovers under her lord,
> So many that there was no end. (ll. 46–8; translation mine)[13]

For a reason that is never explained, at her marriage the queen gives gifts to all of Arthur's men except Launfal, who receives nothing (ll. 67–72). Unlike Marie's king, however, Arthur continues to act the good patron, giving Launfal 'great spending' and his two nephews as companions when he leaves court to bury his father.

Chestre's Logres is much less purely aristocratic than Marie's. After leaving Arthur's court, Lanval lodges with the Mayor of Caerleon. In his poverty he eats with the Mayor's daughter and begs from her a saddle and bridle so he can ride out of the city. Chestre's descriptions of both wealth and poverty are more attuned to the material needs of his hero. Nowhere is this more evident than in his description of the gifts given to Launfal by the fairy mistress, Tryamoure. In Marie's lay, Lanval is given an unspecified, if inexhaustible, wealth. In *Sir Launfal* the hero is given 'an alner':

> A purse made of silk and clear gold
> With three fair images;
> As often as you put your hand into it
> You shall win a mark of gold
> Wherever you may be. (ll. 320–4)

Tryamoure's gifts are specified with the eye of an accountant: a mark of gold, a horse, a servant, a banner. Launfal accepts the gifts as a 'chepe', a good bargain. These materialistic details may suggest less a shift in the class allegiances of the audience that consumed these romances than a shift in the culture from an economy of expenditure to an economy of acquisition. While the focus in Marie's *lai* is almost entirely on Arthur's and Lanval's failures to expend wealth as the patronage system demands, the focus in Chestre shifts subtly to a description of Launfal's acquisition of wealth.

The early fourteenth-century Middle English translation of *Le Fresne* is a more faithful adaptation of Marie's lay, even reproducing her octosyllabic couplets. The translation may have been done by the same poet who wrote or translated *Sir Orfeo*, which appears in the same manuscript (Barratt, *Women's Writing* 40). The manuscript has been severely mutilated and most of the end of the *lai* is missing. *Le Fresne*, which skilfully interweaves several folklore motifs, begins with a woman slanderously accusing a neighbour of adultery because she has given birth to twins (there was a widespread folk belief in the Middle Ages that twins resulted from intercourse with more than one man). The accuser, in turn, gives birth to twin daughters and, rather than face the disgrace her slander would bring her, determines to kill one of the babies. She is persuaded by one of her 'damsels' (*meschine* in the French) to abandon the child instead. The damsel leaves the child wrapped in an embroidered cloth (a 'riche bandekine' in Middle English) with a ring tied to her arm in an ash tree outside a nearby convent. She is taken in and raised by the abbess. When she grows up her beauty is so highly praised that Gurun, the lord of Dole, falls in love with her, though he has never actually seen her. He becomes a patron of the convent so that he can gain access to her; the French text says,

> He gave generously of his goods –
> but he had a motive
> other than receiving pardon for his sins.[14] (80)

Gurun persuades Fresne (named for the ash tree in which she was found) to come and live with him as his 'leman'. After a while, however, his vassals urge him to marry a noble woman from whom he can get a proper heir:

> it would be much to their disadvantage
> if he was deterred by his concubine
> from having a child born in wedlock. (82)

The wife he chooses just happens to be Fresne's twin sister, Codre (Hazel).[15] Fresne's identity is discovered when she leaves the embroidered cloth she had been swaddled in on the marriage bed and her mother recognizes it. The marriage with Codre is conveniently annulled; she is married off to someone else so that Gurun is free to marry Fresne and all live happily ever after.

Hanning and Ferrante argue that most of the action in *Le Fresne* is motivated by the impulse to protect and nurture, and that impulse is represented by the symbol of the ash tree which shelters the infant Fresne and gives her her name (89–90). Though it is tempting to read folktales as if they offered universal wisdom, it would be a mistake to read this *lai* proleptically through our own childrearing practices and beliefs about nurturing. The most curious feature of *Le Fresne* is the extent to which nurturing is constantly displaced. The *lai*'s action is set into motion when the knight whose wife has given birth to twins sends word to his neighbour that

> He would send one to him to be raised
> and name the child after him. (73)

Among the aristocracy throughout the Middle Ages, the practice of fosterage was common, if not universal. Noble children were sent at a very young age to be raised by foster parents. In such a culture, it seems at least possible that an individual's primary affectional ties were not necessarily with biological parents and children, but with foster parents and children. *Le Fresne* seems to represent this arrangement through its constant displacement of nurturing from its source in a biological parent. Fresne's mother would rather get rid of one of her own children than face disgrace. For modern readers this makes her the villain of the tale. Yet, curiously she is never punished for that crime and even she is shown to be capable of deep affection.

> The lady had an attendant [*meschine*]
> who was of noble birth;
> the lady had raised and taken care of her
> and she was very attached to her. (75)

In fact, the French of the last line reads "*E mut amee e mut cherie*' (She loved and cherished her much). It is this *meschine* who conceives of the idea of abandoning the child at a convent where she would be taken care of. There Fresne is first nursed by the porter's daughter and then raised and nurtured in turn by the abbess. Fresne's act of placing her own birth covering on her sister's marriage bed is the last in a chain of displaced acts of nurturing that structures the tale. The tale returns full circle when Fresne is reunited with her family, not for the purposes of nurture and protection but to reclaim her social identity. This restoration of proper social identity is the end toward which romance as a genre tends.

The same themes of social identity and nurturance run throughout the romance cycle that is considered the greatest extant work of Welsh literature, the *Four Branches of the Mabinogion*. No one is really sure how to classify these stories, though they bear some relationships to other medieval romances. One of the problems revolves around the term *mabinogi* whose meaning is obscure. Scholars now believe that the presence of the element *mab* 'boy, child, son' suggests that the word may have once referred to stories about the boyhood deeds of a hero and later came to be a general term for story or legend (Breeze, *Medieval Welsh Literature* 69). The only character who unites all four branches or stories is Pryderi, although he appears only peripherally in the second and fourth branches. As is typical of romance, the first branch begins by telling the story of Pryderi's ancestry by relating the adventures of Pwyll pen Anwfn, his father, and Rhiannon, his mother. The second branch shows Pryderi as one of the seven survivors of the war between the Isle of the Mighty and Ireland. The third branch follows the adventures of Manawydan, son of Llŷr and his wife Rhiannon and Pryderi and his wife Cigfa during a time when Gwynedd is placed under an enchantment. Finally, in the fourth branch, Pryderi is killed in a war between Dyfed and Gwynedd over some pigs from the other world.

In his 1997 book, *Medieval Welsh Literature*, Andrew Breeze makes the audacious claim that these four brief prose tales were written by a woman. He argues that the author of the *Mabinogion* may have been Gwenllian, daughter of Gruffudd ap Cynan and wife of Gruffydd ap Rhys. Gwenllian lived between 1098 and 1136. Her father was king of Gwynedd and her husband, whom she married in 1116, a prince of Dyfed in west Wales (75). The evidence for Gwenllian's authorship is largely circumstantial and it is unlikely that any new definitive evidence will emerge that would either prove or disprove her authorship. Still some of the evidence is tantalizing. Only a woman of Gwenllian's rank would have been likely to have written a vernacular text and have it survive after her death (75). Gwenllian is nowhere identified as a writer, though she came from a family of writers and patrons of literature. Her nephew Hywel ab Owain Gwynedd was a poet and there are some verbal echoes of his poetry in the tales of the *Mabinogion*. Gwenllian's grand-nephew was the historian Giraldus Cambrensis (77). The manuscript that contains *The Four Branches of the Mabinogion*, the White Book of Rhydderch, seems to have passed largely through the descendants of her son, Lord Rhys (77–8). Furthermore, the texts show an intimate familiarity with the landscapes of Gwynedd and Dyfed (both areas in which Gwellian would have lived as a princess of Gwynedd married to a prince of Dyfed), but only a shadowy knowledge of the rest of Britain. Breeze believes that this familiarity with both Gwynedd and Dyfed tends to rule out Gwenllian's nephew, Hywel, as the potential author of the *Mabinogion*; he believes Hywel's general indifference to Dyfed would be hard to reconcile with the pride in Dyfed's expansion expressed in the *Mabinogion*.[16] The second branch, *Branwen, Daughter of Llŷr*, also shows familiarity with the geography of Ireland, which Gwenllian could possibly have known if she accompanied her husband into exile in Dublin in 1127 (78). Finally, none of the linguistic and historical evidence contradicts Gwenllian's authorship. For her to be a plausible author, the text would have to be written in the 1120s, which fits with chronological arguments advanced by Ifor Williams and others (Breeze 78).

None of this is conclusive or irrefutable proof of Gwenllian's authorship; however, little evidence exists that might discredit Breeze's hypothesis either. Breeze argues that to prove conclusively that Gwenllian could not have written the *Mabinogion* would require certain evidence which is simply not available. One would have to show that the author had professional bardic training (which would be extremely unlikely for a woman); however Walter Jackson has argued that the *Mabinogion* was the work of an antiquarian, not a professional poet. It would also be possible to disprove Breeze's hypothesis if one could prove that the author had knowledge of Geoffrey of Monmouth's *History of the Kings of Britain* since that appeared after Gwenllian's death in 1136. Finally if it could be shown that the author had knowledge of biblical or patristic learning or canon law it might rule out Gwenllian.[17]

Breeze points to other arguments in favour of female authorship such as the text's lack of interest in warfare (most of the battles are dispatched in a sentence or less), its emphasis on mothering, childbearing, childlessness, wet-nursing, fosterage and other aspects of childrearing, and the presence of strong female characters who direct the action and often rescue their male counterparts, as in the first branch when Rhiannon has to show Pwyll, who has foolishly given her away to a rival suitor, how to trick his opponent into giving her back. Such arguments about female authorship based on content may seem less convincing, as I have argued earlier, but they do have the advantage of turning our attention to some of the epicene features of these intriguing tales. Perhaps nowhere is the epicene nature of the *Mabinogion* more in evidence than in the tale of the last branch, *Math son of Mathonwy*. In this tale, Math punishes his nephews, Gwydion and Gilfaethwy, for the rape of his maiden by turning them into various male and female animals and forcing them to bear children, each by the other. Like Tiresias in Ovid's *Metamorphosis*, they are forced to experience being both male and female, human and animal. The second part of the tale involves a contest between Gwydion and Aranhrod over Aranhrod's son, Lleu Llaw Gyffes. When Aranhrod is invited to become Math's new virgin foot-holder, she must be tested to discover if she is still a virgin by stepping over a magic rod. When she does so she drops a fine looking boy (who is later baptized as Dylan) and a 'small something' which Gwydion hides in a chest. In due course an infant boy is delivered from the chest and Gwydion raises him. Aranhrod refuses to recognize the child as her own and Gwydion must trick her into bestowing on him a name (Lleu Llaw Gyffes) and arms. When she refuses him a wife, Gwydion creates a wife for him out of flowers and calls her Blodeuedd.

As with *Le Fresne*, I think it would be a mistake to read Aranhrod simply as the 'bad' mother in this tale. Indeed, I have always found her to be one of the most interesting and enigmatic characters in medieval literature precisely because of the way in which, for reasons which are never articulated, she refuses at least twentieth-century notions of proper motherhood. And yet the text does not condemn her for it. What Gwydion seeks from Aranhrod is not protection and nurturing for her son. Gwydion provides all of that, even the chest that serves as a surrogate womb for the child. What he seeks from Aranhrod is her son's social identity; he wants her to recognize the child's status by bestowing on him a name, armour and a wife. This tale may show at least vestiges of a culture in which property and status descended through the mother's rather than the father's lineage; in such a culture, recognition by the mother would be essential to a child's social status. As a result, a curious role reversal takes place from those we usually expect in the genre of romance. In this tale, Gwydion serves in the maternal role, gestating the child, raising him and plotting to force others to recognize the child's true identity. Aranhrod plays the distant paternal role, representing the hero's status and social recognition – whose acquisition is a central feature of romance as a genre – and at the same time withholding it.

HAGIOGRAPHY

One of the most popular genres of medieval literature was the hagiography or saint's life. These tales recounting the lives and exploits of Christian saints appealed to many different kinds of audiences and served several purposes. The documentation of sanctity offered by the saint's life was an important step in the canonization process. In England, the oldest monastic institutions traced their founding back to native saints and the *vitae* of these founders served as documentation of a monastery's property claims (Wogan-Brown, 66). When translated into the vernacular, however, saints' lives were popular recreational reading both for laypeople and those within religious institutions, as evidenced by their frequent appearance in large manuscript anthologies like the Vernon or Auchinleck manuscripts. And, of course, especially when the subject was a contemporary, they functioned as memorials for beloved religious leaders and models of Christian virtue.

This last is almost certainly what motivated the abbess Hugeberc in the eighth century to write the earliest saint's life written by a woman.[18] The Anglo-Saxon nun from Wessex, one of the women who followed St Boniface on his mission to Germany, began in 778 to record in Latin the life and sayings of St Willibald because 'it did not seem right to allow these things to pass into oblivion, nor to be silent about the things God has shown to His servant in these our days' and 'to gather together a kind of nosegay of his virtues and give you something by which you may remember them.' She addresses an almost exclusively male audience, the 'priests, deacons, abbots and brethren beloved in Christ, whom our holy bishop . . . appointed throughout his diocese.' Deprecating her own abilities as a 'weak woman' – 'I know that it may seem very bold on my part to write this book when there are so many holy priests capable of doing better' – she justifies her temerity on the grounds that she is a 'humble relative' (Petroff, *Visionary Literature* 92). Hugeberc's *Hodoeporicon of St Willibald* records not only the life of St Willibald, but his extensive travels as well, thus producing the earliest Anglo Saxon travel book, a guide for pilgrims to the Holy Land including all the shrines along the way (Petroff, *Visionary Literature* 86).

The earliest (and only) vernacular hagiographies that can be attributed to women were written in Anglo-Norman during the last part of the twelfth century. It perhaps says something about the state of neglect of Anglo-Norman literature, especially by scholars of English literature, that none of these saints' lives has been translated into English and so are virtually inaccessible except to scholars of Old French. Two and perhaps all three of these hagiographies were produced by nuns. Yet while hagiographic manuscripts were often produced in religious houses, they enjoyed a much wider audience. Lay women especially seemed to be a target audience for stories of this kind and they frequently appear as patrons and dedicatees of hagiographic manuscripts. The three Anglo-Norman hagiographies written by women include a *Life of Saint Audrée* by a woman named Marie, a *Life of Saint Catherine* by Clémence of Barking, and a *Life of Edward the Confessor* by another, anonymous nun of Barking. These texts describe the lives of three virgin saints; indeed they describe three different types of virgins: the virgin martyr, the virgin abbess and the virgin spouse (Wogan-Brown 65).

A woman named Marie, about whom virtually nothing is known, wrote a life of the Anglo-Saxon abbess Etheldreda (*Vie seinte Audrée* in Norman French), founder of the powerful house of Ely. The author was either a nun (Wogan-Brown 65) or a canoness (Legge 75). This octosyllabic poem is a reworking of a post-Conquest Latin life of Etheldreda. However, none of the vernacular versions of Latin Anglo-Saxon saints' lives like the *Vie seinte Audrée* are simply translations. They served a very different purpose from their Latin antecedents and so must be read as different texts altogether. The Latin lives of native saints were often used to legitimate the property claims of male monastic institutions (like Ely) with which these saints were connected. (By the time of the Conquest, Ely, like other great Anglo-Saxon double monasteries, had become an exclusively male house.) The vernacular versions, because they were less tied to the immediate interests of particular monasteries, offered models of women who held considerable power and authority. For instance, when Audrée escapes from her second marriage she uses the dower from her first chaste marriage to found a new religious community. For the monks of Ely, Audrée's use of her dower becomes the basis of their property claims, a 'symbolic land charter' (Wogan-Brown 66). In a vernacular life written by a woman perhaps for a community of women readers, however, the same incident takes on different significance. Audrée's refusal of marriage and her title to dower lands becomes the basis for a female religious career. Her situation was not all that different from at least a handful of post-Conquest abbesses who still held abbeys as baronial fiefs or from Anglo-Norman noblewomen who could still offer considerable patronage to religious foundations (Wogan-Brown 66).

The remaining two saints' lives were both written in the late twelfth century at Barking Abbey, the most important convent in post-Conquest England. Barking was renowned for its learning; even after the Conquest its inhabitants preserved a tradition of Latin literacy. The nuns of Barking participated in the sophisticated Anglo-Latin and Anglo-Norman culture of the royal court, from which several of its twelfth-century abbesses were drawn, including the wife of Henry I, the wife of King Stephen, the sister of Thomas Beckett and Henry II's daughter (*Life of Saint Catherine 95*). The ties between Barking and the Norman court are nowhere more clearly manifest than in the hybrid text Brigitte Cazelles calls 'hagiographic romance', which enjoyed enormous popularity in the late twelfth and early thirteenth centuries. Clémence of Barking's *Life of Saint Catherine* is one of the finest examples of the genre. In this poem, the author, who confidently identifies herself at the end of the poem (ll. 2689–91), skilfully adapts the octosyllabic couplet used in the *lais* of her contemporary, Marie de France, to recount the life of this popular virgin martyr. Like many Anglo-Norman hagiographers, Clémence draws on the themes, techniques and vocabulary of twelfth-century courtly romances to increase her story's appeal to an aristocratic audience steeped in the sentiments of courtly love or *fin' amor*. Clémence's *Catherine* (along with the other Barking saint's life, the *Vie d'Edouard le confesseur*) is one of the earliest texts in Britain to use the term 'fin'amur' (Wogan-Brown 68). Clémence's *Catherine* distinguishes itself from countless medieval tales of virgin martyrs primarily in its shifting the audience's attention away from voyeuristic displays of gruesome torture (see for instance the Middle-English life of St Julianna in the so-called Catherine group), emphasizing instead the intellectual and emotional consequences of Catherine's choice of 'career virginity' (Wogan-Brown 68).

The third Anglo-Norman hagiography attributed to a woman is anonymous. The author, while at least presenting the appearance of humility, derogating both her French and her skill as a translator, insists that she is not fit to include her name along with that of England's greatest saint. She does, however, clearly identify herself as a nun of Barking (ll. 5304–7). The Barking *Vie d'Edouard le confesseur* offers an interesting variation on the theme of virginity since it deals with a virgin king. In this text, we see the conventional hagiographic chaste marriage from the point of view of a husband, rather than the wife, struggling to maintain his chastity in the face of several obstacles. Unlike *Catherine*, which successfully blends the courtly and doctrinal, the *Vie d'Edouard* dramatizes the tensions between the courtly and the saintly, offering the life of a saint in whom temporal and spiritual power fused. Edward the Confessor, the last Anglo-Saxon king of England, may seem, at first glance, a strange choice for an Anglo-Norman hagiography. Yet, besides the *vita* by this anonymous nun in the late twelfth century, there is a vernacular life by Matthew Paris in the thirteenth century, also written for the royal court, as well as a Latin *vita* by the Anglo-Norman prelate Aelred of Rievaulx which served as a source for both vernacular *vitae*. Given the circumstances of Edward's reign, his marriage, childlessness and the ensuing struggle over English succession, it is perhaps not all that surprising that the Norman kings, especially Henry II and Henry III, would chose to promote a cult of the Confessor (Wogan-Brown 68). Edward spent most of his life before becoming king living in Normandy and brought to England many Norman retainers when he became king. When he died childless, England was left without a legitimate heir to the throne. In the chaos that followed Edward's death, the Duke of Normandy was able to seize the throne for himself. By the twelfth century, however, most European aristocracies based their claims to power and legitimacy on the fiction that they could trace their titles from eldest son to eldest son in an unbroken line back to an originary founder, producing a 'vision of social order as a genealogico-historical continuity' (Durling, 'Hagiography and Lineage' 454; see also Bloch, *Etymologies* 65). Of course, the idea of genealogy as an unbroken line could never be more than a fiction and the nobility was continually faced with the problem of rationalizing ruptures that might be disastrous for one family, but a rich opportunity for another. Edward's childlessness created a rupture in the English succession even as it enabled the Normans' rise to power in England. Ideologically, what the Norman rulers needed in the twelfth century was a history of the English succession that was both 'legitimate and legitimately disrupted' (Wogan-Brown 69).

All of the Norman hagiographies of Edward wrestle with the conflict between the political obligation of a king to produce an heir and the spiritual model of sanctity on which hagiography as a genre is based. The hagiographic chaste marriage offered a means of reconciling legitimacy and disruption, especially since the genre itself was already part of a complex debate between ecclesiastical and aristocratic models of marriage. Throughout the twelfth century the church attempted to exert its control over marriage as a sacrament by stressing the indissolubility of marriage and demanding the mutual consent of both partners to legitimate marriage. This view contrasted with the aristocracy's conception of marriage as a tool for furthering dynastic expansion. The chaste marriage, in which both partners mutually consent to a life of chastity within marriage, dramatizes the refusal of the obligations of lineage. The Barking *Edouard* depicts such a marriage between Edward and Edith, the daughter of Edward's most rebellious earl. Edward's insistence on a chaste marriage interestingly places him in the position usually occupied by female virgins. It might also seem to present a challenge to the politics of linear succession. But hagiographies like the Barking *Edouard* contain such challenges by displacing the source of rupture from Edward's chastity to the sins of the English people. The hagiographic romances served in twelfth-century England not solely as a devotional genre designed entertain and instruct an unsophisticated laity; they were very much a part of the political landscape of Norman England, serving to justify both monastic property rights and the dynastic expansion of secular rulers.

DRAMA

The drama developed in English only relatively late. It tends on the whole to be anonymous and communal. For these reasons, it is difficult to assess the extent to which women contributed to the growth of this increasingly popular means of religious education and entertainment. Most scholars believe that English drama evolved in the late Middle Ages out of liturgical dramas that were enacted inside churches during holy day celebrations. The Easter liturgy especially seemed to spawn a series of Latin plays dealing with subjects like the harrowing of hell, the resurrection, and the visit of the three Marys to Christ's tomb. The survival of one such liturgical play from a medieval convent, almost certainly written by a woman, offers clues as to why church officials might have used drama to illustrate religious doctrine.

At Easter, some time in the mid-fourteenth century (between 1358 and 1377), Katherine of Sutton, Abbess of Barking, fearing that those attending services were becoming increasingly cool in their devotions, produced a series of liturgical dramas enacting the events of the Easter drama (Cotton, *Women Playwrights* 27; Faulkner, 'Harrowing of Hell' 141). Lady Katherine's purpose in producing these 'unusually lively adaptations of the traditional liturgical plays' was to 'excite devotion at such a crowded, important festival' (Cotton, *Women Playwrights* 27). There is no good reason to suppose, given the literary output of this important English convent and its tradition of Latinity, that Katherine herself or one of her sisters did not write these plays. Of particular theatrical interest is the *elevatio crucis*, which is one of the few surviving liturgical plays that contains a representation of the harrowing of hell. The stage directions in the single extant manuscript (*The Ordinale and Customary of the Benedictine Nuns of Barking*, University College, Oxford MS 169) are specific in allotting central roles to the nuns as well as to officiating clergymen. In the *visitatio sepulchri*, the three Marys are played not by male clerics, which was customary elsewhere, but by nuns (Cotton, *Women Playwrights* 28). The harrowing of hell play involves the abbess and resident nuns in the procession of souls to be led from hell. It opens with the following instructions: 'first the lady abbess shall go with all the convent and with certain priests and clerks dressed in copes, and with each priest and clerk carrying in his hand a palm and an unlighted candle. They shall enter the chapel of St Mary Magdalene, signifying the souls of the holy Fathers descending into hell before the coming of Christ' (Faulkner, 'Harrowing of Hell' 145). Later this same procession is led out of the chapel by the priest who figures Christ leading the souls of the fathers into heaven: 'Then the officiating priest shall lead out all those who were inside the aforesaid chapel . . .' (Faulkner, 'Harrowing of Hell' 149).

The Barking plays are not unique, however, in showing the active participation of nuns in liturgical drama. On the continent both Hrotsvitha of Gandersheim and Hildegard of Bingen wrote Latin religious plays and there is evidence that women in religious houses on the Continent sometimes acted in church dramas (Cotton, *Women Playwrights* 28). They are, however, unique in England where the destruction of many liturgical texts during the Reformation makes it extremely difficult to assess the contributions English convents may have made to the 'slow, anonymous, communal growth of the medieval religious drama' (Cotton, *Women Playwrights* 28). Lady Katherine's work suggests, however, that to continue to assert that religious women were not educated enough to participate in the development of medieval drama is to perpetuate misinformation born of ignorance and biased assumptions.

EPISTOLARY

It may seem, at first glance, peculiar to treat letter-writing as a literary genre on a par with, say, the lyric poem or romance. The modern reader is apt to view letters as the most ephemeral of written speech acts. We think of letters as an immediate form of self-expression, unadorned by literary artifice. They are one of many substitutes for face-to-face communication. But the Middle Ages must have understood letters very differently. In the first place, in a world without telephones, telegraphs, computers, television, radio, fax machines and email, letters were the *only* means of communicating with someone who was absent and so they tended to take on an importance they lack for modern readers. In the Middle Ages, letters were, in the words of Giles Constable, 'for the most part self-conscious, quasi-public literary documents, often written with an eye to future collection and publication' (cited in Cherewatuk and Wiethaus, *Dear Sister* 4). They often abandon the fiction of a single recipient, addressing a wider audience. The correspondence of the English missionary, St Boniface, was collected shortly after his death and copied in several manuscripts, presumably so it could be read more widely. Even more intimate correspondence in the vernacular, like the Paston Letters, seems to have been saved as evidence for legal proceedings, or in the case of the Stonors seized for legal purposes. The consciousness of a larger audience calls forth a style that is much more rhetorical and crafted than we might expect in a letter. At times medieval letters abandon altogether the fiction of intimate discourse. Occasionally the epistolary context itself is lost and the letter circulates as an independent literary text. Perhaps the most famous examples are the epistles of St Paul in the Bible. It is easy for the modern-day Christian to forget that these oft-quoted texts were initially letters written by Paul to his far-flung disciples in struggling new churches. In the fifteenth century, Christine de Pizan frequently adopted the epistolary mode in her writing, sometimes address-ing real people, as in her *Epistre a la Reine*, written to Queen Isabeau de Bavaria, sometimes creating fictional writers and addressees as in her *Epistre de Dieu d'Amour* or the *Epistre d'Othea*, in which the Goddess Othea address the fifteen-year-old Hector.

Of course the most famous medieval letter-writers were the star-crossed lovers Abelard and Héloise, whose erotic relationship is preserved in a series of Latin letters written while Héloise was the abbess of the Paraclete, the monastery Abelard founded for her. Controversy continues to rage over the authenticity of Héloise's letters, the argument being, that, despite Abelard's claims about Héloise's great learning, no woman could have been educated enough to write such erudite letters in Latin.[19] Therefore Abelard must have fabricated them. If we place those letters in a tradition of medieval women's epistolary writing, however, Héloise's accomplishments seem less suspect. Héloise, like Christine after her and like most formal letter-writers of the Middle Ages, knew something of the tradition of the *ars dictaminis*, the rhetorical study and practice of epistolary compositions that dictated the form of letters. Collections of sample letters illustrating the various conven-tions of letter-writing circulated widely throughout Europe, first in Latin and by the fourteenth and fifteenth centuries in the vernacular. Many women writers, undoubtedly including Héloise, modelled their letters on such formularies (Cherewatuk and Wiethaus, *Dear Sister* 5). Héloise's letters occasionally illustrate her knowledge of epistolary conventions. In her second letter, Héloise chides Abelard for violating the conventions of the *salutatio* or epistolary greeting which is designed to recapitulate the relative social positions of the writer and recipient. He had opened his letter 'To Héloise, his dearly beloved sister in Christ, Abelard her brother in Christ' (Radice, *Letters* 119; Kamuf, *Fictions* 9). Her response could be right out of an *ars dictaminis*. 'Surely,' she writes, 'the right and proper order is for those who write to their superiors or equals to put their names before their own, but in letters to inferiors, precedence in order of address follows precedence in rank' (Radice, *Letters* 127, Kamuf, *Fictions* 9). To understand why it would be perfectly believable for someone of Héloise's rank and position to have written Latin letters, we need to uncover a tradition of women's epistolary writing that demonstrates the possibility of women's familiarity with the conventions of letter-writing in the Middle Ages. Fortunately, evidence of such a tradition is available both for continental and English women.

The oldest surviving letters written by English women are preserved in the eighth-century correspondence of St Boniface. Boniface, born Winfred, was an Anglo-Saxon priest who went as a missionary to Germany to convert the Franks. He corresponded with a group of supporters in England, which included the Abbesses Eadburg and Eangyth, Eangyth's daughter Heaburg (or Bugga), Leoba, and the Abbess Cyneburg. Also included in his correspondence are three letters from an Anglo-Saxon nun, Berhtgyth, to her brother, Balthard, in which she describes her situation in Thuringia where she had gone with Boniface. The women's letters cover several subjects. They convey gifts in support of Boniface's mission. The English St Leoba, who would later join Boniface in his German mission, writes to ask for his prayers for her mother. Eangyth's and Bugga's letter of 718 requests Boniface's advice about a proposed pilgrimage to Rome.

We can only assume that when the women refer to their 'rude unpolished speech', it is a conventional nod to the humility topos. These letters are written in a sophisticated, even erudite Latin. Their syntax is complex, their vocabulary learned. Even the most personal letters are impressive rhetorical performances. The Abbess Egburga writes to Boniface between 716 and 718, lamenting the death of her brother, Oshere, and the departure of her only sister, Wethburga, 'whom I adored and who was nursed at the same mother's breast' (*Boniface* 34), to become a recluse in Rome. She expresses her grief and her longing for Boniface's comfort through an elaborate set of classical similes, expressed in a complex series of balanced clauses: 'Wherefore, believe me, more than the storm-tossed sailor longs for the harbor, more than the thirsty fields desire rain, or the anxious mother watches the shore for her son, do I long for the sight of you' (35). This ornate style is typical of the entire letter, and indeed of several of the women's letters. When the Abbess Eangyth and her daughter Bugga write to Boniface between 719 and 722 to complain about the 'load of misery' and the 'crushing burden of worldly distractions' that weigh them down, they too employ lavish extended similes to describe their misfortunes:

> As when the whirlpools of the foaming sea draw in and out the mountainous waves dashing upon the rocks, when the force of the wind and the violence of the storm drive through a monstrous channel, the keels of ships are upturned and masts are shattered – even so the frail vessels of our souls are shaken by the mighty engines of our miseries and by the multitude of our misfortunes. (36)

This lengthy letter is characterized throughout by such long Ciceronian periods whose balanced clauses in the Latin delay sentences' main verbs until the very end of the clause. This is the kind of Latin prose produced by someone who is at ease reading and writing the language. It is possible to argue that these letters were the work of some male secretary, but given what we know about the education of eighth-century Anglo-Saxon nuns it is just as reasonable to suppose that the women wrote these letters themselves.

Even after the Conquest, when Latin education in the convents was supposed to be deteriorating, the convent-educated Matilda, queen of Henry I, could carry on a Latin correspondence with Anselm, the Archbishop of Canterbury. That correspondence provides some insight into the queen's education and tastes. In one letter dated around 1100, she chides the archbishop for his too-severe fasting, fearing that 'his body may wither away, that the windows of his eyesight and hearing and other senses will grow dull, that his spiritually edifying voice will grow hoarse, that his voice – which once gave to quiet gentle discussion the qualities of song and speech most sweet to God – may grow quieter from now on.'[20] What is striking is the rhetorical self-consciousness of the elaborately balanced periods. In her letter, Matilda cites not only scriptures – both Old and New Testament – in support of her argument, but Cicero's 'On Old Age', Pythagoras, Socrates and other philosophers as well. In other letters, she expresses grief at Anselm's exile, the result of a quarrel with the king over investiture, and offers to act as a mediator in the dispute, even writing to the Pope. Matilda read and admired Anselm's work, comparing his style to that of Cicero, Quintilian, Jerome, Gregory and others she had read (Eckenstein, *Women Under Monasticism* 210). Anselm also counted several other abbesses of Wessex institutions among his correspondents, so that it would be a mistake to view Matilda's letters simply as an anomaly.

The first vernacular letters survive from the fifteenth century, letters written not by aristocratic and convent-educated women, but by women of the merchant and gentry classes who wrote in English about the mundane affairs of their lives: their marriages, their children, their husbands' business affairs, local gossip. Three great collections of English letters from the fifteenth century have survived, written by the Celys, a merchant family that traded in London and Flanders, the Stonors, another merchant family from Oxfordshire, and the Pastons, lawyers and estate-owners in Norfolk. The Paston correspondence is by far and away the largest and most significant collection, including the largest number of letters written by women: it includes 930 letters, including 174 by women. The Cely letters include only 2 letters by women, while the Stonor correspondence includes 36 letters by women (Watt 136–7).[21]

The Stonor Letters, after the Paston Letters, are the second largest collection of private correspondence from medieval England. The correspondence includes some 600 documents, including 256 letters written between 1290 and 1483. The principal figure in the Stonor correspondence is William Stonor, who was born around 1449. He was twenty-four when he inherited the family estates in Oxfordshire. In 1475 he married Elizabeth Riche, the daughter of a London alderman. William outlived Elizabeth to marry twice more, to Agnes Wydeslade, an heiress and the widow of the son of a Devonshire squire and later to Anne Neville, eldest daughter of the Marquis of Montagu, a cousin of the King. Stonor joined Buckingham's rebellion against King Richard and was attainted in 1483. The Stonor Letters survive because they were confiscated at the time of his attainder and preserved in the Tower (Kingsford, *Stonor Letters* xxiv–xxxvi).

Elizabeth seems to be the most prolific of the women correspondents; most of her letters are written from London to her husband who seems to have remained in Oxfordshire. She was not a lady of rank, but Kingsford suggests that her connections with London wool merchants may have appealed to a family whose wealth was largely in sheep (xxvii). Her letters imply that the family may have seen her as something of a *parvenue*. She seems particularly angry and defensive about her brother-in-law, Thomas Stonor. In a letter dated 7 November 1476 she writes 'I pray you to greet well my brother Thomas Stonor for me, desiring you to say to him that I wonder greatly what moves him to say such things about me as he does, that I would pluck all that I could from your livelihood. . . . I know you can answer for me well enough' (Kingsford, *Stonor Letters* 175).[22] A few months later in March of 1477 relations between Elizabeth and her brother-in-law seem, if anything, to have deteriorated into name-calling. She writes 'And touching my brother Stonor, truly sir there was no one who told me precisely that it was he, but I know well that it was, for it was said to me that I kept you here [in London] among such a retinue of boys, who used language which is not fitting for any servant that belongs to you or me. . . . He has no cause to say of me anything except good for I never said anything intentionally to displease him' (180).

In a letter dated 22 October 1476, Elizabeth describes herself in the retinue of the Duchess of Suffolk with whom she is trying to curry favour:

And sir, you shall understand that I have been with my Lady of Suffolk on last Thursday, and waited upon her to my lady the King's mother and hers by her commandment. And also last Saturday I waited upon her thither again, and also from there she waited upon my lady her Mother, and brought her to Greenwich to the King's good grace and the Queen's. And there I saw the meeting between the King and my lady his Mother. And truly I thought it was a very good sight. And sir, I was with my lady of Suffolk this day, hoping that I might have had her at leisure so that I might have spoken to her for the money, but truly she was very busy getting ready, for she is riding to Canterbury this same day; but she will be here again next Saturday, for she told me so herself. (172)

Elizabeth took an active interest in her husband's business affairs. That interest is reflected in her attempts to ingratiate herself with 'my lady of Southfolke', and perhaps accounts for her reputation as a social climber. However, judging from the Paston Letters, this behaviour seems common enough in both men and women of her class (see below pp. 187–97).

Elizabeth's letters also tell us something about her relationship with her husband. She is concerned that he will catch 'the poxe' from his brother who is ill; she is weary of their continued separation. She mentions his relationship to her four children (three daughters and a son) from her first marriage to Thomas Riche: 'As touching my children, I heartily thank you that it pleases you to tend them, but yet, Gentle Cousin, if it pleases you send them up with such horses as you like to send for me, I heartily pray you' (169, 12 September 1476). But, like most of the women of her class whose letters have survived, Elizabeth is rarely sentimental and always practical, even when discussing 'affairs of the heart'. In a letter dated 11 December 1476 she describes negotiations for the marriage of one of her daughters:

on Friday last I dined with my father and mother. And there was at dinner with them the friends of the child who was proposed for one of my daughters the last time you were here. And so after dinner they had their communication about the said matter, whereby I understood their disposition and how they were disposed in the said matter. And truly it was nothing as it was spoken of at the beginning, wherefore I answered and said in this wise: that though she were my child, as she is, I could not answer that matter without you nor would I do so. Albeit I answered on your behalf: that I knew right well that you would be a right kind and loving father, if God fortuned that you and they should deal. (176)

This passage exemplifies the businesslike rhetoric that marks most women's vernacular letters. Though Elizabeth appears to be describing the approaching marriage of her daughter, her prose is disinterested, legalistic, even calculating. The proposed match is referred to as the 'said matter'; it is 'moved' by the groom's 'friends'. Elizabeth must understand their 'disposition' in the matter. While the prose of Elizabeth's letters is generally paratactic, that is, sentences are juxtaposed with no connectives or loosely connected by 'and' (as in the first two sentences of this passage), when she uses connectives they add an imposing legalistic weight: 'whereby' or 'albeit'. In this passage, Elizabeth's syntax shifts markedly at the moment she understands that the 'deal' being proposed is not what she expected. Straightforward reporting conveyed in simple sentences gives way to indirect discourse and a more complex sentence structure. Elizabeth is reporting her negotiating strategy to her husband, which consists of simultaneously denying ('I could not answer the matter without you') and asserting ('I answered on your behalf') her authority in the matter.

The epistolary form represents an important moment in the evolution of English prose. As the genre was developed by pragmatic readers of the fifteenth century (see above p. 67), its vocabulary and syntax tended to reflect a utilitarian approach to literacy. For the moneyed and propertied classes, Georges Duby and Phillipe Braunstein have argued, the acquisition of wealth was the primary motivation for writing. It 'was associated with a concern that one's property be administered well' and properly transmitted to heirs. As these pragmatic readers began 'to catalogue and arrange . . . material in . . . family archives' they made little distinction between commercial and personal accounts (Duby, *Private Life* 459). Late medieval epistolary prose does not support a distinction between a public realm of business affairs dominated by men and a private domain of emotion and sentiment presided over by women, a distinction that more readily distinguishes women's letters from men's in later centuries. Fifteenth-century vernacular letters are much less revealing of an individual's interiority than they are a record of the social networks in which that individual located herself.

PRACTICAL TREATISES

As the previous section suggests, any attempt to uncover a tradition of women's intellectual accomplishments during the Middle Ages must account not only for the literary but also for the utilitarian ends to which language might be put. Of course, this distinction between practical and fanciful, between fiction and non-fiction, is largely a modern one so that texts lumped together under a catch-all category called practical treatises are bound to be diverse. The works of the two women I examine in this section have almost nothing in common with one another except their choice of 'practical' subjects and their somewhat less self-conscious literary use of language. Trotula, or Trotta, was an eleventh- or twelfth-century Salernitan physician who may have been the author of three Latin prose treatises on women's diseases. These treatises survive in several Middle English translations from the fifteenth century and whether these particular texts were or were not written by Trotula, they were almost universally attributed to her. Juliana Berners, identified by William Burton in the seventeenth century as 'the daughter of Sir James Berners, of Berners-Roding, in Essex, Knight, and Sister to Richard Lord Berners . . . Lady Prioresse of Sopwell Nunnery neere St. Albons', is credited with producing a verse translation that conflates two fourteenth-century French prose treatises on hunting: William Twiti's *L'Art de Venerie* and Gaston de Foix's *Livre de Chasse* (Barratt, *Women's Writing* 232).

Virtually nothing is known about the female physician Chaucer's Wife of Bath lists as one of several authorities on the 'woe that is in marriage' in her husband Jankyn's book of wicked wives. While some historians dispute her existence, a woman named Trotula or Trotta appears to have practiced medicine in the town of Salerno in Italy in either the eleventh or twelfth centuries (scholars argue for dates ranging from 1050 to nearly 1200; see Benton, 'Trotula'). Though women were excluded from universities throughout the Middle Ages and hence from the formal study of medicine, there were a number of female healers in Salerno, which was an important site for the introduction of Arabic medicine into western Europe in the eleventh and twelfth centuries.[23] These women are frequently cited collectively as the Salernitan women (*mulieres Salernitane*). The documented existence of a group of women healers certainly makes plausible the case for a real figure behind later medieval representations of Trotula, although the truth is perhaps less lurid than the fiction of a woman who reveals all the 'secrets of women'.

Trotula is credited in the later Middle Ages with the authorship of three Latin treatises that deal with women's diseases, medical problems and cosmetics. Initially these three works – the *Cum auctor*, which is exclusively concerned with medicine, *Ut de curis*, which includes information about both medicine and cosmetics, and *De ornatu*, which deals exclusively with cosmetics and beauty aids – circulated independently. Eventually they were combined into two treatises that became know as the *Trotula major* and *Trotula minor* and, in the sixteenth century were compiled into a single text by Georg Kraut (Benton, 'Trotula' 32–4). These texts were enormously popular between the thirteenth and fifteenth centuries; John Benton has located nearly one hundred extant manuscripts that contain one or more of the texts. By the fifteenth century they were translated into most of the vernacular languages (Benton, 'Trotula' 35). Middle English translations of these texts occur in several fifteenth-century manuscripts, including three I will examine below, the *Liber Trotuli* (BL MS Additional 34111), *The Diseases of Women* (BL MS Sloane 421a), and *The Knowing of Women's*

Kind in Childing (Oxford Bodley MS Douce 37). Benton believes that none of the treatises attributed to Trotula were actually written by her. Rather, he argues that she was the author of the much less popular *Practica Secundum Trotula*, which was never translated out of Latin and exists today only in fragments (Benton, 'Trotula' 41–2).

The truth behind medieval myths about Trotula may remain murky, though much light has been shed on the subject by the recent work of historians like John Benton and Monica Green. As literary critics, however, we might take a bit more licence to explore the myths themselves. What does it mean that a particular group of popular texts were routinely grouped under this woman's signature? Here Michel Foucault's meditation on authorship in 'What is an Author?' might point us away from the task of locating a particular historical individual we can credit with the production of a work and so limit the proliferation of its meaning. In this essay, he asks how the sign of the author enables the circulation of a text and determines how it will be read. This process of characterizing the mode of existence, circulation and functioning of a text Foucault calls the 'author-function'. To speak of an author-function rather than authorship recasts the questions we ask of a particular text. Instead of 'Who really spoke?' and 'Was it really she and not someone else?' we now ask 'What are the modes of existence of this discourse? Where has it been used, how can it circulate, and who can appropriate it for herself? What are the places in it where there is room for possible subjects? Who can assume these various subject-functions?' (Foucault, 'What is An Author?' 160).

Foucault's second set of questions prompts us to ask how the circulation of a group of fifteenth-century Middle English manuscripts on women's health bearing a woman's signature determined how the text would be read and who could assume the various subject-functions the texts created. One answer, outlined by Benton, is that Trotula's signature contributed to the misogyny of medieval medicine, excluding women from the practice of medicine while simultaneously invoking a woman's knowledge of the secrets of her sex. The Trotula texts were becoming widely accepted among male physicians at the same time that actual women practitioners were being prosecuted and driven from the profession. He argues that the emphasis on Trotula's gender by scribes and rubricators of the manuscripts suggests that it was not merely plausible that a woman wrote these texts, it was necessary. Men, even authoritative male physicians, were not supposed to have access to women's physiology; medieval canons of modesty at least gave lip service to the belief that it would be improper for a man to examine a woman intimately. The advantage to a male-dominated medical profession of attributing to Trotula texts that, ironically, contained nothing that could not be found in other medical texts written by men, was its fiction of presenting information that only women could know. These texts could speak with an authority about women's physiology that men lacked without having to concede any real expertise to women practitioners (Trotula being safely dead). Benton quotes one thirteenth-century scientific encyclopedia that argues that physicians 'who know nothing, derive great authority and much solid information' from Trotula because she wrote what she had 'felt in herself, since she was a woman' and 'because she was a woman, all women revealed their inner thoughts more readily to her than to any man and told her their natures' (Benton, 'Trotula' 51). Benton assumes that female authorship confers on the male physician – the only readers he can envision for these texts – an authority to speak about women's bodies he would otherwise lack.

Benton's analysis, as Monica Green suggests, is not so much wrong as incomplete. She adds that the texts' reduction of women's health to women's reproductive health may be another sign of the texts' misogyny. Reproduction was certainly not women's only, or even most urgent, health concern (Green, 'Women's Medical Practice' 434–8). However, even if the texts that circulated under Trotula's name were initially intended to be read primarily by physicians (a reasonable assumption for texts written in Latin), their wide translation into vernacular languages during the late Middle Ages suggests the works were being appropriated by other audiences perhaps not originally intended. Surely any physician, even in fifteenth-century England, could still read a medical treatise in Latin; physicians were educated in Latin. The fact that the Trotula texts were translated not once but several times into English in the fifteenth century certainly suggests that these texts were regularly used by non-physicians. It would also suggest that physicians were not the only – or even the primary – source of medical care for most people. In fact, health care would have been the primary responsibility of the woman in charge of a household, whatever its size or income. She would, of necessity, have some rudimentary knowledge of health care – or access to information about it.

The existence of vernacular translations of the Trotula texts, then, suggests another view of their circulation among readers who were not trained as physicians – and that some members of this audience were women. Two closely related Middle English manuscripts (Oxford MS Douce 37 and BL MS Sloane 421a) contain a translator's preface that encourages female readers to take up a subject position within the text.

> Wherefore, for the worship of our Lady and all the saints, I intend to
> try diligently to translate from Latin into English the diverse causes of
> [women's] maladies, the signs by which they are known, and the cures
> for them, according to the treatises of various masters who have translated
> them out of Greek into Latin. And because women can read better in our

own tongue and can understand this language better than any other, and so that every literate woman may read it to others who are illiterate and help them and counsel them in their maladies, without showing their diseases to man, I have translated this into English. (Barratt, *Women's Writing* 30; translation mine)

It is impossible to tell if this preface is merely a conventional *topos* or if it accurately describes the circulation of this work among a group of female readers both literate and illiterate. To be sure, the translator imagines other, more traditionally misogynist, uses to which the work might be put by other readers: 'And if any man reads it, I pray him and charge him on Our Lady's behalf, that he does not read it for any contempt or slander of any woman, or for any other reason except their healing and help, dreading the vengeance that might fall to them as it has to others who have revealed their [i.e. women's] private parts to slander them' (Barratt, *Women's Writing* 31).[24] Either appeal to an intended audience might be merely conventional. Yet this translation seems, at least, to create a subject position women might occupy, imagining them not merely as readers of this book but as the very individuals who might put its advice to use.

The physical state of the manuscripts offers some clues to their function. The Douce and Sloane manuscripts both contain a single text, called variously 'Of the Diseases of Women', 'Regiment of Health' and 'The Knowing of Women's Kind in Childing' and contain almost exclusively practical information about reproduction and childbirth. They cover such topics as the differences between male and female anatomy, menstruation, pregnancy, delivery, problems with deliveries and reproductive disorders. They are small portable books, made from relatively inexpensive materials, which appear capable of being used at a bedside. And their advice is consistently practical, even hands-on. For instance, both describe several versions which could be tried when a child presents in a breech position or other position that might make delivery difficult (BL MS Sloane 421a, ff. 9v–12r). They describe in great detail how to cut the umbilical cord.

After the child is born bind his navel [with a thread] a little way from the womb and a little way from thence beyond it with another thread so that he does not bleed too much and when he has rested a little out of his mother's womb then let his navel be cut this way: lay it upon a board and then take with your two fingers the two bindings in your hand & with your other two fingers take the other binding. Then with a razor or a sharp knife cut the navel between the binding & pay no attention to the folly of old women that preferred to cut them with glass or a piece of a pot of earth or a sharp stone for that is but foolish & witchcraft. (BL MS Sloane 421a, 11v)

The simple paratactic prose is characteristic of this spare text, and indeed of all of the Middle English Trotula texts. But it also, as Alexandra Barratt suggests, seems 'based on, and sympathetic towards, women's experience of sexuality and childbirth' (*Women's Writing* 27). It avoids sensational revelations about women's sexuality (as, for instance, the *Liber Trotuli*'s advice on how to restore virginity, BL MS Additional 34111, f. 212) in favour of practical advice, while at the same time claiming its own authority, dismissing 'old wives tales' as folly and, worse, as witchcraft.

The *Liber Trotuli*, on the other hand, is one of a series of medical texts in a larger medical miscellany (BL MS Additional 34111) that might have belonged to a Master William Somers. It is almost exclusively concerned with cures for various ailments, including amenorrhea (f. 199), heavy menstrual bleeding (200), wandering womb (202), haemorrhoids (207) and constipation (206v), as well as cosmetic information for making the hair curly, long or thick, the face or teeth white (207v) and curing bad breath (214) or foul odours (211). Though all the Middle English Trotula texts contain recipes for various medications, the *Liber Trotuli* is almost exclusively concerned with herbal pharmacology. Its various recipes for restoring virginity, beautifying hair and face and eliminating foul odours presents a much less sympathetic view of women's bodies than either the Douce or Sloane manuscripts. It suggests that the conflation of women's health with women's beauty that marks most popular discussions of women's health is of much older date than we might have imagined. Taken together, these three Trotula manuscripts suggest that in England, at least, the Trotula author-function (the maintenance of the myth that these texts were authored by a woman healer) could simultaneously reinforce misogynist beliefs about women's bodies and empower women as healers.

If the Trotula author-function gave authority to texts about women's bodies that were in all probability translated by men, what function might the attribution of a verse treatise on hunting to 'Dame Julyans Barnes' in the *Book of St Albans* serve? The *Book of St Albans* was first printed in 1486 by the 'schoolmaster printer' at St Albans press. It contains four treatises, one on hawking, one on hunting and two on heraldry, each preceded by a short introduction by the printer or compiler. Dame Julyans Barnes, or Juliana Berners, is named at the end of the second text, called 'The Book of Hunting': 'Explicit Dam Julyans Barnes in her boke of huntyng' (f iiii). For this reason, modern scholars have identified her only with this treatise and not with the entire book, as a 1595 prose redaction, called *The Gentleman's Academe* (which pretty well describes the book's contents), did. 'The Book of Hunting' exists independently in two other fifteenth-century manuscripts, although Berners is not named in either.[25] Nothing certain is known about the woman referred to in this colophon. A 1496 edition printed by Wynkyn de Worde renders the name 'Bernes' and, in a note written before 1612 in his copy of the *Book of St Albans*, William Butler identifies the author as 'the daughter of Sir James Berners, of Berners-Roding, in Essex, Knight, and Sister to Richard Lord Berners . . . Lady Prioresse of Sopwell Nunnery neere St Albons' (Barratt, *Women's Writing* 232). While it is impossible to corroborate this identification, the name Juliana Berners continues to be associated with this text.

Rachel Hands, the editor of the facsimile edition of the *Book of St Albans*, has argued that Juliana Berners could not have been the author of 'The Book of Hunting', but instead identifies her as 'the compiler of the miscellaneous material, of the sort often preserved in commonplace books, found at the ends of both *The Book of Hawking* and *The Book of Hunting*' (Barratt, *Women's Writing* 232). She bases her argument on the possible appearance of Berners' name in two other manuscripts containing this kind of miscellaneous material, mostly lists of various kinds. Pepys Library MS 1047 identifies this material with 'Iulyan Barne', while BL MS Harley 2340 makes a reference to a 'J.B.' in an explicit (a manuscript rubric indicating the end of a textual unit) following similar material. But her argument for Berners as a compiler of lists rather than author of 'The Book of Hunting' also rests heavily on assumptions about what it would be proper for a woman to write: 'It is curious to find a woman both issuing instructions of this kind and having such a detailed knowledge of the subject' (Hands, 'Juliana Berners' 381). She goes on: 'The heterogeneous material of the manuscripts [Harley 2340 and Pepys 1047] seems much more likely to have been assembled by a woman. On the whole its contents are much less detailed and technical, and are very much more like the kind of semi-practical, often mnemonic lore collected in commonplace books' (382).

But, as Barratt points out, the assumption that a woman could not have written a treatise on hunting because the activity was considered inappropriate for a woman cannot stand close scrutiny. It would not take a first-hand or even detailed knowledge of hunting to produce this text, which is a verse translation of two French prose treatises on hunting (Barratt, *Women's Writing* 232). While she would need to familiarize herself with the vocabulary, learn how to 'talk the talk', she would not need actually to have hunted herself. Presumably the French authors, William Twiti and Gaston de Foix, would have supplied whatever expertise might be necessary to such an enterprise, though no doubt their information was also culled from some other source. For instance, in the section titled 'Note here the age of an Hart', she enumerates the names used to designate a hart at different ages:

And to speak of the hart if ye will it hear
Ye shall call him a .*Calf*. at the first year
The second year a .*Bracket*. so shall ye him call
The third year a *Spayad* learneth this all

> The fourth year a .*Stag*. your dame bids you say
> The vi. year call ye him an .hart. [e.i^v; translation mine]

These lines suggest a working knowledge of the proper terminology but do not call for anything other than a 'bookish' familiarity with deer hunting. The difficult task in translating French prose into English verse would require not expertise in hunting, but expertise in versification and, as the above passage suggests, the poet is clearly an amateur. The lines contain irregular feet, sometimes 12, sometimes 10 or fewer syllables (my translation does not accurately reflect versification). The poem is more or less stanzaic, but the number of lines per stanza is haphazard. The poet generally uses rhyming couplets though, as in this stanza, there are many stray lines that do not rhyme. The verse relies on set phrases like 'if ye will it hear', and 'your dame bids you say' to fill out the lines.

The first part of 'The Book of Hunting', which draws on Twiti's *Art of Hunting*, takes the form of a woman instructing her son:

> Wheresoever ye fare by frith or by fell
> My dear child take hede how Tristram doth you tell
> How many manner beasts of venery there are
> Listen to your dame and she shall teach you. (e.i)

The romance hero Sir Tristram is presented as the ultimate authority on hunting and the source of the lore, which, like all of the material in the *Book of St Albans*, is the sort of knowledge a young gentleman would be required to master. The second part, based on Gaston de Foix's *Master of the Game*, presents a dialogue between a master and his man, suggesting a closer link to the actual experience of hunting. It begins 'The boast that the master hunter maketh to his man now here following ye may hear' (e.vi). This imaginary dialogue relieves the poem's constant recitation of classifications and nomenclature with occasional passages of direct discourse.

> 'What is the cause,' quod the man, 'master I thee pray
> That the hart before the hounds when they hunt him
> That then to the River he will go.'
> Quod the master to the man, 'there are two causes.' (e.vii)

Taken together, the two sections of the treatise suggest two different models of authority for the education of young aristocratic men. The first is characterized by the relationship of mother and child. Authority in this model is female; it is always softened by the affection inherent in a close bond: 'My dear child'. The dryness of the material is from time to time broken up by the speaker's expressions of affection for the child. The second model is clearly male, representing the relationship between master and man. This relationship is marked by distance and deference: 'master I thee pray'. Since hunting is an activity best learned in actual practice, we might conclude that young gentlemen did not turn to primers like these to learn how to skin a deer. We might speculate that texts like those preserved in the *Book of St Albans* served a different function altogether, that they had some rhetorical purpose in the schooling of young gentleman. Such a book was more likely used to teach the art of gentle discourse, to educate the young in the orderly and pleasing arrangement of material within discourse and the nature of the authorities that directed such discourse. That these authorities are both male and female, that women had a distinct role to play in the transmission of knowledge, lends credibility, at least, to the belief that the translator of 'The Book of Hunting' was a woman.

DEVOTIONAL AND VISIONARY LITERATURE

Without doubt, the largest single genre of women's writing throughout the Middle Ages was devotional, which we may take to include 'the entire range of piety from simple, affective prayer to works describing, or inciting to, contemplative union' (Sargent, 'Minor Devotional Writings' 147). Religious writing by women takes a variety of forms during this period including prayers, meditations on scriptures, commentaries on biblical texts, religious rules, devotional texts, mystical writing and visions of every kind, including narrative visions recounting the visionary's experiences, narratives of scriptural events and didactic visions. Women even produced heretical texts that challenged the authority of the institutional Church. While these works may seem alien to the aesthetic sensibilities of the modern reader, if we ever hope to understand women's participation in medieval culture, we must understand their contributions to its religious life and we must understand the considerable appeal that these texts had for medieval readers of both sexes. Religious writing dominated writing of all kinds during the Middle-English period, including the canonical writing that shapes our own perception of the Middle Ages. Peter Jolliffe, in his *Check-List of Middle English Prose of Spiritual Guidance*, lists 349 separate works that fall into this category. Given the dearth of what modern readers would consider 'literary' prose before the fifteenth century, this output is remarkable; religious prose must certainly figure heavily in any analysis of the development of English prose. Alexandra Barratt has suggested that it might help modern readers understand the popularity of devotional writing to compare it to best-selling self-help books today.[26] While such comparisons are helpful, enabling readers to understand the popular and practical nature of these texts, they run the risk of obscuring important and interesting aesthetic questions, particularly about the role devotional writing might have played in the development of prose as a vehicle for English literature.

The reasons for the relative abundance of women's religious writing are doubtless many. Even in the fifteenth century, when lay literacy was increasing (see above p. 66), those in the religious life were more likely than the laity to possess the leisure time and materials necessary to literary production; in this regard, textual production simply followed the interests of those best equipped to produce it. The reading materials of most women, however, religious and lay, literate and illiterate, would have been heavily devotional in nature. Religion enjoyed enormous authority in the medieval world and women who were unlikely to be able to speak authoritatively on their own (women were forbidden to preach or teach during this period) could claim authority by speaking through God. We see this most explicitly in the visionary writers of the period.

Visionary writing

Evelyn Underhill has defined mysticism as 'the direct intuition or experience of God', and a mystic as 'a person who has, to a greater or lesser degree, such a direct experience' (Underhill, *Mysticism* 10). The thirteenth, fourteenth and fifteenth centuries produced a significant body of works by and about women whose mystical visions imbued their speech and writing with an authority of divine origins. 'This is the only place in the West', Luce Irigaray writes rather hyperbolically in 'La Mystérique', 'in which a woman speaks and acts so publicly' (*Speculum* 191). This section examines women's participation in visionary disciplines as a public, not solitary and isolated, activity which was very much a part of medieval culture by examining five continental mystics whose visions were translated into Middle English during the fifteenth century and one homegrown British visionary.

The Book of Ghostly Grace is a fifteenth-century Middle English translation of the visions of the German visionary Mechtild of Hackeborn, which were compiled in the *Liber Spiritualis* (or *Specialis*) *Gratiae* between 1291 and 1298 by Gertrude the Great. The original Latin, which Barratt describes as 'fluent and elaborate' (*Women's Writing* 49), illustrates the vitality of Latin literacy and culture among well-educated religious women as late as the thirteenth century. The Benedictine convent of Helfta, under the forty-year rule of its Abbess Gertrude of Hackeborn (Mechtild's elder sister), was renowned for its learning and piety. It produced two saints and three visionaries: St Gertrude the Great (not to be confused with the abbess), Mechtild of Hackeborn (called in English either Maud or Matilda), and

Mechtild of Magdeburg, who was a beguine before retiring late in life to Helfta. Gertrude the Great and Mechtild of Hackeborn were both oblates, that is, children given to the convent at a very young age – Gertrude came to Helfta at four or five, Mechtild at age seven (BL MS Egerton 2006 f. 22v). They spent their entire lives in a community made up exclusively of enclosed women actively engaged in the pursuit of learning.

Gertrude came to write down Mechtild's visions because of Mechtild's reluctance to reveal them:[27] 'And of her own lowness she held herself so unworthy that she would not tell [of her visions] unless she were compelled by those who were familiar with her spiritual [ghostly] secrets. And yet of those she told only part; some she withheld and some she described for the worship of Our Lord, but only when she was constrained by the virtue of obedience' (*Visions of St Matilda*, BL MS Egerton 2006, f. 21; translation mine). Mechtild's diffidence highlights several important features of visionary literature. The first is the ambivalence many female visionaries express about the publicity their visions bring. Mechtild seems to have tried to avoid publication, perhaps not so much because of her modesty, but because she felt writing would put them beyond her control – 'what shall befall this book after my death?' (f. 136). She asks God, 'how may I know if all they write of these showings is true when I have not read them and I have not approved them?' (f. 202). She certainly does not shy away from the public roles that her visions create for her: 'She gave doctrine and teaching in so great abundance that there was never anyone like her in that monastery and, I fear, there never will be. Everywhere she was her sisters gathered together about her as they would about a preacher to hear God's word' (f. 208). Despite the Church's injunctions against women preaching, Mechtild seems comfortable in the public roles of teaching and preaching so long as that teaching is tied to her person. What she fears is the loss of authorial control that writing brings.

This fear reminds us that visionary literature is always belated. Any visionary experience made public is always a re-visioning of that experience, an attempt to represent through physical forms the unrepresentable spirit. Both Mechtild and Gertrude are conscious of this gap between the presence implied by the vision and the absence implied by writing: 'but you should understand that all the revelations that are written in this book are but few in number, considering all the others that have been left unwritten. For many more were shown to her by Our Lord which she would not tell. Also sometimes what she saw was so spiritual that there was no way she could or would show it in words' (f. 136v). The ineffable recedes in the violence of writing. The visions become literary constructs which attempt to move the reader beyond words, beyond the physical to the spiritual. Yet the physical continues to reassert its claims if only because vision, and accompanying sensory experiences, such as sound or smell, are rooted in physical sensation. Mechtilde's visions, at times, evoke a palpable physicality.

The reader of Middle English *The Book of Ghostly Grace* encounters Mechtild's visions as literary artifacts at three removes: Mechtild has related them to Gertrude who writes them in Latin which is then translated by an anonymous fifteenth-century writer into English. Nothing is known of this translator, though it seems likely the translation was done in the first half of the fifteenth century. The original audience appears to have been religious, as the prologues refer at one point to 'devout sisters' (f. 20v) and at another to 'brethren and sisters' (f. 21). Several fifteenth-century monastic houses in England appeared to have owned copies of the text, including Syon Abbey (see above pp. 49–53), whose library catalogue lists four manuscript copies, including one in English (Halligan, *Ghostly Grace* 51). The appearance of the names 'Anne warrewyk' and 'R. Gloucestre' on the flyleaf of Egerton 2006 suggests that this particular manuscript might have at one time been owned by Richard III and his wife, Anne Warwick, indicating that the book enjoyed a popularity among the laity as well. That Richard might have owned this volume is not as farfetched as it may seem (if we rely only on Shakespeare's characterization of the villain in *Richard III*). His mother, Cecily, Duchess of York, who was renowned for her piety, owned a copy, mentioned in her household ordinances, which she bequeathed to her granddaughter Brigitte (see above p. 78).

Theresa Halligan, the editor of *The Book of Ghostly Grace*, claims that one explanation of the text's popularity in fifteenth-century England is that, during a period of intense religious controversy, it contained nothing heterodox (55–7). Yet it is not difficult to discern in many of Mechtild's visions some resistance to the monopoly of the priesthood over the liturgy and sacraments. On more than one occasion, when she desires to receive communion but has not confessed herself, she is allowed to confess her sins directly to God 'the most high and worthy priest' (f. 114), by-passing the authority of the male clergy. At times she even assumes the function of the clergy. In one Eucharistic vision, Christ gives her 'his heart in the likeness of a cup of gold wondrously and richly arrayed and of curious work'. She then offers the cup in turn to the angels, the patriarchs, the prophets, apostles, martyrs, confessors and virgins, using words reminiscent of those the priest speaks over the Eucharist. Most of Mechtild's visions take place in church during mass and are tied to particular liturgical feasts – the Nativity, the Circumcision, the Epiphany, Palm Sunday – and particular moments in the service. Since women were excluded from active participation in the rituals of the mass (they could not be priests), and were not even allowed to view the climactic performance of the mass, Mechtild's visions create for her a means of participating actively in liturgical rituals. They also, intentionally or not, challenge clerical authority.

The participatory quality of Mechtild's revelations invoke a characteristic way of looking that is shared by many medieval visionaries. It creates a visual regime that is, as Sarah Stanbury has noted, quite different from 'the scopic regime of modernity'. Much feminist analysis of the visual has relied on a theoretical approach that emphasizes a specular gaze that splits subject and object, using distance to objectify and control (Stanbury, 'Regimes' 279). Medieval visionaries gazed at the divine, but not voyeuristically to possess and control it. Instead, by looking, they ran the risk of annihilation: 'Suddenly she saw our lord Iesus on high sitting on his throne and with that delectable sight she fell from herself into nothing as burning wood turns to ashes' (f. 24). The visionary gaze 'fractures distance, fusing self with the objects of devotional desire in a hybridized mix of maternal, infantile, and erotic impulses' (Stanbury, 'Regimes' 267). It is this intersubjective gaze that gives Mechtild's visions much of their charm and emotional force. One vision of the Nativity, for instance, illustrates both the participatory and intersubjective nature of the mystical gaze, as well as its melding of the infantile and maternal:

> This holy maiden, sitting beside Our Lady, as it seemed to her, beheld that holy vision [of the nativity] and the blessed countenance between the mother and the son. Greatly she desired to kiss the lovely child. Suddenly, that glorious mother and maiden took her son and spoke to him meekly and embraced him between her arms softly, and took him to the maiden so that she might have him in her arms as she desired. That blessed nun took him from Our Lady with great love and held him between her arms and with her hands pressed him to her heart. (f. 29; Barratt, *Women's Writing* 52–3)

It would be a mistake to read this passage as the expression of longing for a peculiarly female experience like motherhood which has been denied to the career virgin. As Carolyn Bynum has persuasively shown, this maternal imagery is far too widespread in devotional works by both men and women (Bynum, *Jesus as Mother*). It is especially representative of Cistercian piety, which greatly influenced the spirituality of the nuns of Helfta. Rather than try to characterize this imagery as peculiarly female, it seems more productive to examine this maternal vision as an example of what Stanbury calls 'tactile visualization', a way of seeing quite alien to the kind of analytics of vision developed by theorists like Foucault (*Discipline and Punish*) or John Berger (*Ways of Seeing*). In this visual scheme, the gaze on the object of devotion – in this case the infant Christ – and the desire to participate in the events of Christ's life efface the emotional and aesthetic distance characteristic of post-Enlightenment, scientific optics, disrupt boundaries between subject and object, transform the viewer from a passive onlooker (even a voyeur) to an active participant in the drama she watches, and, at times, even displace gender as a fixed category (as it does, for instance, in the visions in which Mechtild takes on priestly roles).

If visionary writing provides modern readers with a challenge to post-Enlightenment optics, it also offers a unique space for exploring representations of interiority or what contemporary theory calls 'subjectivity'. By their very strangeness, mystical visions highlight what Foucault called the 'technologies of the self', those strategies by which the self represents itself to itself and to the world, those strategies by which the self literally fashions itself. These technologies are nearly invisible to analysis because they are so naturalized (Foucault, 'Sexuality and Solitude'). Medieval literature is not known for its interiority. It has a tendency to externalize what the Russian critic V. N. Vološinov calls the 'inner voice' (Vološinov, *Marxism* 28–9, 37–9).[28] This tendency is reflected in the period's preference for allegory as a mode of expression, which tends to render the internal dialogue as exterior form. Yet, as Foucault noted, in techniques like the confessional the Middle Ages would lay the groundwork for those psychological processes of interiority that we take for granted in modern literature and life.

By way of an example of the medieval preference for exteriority we might turn to a Middle English translation of yet another continental mystic of the thirteenth century, St Elizabeth of Hungary. The identity of this mystic has not been established with any certainty, but if we accept Barratt's suggestion that the revelations preserved in Cambridge MS Hh.1.11 are those of Elizabeth of Toess (1294–1336), a Dominican nun at the convent of Toess, then we may have a text produced almost exclusively by women. Elizabeth dictated her revelations orally to another nun, perhaps Elsbeth Stagel, author of a Middle High German life of the nuns of Toess and close friend of the German mystic, Henry Suso. The Middle English version, which was produced from a Latin text, may have belonged to a convent of nuns, perhaps the Franciscans at Bruisyard in Suffolk; some of the text's scribes may have even been nuns (Barratt, *Women's Writing* 71–2).[29]

Elizabeth's visions, which consist mostly of dialogues with the Virgin Mary, tend to externalize the mystic's subjectivity, primarily by insisting on the corporeality of her visions. The Virgin Mary appears to her, 'not in sleep but in waking' (CUL MS H.1.11, f. 122; translations mine) and later 'visibly' (f. 122v), stressing that the event is not a dream, an internal state, but an event in the external world. While occasionally the text makes reference to interiorized states of mind – 'I thought in my heart' (f. 122v), 'she thought' (f. 126), 'she saw secretly with the eyes of her soul' (f. 127v) – the text tends to externalize the interior process of the soul's progression toward perfection in God. Many of Elizabeth's visions occur while she is praying, which is surely as much an interior as an exterior activity, that is, one's state of mind is more important than the external signs of prayer (kneeling, crossing, reciting). Yet this activity is represented through external and corporeal images. For instance, when the Virgin Mary describes the proper way to pray, she does so by comparing it to a man who will dig a new well:

> When I prayed I did as he that would make a new well. First he goes to that part of a hill where the water runs and searches busily for the vein of water. And when he has found it, then he begins to dig in that part of the hill until he finds the spring of the water running. And then after he brings the water to the place of the well which he makes fairly large to ensure that enough clean and clear water may be kept there ever more. Afterwards he walls the well on every side and in the middle of the well he makes a pillar of stone, and fastens to it cane on every side so that the water now goes through it the more plenteously on every side. (f. 126)

She continues, 'Right so to speak spiritually I did.' She goes to the hill when she learned the law of Moses and the commandments; she finds the vein of water in praying. 'The spring well of all good', she says, is 'to love God with all my heart and with all my might.' The water flows into the well when she 'desired and assented to love all things that God loves and to hate all things that he hated.' 'Then I kept bright and clear water when I studied to keep the desire of my heart and the affection of my wits from all filth and sin. Then I raised a wall about the well when I was busy to keep all virtues and especially meekness and patience with faith, hope, and charity' (f. 126). Throughout this passage Mary, Elizabeth's spiritual guide, casts internal spiritual disciplines like prayer, study, even self-examination, and emotions like desire, love and hate, only in terms of external corporeal processes like searching for water or digging a well. If modern readers find comparisons of this kind a bit strained and alienating, it is because of their ostensible avoidance of the techniques of internal self-examination with which we have become so familiar.

To be sure, as Foucault argues, techniques of self-examination were available to medieval men and women. 'Everyone in Christianity', he writes, 'has the duty to explore who he is, what is happening within himself, the faults he may have committed, the temptations to which he is exposed. Moreover, everyone is obliged to tell these things to other people, and hence to bear witness against himself' ('Sexuality and Solitude' 367). But the hermeneutics of the self Foucault attributes to early Christianity bear little resemblance to post-Enlightenment technologies of self-examination. The modern reader, accustomed to technologies of the self that presuppose a transcendent subject already there to be examined, will invariably find medieval technologies of the self remote and unappealing precisely because they seem to be fashioning the very subject they purport to be examining.

An example from another Middle English mystical text will illustrate this point. The *Liber Celestis* of St Bridget of Sweden (1303–73), a collection of more than 650 of the saint's visions, achieved wide popularity in England among both religious and lay readers. It survives in seven Middle English manuscripts (though none are complete) and is mentioned in several fifteenth-century wills, including that of Cecily, Duchess of York, who bequeathed a copy to her daughter, the prioress of Syon Abbey, the only Bridgettine house in England (see above p. 78). A Swedish noblewoman and the mother of eight children, Bridget was the first woman to found a religious order, though she herself never became a nun. Bridget seems to have taken a more direct hand in the publication of her visions than the other mystics we have examined so far. She either wrote or dictated her visions in Old Swedish immediately after the event. They were then translated into Latin by one of her confessors and read back to her so she could correct any errors, 'so that not one word was added or left out, unless it was seen or heard in a divine vision' (*Liber Celestis* xiii). Though the originals were destroyed, Peter of Alvestra recorded the Latin in a book which later became the *Liber Celestis* (Cumming, *Revelations* xxvii).

Like Elizabeth of Hungary's visions, Bridget's revelations often raise the problem of interiority most complexly when they attempt (and fail) to articulate the nature of the mystic's vision: 'It seemed to a person waking in prayer and not sleeping, as though she had seen in a spiritual vision a palace of incomprehensible greatness' (Cumming, *Revelations* 43). Later she describes seeing a pulpit within a house, surrounded by an angel and a fiend: ' "when I," said Saint Bridget, "beheld attentively with all consideration of my mind the same pulpit, my understanding was not sufficient to conceive it as it was, nor might my soul comprehend the fairness of it, nor my tongue express it" ' (*Liber Celestis* 68). These attempts to communicate the nature of the mystical vision are striking in the way they simultaneously engage both interiority and exteriority, deconstructing the opposition between inside and out. Bridget insists that the vision is an interior event, separate from the exterior physical world, engaging her mind, her conscience, her soul. But she also insists that it is real, that it happens to a person who is awake. It can be externally validated and so is not merely a solipsistic event, like a dream. This, God informs her, is the only way humans can understand the divine: 'these things that are shown to you are not corporeal but spiritual. For neither angel nor fiend has body; but they are shewn to you in such a way, for you may not understand spiritual things but by bodily likeness' (Cumming, *Revelations* 69).

Bridget's revelations illustrate the spiritual techniques that Foucault discusses but demonstrate how that interiority is fashioned rather than revealed by these techniques. Early in Book 1, Christ teaches Bridget how to tell a divine vision from one inspired by the devil. Distinguishing the two must have been a source of great anxiety to Bridget's spiritual advisers. The audacity with which mystics like St Bridget proclaimed divine inspiration must have been frightening to the orthodox Church; it certainly challenged their monopoly on technologies of the self, allowing, in Foucault's words, 'individuals to affect, by their own means, a certain number of operations on their own bodies, their own souls, their own thoughts, their own conduct, and this in a manner . . . to transform themselves, modify themselves, and to attain a certain state of perfection, happiness, purity, supernatural power' ('Sexuality and Solitude' 367). Enumerating the ways in which the 'unclean spirit' may tempt her, Christ reminds her that the 'unclean spirit' often deceives under 'the colour of good': 'and therefore I bade thee discuss thy conscience and open it to spiritual wisemen' (*Liber Celestis* 10). Bridget's careful account of her visions, then, records not only her own self-fashioning, but the process by which the Church attempts to wrest back some control of Bridget's audacious claims to self-definition as well.

The central metaphor permeating the *Liber Celestis* by which Bridget fashions herself is the image of the bride of Christ. In the second chapter of Book I, Christ marries Bridget: 'I have chosen you and taken you as my spouse, for it pleases me to do so and I will show you my privy secrets' (*Liber Celestis* 8). In her revelations, the widowed Bridget is always identified by her role as bride of Christ or daughter-in-law of the Virgin Mary; she is always referred to as 'the spouse' or 'the daughter', depending on whether she is talking with Christ or the Virgin. The external role of spouse is used throughout to define the saint's inner state – her devotion to God: 'you assigned your will into my hands at the time of your husband's death, after whose burying you had great thought and made prayer as to how you might be poor for me, and you desired to forsake all things for me. . . . Wherefore I take you as my spouse for my own proper delight, as it is proper that God have his delight with a chaste soul' (*Liber Celestis* 8). Bridget's will, her desire, her thoughts and prayers are made manifest, enumerated, and even called into being, by the social role of bride. It is proper, Christ tells her, for a bride to be 'honestly and seemingly arrayed and to be ready when her husband will make the wedding'. Just so, 'you are made clean when, with knowledge that you have sinned, you call to mind how, in baptism, I cleansed you from Adam's sin, and how afterward, when you were fallen into sin, I suffered you and supported you' (*Liber Celestis* 8). And just as a wife is supposed to have some token of her husband's upon her breast, 'so you shall ever be fresh in the knowledge of the benefice and the works I have done for you: how nobly I made you, how largely I gave my gifts to you, how sweetly I bought you, and how goodly I restored you to your heritage' (8).[30] In these passages, the bridal imagery enables Bridget to participate in precisely the sort of self-examination that Foucault argues was the primary obligation imposed on the individual by Christianity.

Bridget, however, does not wrest from her visions the power to define only herself; they also give her power to act in the world, even to give advice to the powerful. An illumination at the beginning of Book III of BL MS Cotton Claudius B.i, the only complete Middle English translation of the *Liber Celestis*, illustrates this point nicely. It shows Bridget seated next to a bishop who is standing over her (f. 116 a). While the iconography of a magnificently dressed cleric towering over a slight, humbly dressed woman might initially suggest the bishop's power over the woman, there are subtle cues that work against this interpretation. While the bishop seems to be either admonishing or blessing the woman, with his right hand raised, the saint, seated in a thronelike seat with a nimbus around her head, is writing in a book, presumably the *Liber Celestis*. What the text reveals is that the serene-looking woman in the illumination is actually admonishing the bishop in proper and temperate clerical behaviour. The external trappings of their relationship are reversed by the power of the saint's visions. Similarly in a series of chapters in Book IV (103–5), Bridget admonishes the French and English kings to find some peaceful resolution to their conflicts (this would be in the midst of the Hundred Years War) by relating a vision she had of Mary's and St Denis's intercession and Christ's response to their prayers (*Liber Celestis* 341–5).

The Church did not always, however, willingly cede such power either to women or to the laity. Those mystics who were given the Church's approval were few and they were carefully scrutinized for doctrinal purity. Others who made such audacious claims did not fare so well; they are not memorialized as saints and their works are little known. In *Women Writers of the Middle Ages*, Peter Dronke calls Marguerite Porete 'the most neglected of the great writers of the thirteenth century' (202). Author of a book of poetic prose, dialogues and lyrics written around 1285–95 called *Le mirouer des simples ames anienties et qui seulement demourent en vouloir et desir d'Amour*, this French visionary was condemned at Valenciennes in the last years of the thirteenth century and when she persisted in her heresy was imprisoned, tried and publicly burnt as a heretic in Paris on 1 June 1310. Copies of her book were also ordered destroyed; to possess one was considered an act of heresy, punishable by excommunication. Yet, despite this inquisitorial ban, surviving copies of *The Mirror of Simple Souls* in French, Latin, Italian and English testify to the life of this visionary text long after its author's ignominious death. Today the *Mirror* is significant not only because its author was a woman but also because it is one of the only documents to offer evidence independent of inquisitorial testimony of the beliefs that marked the heresy known as the Free Spirit (*secta spiritus libertatis*).

The Mirror of Simple Souls was translated into English some time during the fifteenth century by a Carthusian monk. It survives in two manuscripts, MS Bodley 505 and British Library MS Additional 37790 (which contains, among other things, the sole surviving copy of the short text of the Revelations of the fifteenth-century English mystic Julian of Norwich; see below Chapter 4). Because of its heretical status, the English translation of *The Mirror* is a fascinating instance of what the Russian cultural theorist Mikhail Bakhtin would call a dialogic text, a text without a single controlling authorial 'voice'. Instead it is a site of struggle over authority that in many ways re-enacts Marguerite's own struggle to articulate her beliefs in the face of inquisitorial intimidation. While it is possible to read the English translation as an appropriation of the *Mirror* that serves the ends of a conservative Christian doctrine, eradicating the call for radical freedom and pleasure that marks the original (Vaneigem, *Movement* 129), such a reading would be monologic; it would misunderstand the extent to which the English translator fails to domesticate the *Mirror* for orthodoxy.

The two manuscript copies of the English *Mirror* are nearly identical, suggesting that both manuscripts were produced under strict clerical supervision. The translator appears not to have known that *The Mirror* was written by a woman nor that it had been condemned as heretical. But he is nevertheless very anxious about the doctrinal soundness of the text he is reproducing. That anxiety displays itself throughout the translator's prologue where he attempts to recuperate the text for orthodoxy. He begins:

> This book, which is called *The Mirror of Simple Souls*, I, most unworthy creature and outcast from all others, for many years worked to translate out of French and into English after my ignorance in hopes that by the grace of God it would perfect those devout souls that read it. . . . But now I am stirred to labour with it anew because I am informed that some words in it have been mistaken. Therefore, God willing, I shall declare those words more openly for though Love declares those points in the same book, they are but briefly set out and may be taken in ways other than they were intended to be by those who read it suddenly and take no further heed. (BM Add. 37790, f. 137; translation mine)

Because the text is so elusive, so difficult – it is 'of high ghostly feelings and cunningly and full mistily it is spoken' – it may easily be misunderstood by its readers. The translator does not see himself simply as 'carrying over' the sense of the French words into the English language, but rather functions as an active participant in the text's construction. At times, he adds his more authoritative voice to the author's as a form of choral support, praising the text's 'high ghostly feelings' and cunning language; at other points, he rejects the author's sense altogether and attempts a counter-argument. At such moments the text most clearly reveals its struggles around issues of authority and orthodoxy.

The translator's anxiety is perhaps most clearly marked by his attempt to gloss those passages that seem to him doctrinally questionable. Because the translator has marked his rather lengthy glosses of Marguerite's text with his own initials (M.N.), it is possible to reconstruct the text as an actively double-voiced text in which two powerful and contradictory voices struggle for recognition. Neither is able to drown out the other. The translator is not willing to allow Marguerite's words simply to be relayed to even the most orthodox and discriminating reader without comment. But neither is he able to erase the radical import of those words; they actively resist such appropriation. The translator's method of marking his textual interpretations of the *Mirror* with his initials sets the two styles into sharp relief.

This double orientation is realized in the text's style, intonation and syntax, or the text's two styles, intonations and syntaxes. Just as we noted in the translator's language an anxious glance in the direction of possible clerical superiors, in Marguerite's style and syntax we can note sideward glances at the hostility of the Church. This is especially prominent in her appropriation of the style and intonation of biblical discourse, especially the gospels and St Paul's epistles, as in the following passage:

> Charity obeys nothing that is made, but only love. Charity owns nothing, not so much that she will ask for anything that is hers. Charity leaves her own work and goes to do others. Charity asks no allowance of any creature for anything she has done. Charity has no dread, nor disease. She is so righteous that she may not flit for anything that falls. (f. 141)

Marguerite borrows the intonations of Paul's epistle (1 Corinthians 13), drawing on the power of its balanced repetition and anaphora, but substituting words of her own choosing, words that allow for a more radical interpretation of Paul's message. Marguerite's biblical lyricism contrasts sharply with the rational, even prosaic language of the translator in his commentaries.

An example may help to clarify this point. Discussing the nature of love and the perfected soul, Marguerite audaciously insists that the annihilated (or 'nouȝted') soul has no need of the virtues.

> 'The soul of such love,' says Love, 'himself may say thus to virtues: "I take leave of you," to which virtues this soul many a day has been servant to.'
> 'I assent, lady love,' says this soul. 'So it was then but now it is thus that your courtesy has thrown me out of her danger. Therefore I say, virtues, I take leave of you and more in peace than it has been because I know well that your service is too laborious. For some time I laid my heart in you without any deception. You know this well. I was obedient to you in all things. O, I was then your servant, but now I am delivered out of your bondage. I know well that I laid my heart in you, so I had long endured in great servitude in which I have suffered many grievous torments

and endured many pains. It is a marvel that I have escaped with my life. But now I do not care because I am parted from you and therefore I dwell in peace.' (f. 143)

In this passage, Marguerite expresses one of the tenets most frequently associated with the sect of the Free Spirit – and the one most noxious to spiritual authorities – that the annihilated soul has no need of virtue. The *Determinatio de novo spiritu*, attributed to Albertus Magnus and written toward the end of the thirteenth century, attributes to heretics of the Free Spirit the belief that 'Man can be united with God in such a way that he no longer sins, whatever he does' (Vaneigem, *Movement* 119). The inquisitor Ubertino of Casale writes around 1305 of similar beliefs: 'They say that men who have the grace of God and charity cannot sin' (Vaneigem, *Movement* 128). In this passage, Marguerite's rejection of virtue is expressed through metaphors of feudal servitude, metaphors that invoke traditional descriptions of Adam's fall into sin and the subsequent bondage of all humanity. Words like 'thralldom' and 'servage' often appeared in narratives of the fall (see for instance Langland's *Piers Plowman*). Terms like 'grievous tormentis', 'paynes' and 'travelous' which would have been appropriate to describe the pains of hell are here attributed to the virtues. It is interesting to speculate to what extent such metaphors expressed resistance not only toward the restrictions imposed by spiritual authority, but also resentment toward temporal authority as well, toward the 'servage' inherent in feudal relations.

The translator is all too aware of the conventional uses of these figures. At this point in the text, he interjects a gloss, marking his dialogue with the text carefully, not only with his initials, but also by addressing his readers, 'Ye auditors of this book', with phrases like 'Touching these words that this soul says'. He restores the 'proper' tenor of the metaphor, claiming that when the soul gives itself to perfection it labours day and night to 'get virtues by counsel of reason' and strives with vice at every point. M.N. restores an orthodox reading to the passage, reinstating the traditional substance of its metaphors of servitude. The virtues are once again the 'mistresses' who impose both spiritual and physical suffering on the soul [f. 143]. He can achieve this interpretation, however, only by doing severe violence to the sense of Marguerite's text.

This is a tactic that is repeated throughout the English *Mirror*. When Marguerite proclaims that the 'annihilated soul' should give 'to nature all that he asks without complaining', M.N. must at least suspect that the author is expressing the heretical belief that (again in the the words of the *Determinatio*), 'Whoever is united with God, can assuage his carnal desire with impunity and in any way, with either sex, and even by inverting the roles' (Vaneigem, *Movement* 118). He counters with a shocked reply: 'Now God forbid that any would be so worldly to think that this means to give to nature any lust that tends toward fleshly sin, for God knows that is not what is meant' (146r). When she argues that 'this soul desires neither despite, nor poverty, nor tribulation, nor disease, nor masses, nor sermons, nor fasting, nor orisons', she again expresses sentiments that are attributed to Free Spirit heretics, that, in the words of the *Determinatio*, 'Man united with God . . . is not bound to accord honor or respect to the saints, nor to observe fasts and similar things on the day of the Lord' (Vaneigem, *Movement* 118). Her words, for M.N., 'seem fable or false, or hard to understand'. M.N. argues that the 'nouȝted' souls in fact really do desire 'for God's sake' despite, tribulation, disease, masses, sermons, fastings and orisons. Love's statement that they don't desire these things provokes a two and one-half page commentary designed to demonstrate that the author of the text meant exactly the opposite of what her text quite plainly says. When love says that these souls don't desire masses or sermons, fastings or orisons we shouldn't take her to mean that they should leave these undone: 'He would be blind to take it in that way.' Rather these souls simply cannot will or desire; instead God wills or desires in them.

In a superficial reading, such diatribes might seem, and no doubt were intended as, a heavy-handed reassertion of monologic authority designed to 'correct' a flawed text and save it for orthodoxy. Yet as a monologic reading, the translation fails utterly. Even as the translator attempts to assert his control − and that of the institutional Church − over the text's authorial voice, even as he tries to manipulate that voice for his own purposes, the text resists appropriation and disputes his intentions. If M.N. attempts to gloss Marguerite's 'misty' text, that text itself glosses the translator's words. Two voices and two accents compete within the text for hegemony. Because M.N.'s role as faithful translator conflicts with his role as representative and guardian of Christian orthodoxy, the English *Mirror* brings together in a single text the rebel and the conformist, the powerless and the powerful, the heretic and the monk. In such a text 'the author's thought no longer oppressively dominates the other's thought, discourse loses its composure and confidence, becomes agitated, internally undecided, and two-faced' (Bakhtin, *Dostoevsky's Poetics* 198). In this loss of composure, we can begin to read something of the complexity − the heterodoxy − of late medieval religious discourse.

A dialogism of a different sort between author and translator marks the Middle English translation of a much more orthodox, yet no less difficult text, *The Dialogue* of St Catherine of Siena. The circumstances both of writing and translation are very different. Catherine of Siena, a charismatic Italian mystic who became the first and only female Doctor of the Church, was neither a heretic nor an enclosed nun. At fifteen she refused the marriages her parents had arranged for her, pledging her virginity to God, like

Bridget, in a mystical vision of marriage to Christ. She lived a life of solitary piety at home until some time around 1363 when she joined the Dominican Third Order or Tertiaries, an Order designed for women who wished to take vows but remain in the world. At about this time she learned to read (she never learned to write) and began to travel and preach, attracting a group of disciples. She became a figure of no small spiritual authority, who used her influence to convince Pope Gregory XI to return the papacy to Rome from Avignon.[31] *Il Dialogo*, a long didactic treatise, was dictated in 1378 to her three secretaries 'when her soul was ravished from all bodily feeling, as was witnessed by her clerks & all her disciples' (Hodgson and Liegey, *Orcherd of Syon* 2; translation mine). The result is unlike anything a modern reader might expect from writing produced in an ecstatic state; it certainly lacks the visual splendour of Mechtild's or Bridget's visions. Its didacticism reminds us that the mystical experience for medieval women and men was not an outpouring of spontaneous emotionalism; it was a discipline. That is, these texts both illustrate the kinds of disciplines mystics undertook as part of their religious practice and are themselves a form of discipline (Petroff, *Visionary Literature* 6–19). The latter is particularly true of Catherine's long treatise. Unlike the mystical texts examined so far, it is not a narrative account of mystical visions, but a long treatise of orthodox moral instruction – abstract, philosophical and theological – an attempt to discipline the mind to the service of God. At first glance the title given this treatise, *The Dialogue*, may seem ironic, given that the text reproduces God's voice as pure monologue. But Catherine's treatment of voice in the text – attributing her words to God – suggests the ambivalence of her position as charismatic religious leader. If women, in the fourteenth century, were not allowed to instruct and preach, Catherine could get around this prohibition by claiming that God spoke through her. Ironically, her ecstatic visions enabled her to produce a work of almost scholastic rationalism that earned her the title of Doctor of the Church.

The fifteenth-century Middle English translation of *Il Dialogo* called *The Orcherd of Syon* extends Catherine's dialogue with religious authorities to include a new audience. This translation was made by an anonymous translator, 'I sinful, unworthy to bear any name' (1), for the nuns of Syon Abbey:[32] 'Religious mother and devout sisters, chosen to labour busily at the house of Syon' (1). How was the translator to adapt this abstruse and abstract treatise for the use of the 60 enclosed women who made up the first generation of nuns at Syon? The earliest Italian and Latin manuscripts of *Il Dialogo* were transcribed without any divisions into parts and chapters. These were added later to an official Latin redaction, presumably to impose some kind of order on an unruly text and to provide smaller portions for its readers to digest, to give it 'clarity and precision' (Hodgson and Liegey, *Orcherd* vii). The Middle

English redactor improves on earlier versions. Picking up on the remark that the sisters labour 'in the blessed vineyard of our Holy Saviour', he or she[33] designs the book as an orchard where the sisters could wander and be comforted: 'You may walk and see both fruit and herbs. And although some fruit or herbs seem to some sharp, hard, or bitter, yet they are necessary and profitable to the purging of the soul' (1). The translator urges the sisters to 'disport and walk about' in this 'ghostly [or spiritual] orchard at a reasonable time ordained'. They may choose where to walk among the thirty-five alleys provided, by which he or she means the thirty-five chapters, divided into seven parts of five chapters each. 'But first my counsel is clearly to try and search the whole orchard, and taste of such fruit and herbs reasonably after your affection, and what you like best afterwards chew it well and eat of it for the health of your soul' (1).

The translator's use of the extended metaphor of the orchard seems particularly appropriate for the sisters of Syon. In Chapter 1 I noted the careful partitioning of time and space in the convent, as well as the contrast between earthly and spiritual space and time (pp. 49–53). The intense regionalization of space and time in *The Orchard of Syon*, its division of Catherine's treatise into alleys, physical spaces, which can be explored at appropriate times, corresponds to the regionalization of monastic time and space that marked the organization and routine of the Bridgettine abbey. At the same time, the religious symbolism of the orchard and the numbers of the alleys, 5 and 7, with their invocation of the chronotope of salvation history, cannot have been lost on its readers. *The Orchard of Syon* seems a perfect example of the medieval aesthetic that Robert M. Jordan calls the 'inorganic' (Jordan, *Chaucer* 10–43). Jordan's exploration of this aesthetic that values structure over expression may provide the modern reader with a means of approaching this alien and somewhat off-putting text.

The inorganic aesthetic values above all harmony and proportion, reason and ratio. It explores 'the aesthetic possibilities of fixity, divisibility, and juxtaposition' through such quantitative means as amplification, division and embellishment (Jordan, *Chaucer* 14, 34). The Middle English translator adopts this aesthetic procedure, using division as a means of explicating the meaning of Catherine's treatise, delineating its parts. What is fascinating about this aesthetic is that it enables a complete split between substantive content and structural form (38). The translator's addition of 35 'alleys' to the original leaves the substance of the treatise untouched. Even when they encourage meditation on Catherine's words, enabling readers to encounter them within a manageable space and time, the translator's divisions bear no obvious or 'organic' structural relation to Catherine's words. The separation between translator and author in *The Orchard of Syon* seems as marked as that in the Middle English *Mirror of Simple Souls*.

And yet the translator's partitioning does not seem to wrench the sense of Catherine's text because she shares this inorganic sensibility, this preference for structure over expression and quantitative rhetoric over qualitative. There is in Catherine's visions none of the emotionalism that characterizes late medieval piety. She is told by God to 'open the eyes of thy intellect, and thou shall see' (62). This intellectualism sets her visions apart from those of a St Bridget, a Margery Kempe, or even a mystic whose theology was as sophisticated as Julian of Norwich (see pp. 165–76). Catherine's style is marked by inorganic metaphors and allegories that are often just as strained – just as constructed – as the translator's conceit of the orchard. In the beginning of Part 2, Catherine portrays the Incarnation through the metaphor of a bridge: 'But first I will that you look at the bridge of my son, and that you behold the greatness of that bridge which stretches from the height of heaven down to the earth. That is to say that the earth of your humanity is joined to the greatness of the godhead. And therefore I say that that bridge stretches from this high heaven to the low earth' (62). The oddly surreal character of this image is rendered quite literally by woodcuts in Wynkyn de Worde's 1519 edition that depict St Catherine on the right side praying, God in heaven connected to earth with a bridge across which souls are climbing. Other, presumably lost, souls are in the water passing under the bridge. In the upper left there is a dying man being tormented by a demon. The bridge metaphor conveys none of the passion that marks other late medieval discussions of Christ's Incarnation. Instead its vehicle calls attention to the logic of structure. The reader is not invited to identify with the humanity she shares with Christ; rather she is asked to recognize the inherent rationality of God's connection with humanity.

Other aspects of Catherine's style conveyed by the translation reinforce her rationalism and intellectualism. The text is marked by a degree of hypotaxis, subordination and complexity of sentence structure unusual in Middle English prose. Middle English is most comfortable making connections through juxtaposition. Such parataxis is responsible for some of the most marked effects in the styles of canonical Middle English writers like Chaucer or Malory. Catherine's prose at times seems to tax the resources of Middle English. One might choose a sample almost at random to examine the density of logical connectives – and hence of cause and effect – in her prose. For example, Adam's fall, God tells her at the beginning of Part 2, has the effect of breaking the bridge between God and the world. Adam becomes 'as an unreasonable beast': 'All the other creatures rebelled against him, where before they should have fully obeyed him, if he had kept that innocence in him in which I had made him. But since he kept him not in that state, but trespassed against my obedience, therefore he deserved everlasting death in soul and in body' (61). I have translated here literally and infelicitously to show both the frequency of subordinating connectives like 'but', 'if', 'since', and 'therefore', as well as the confusion that they occasionally cause. In the first sentence, it is difficult to tell whether one should translate the verb as a simple past tense – 'before [the fall] they obeyed him' – or as a future conditional – 'they should have obeyed if he had kept his innocence'. One might translate the Middle English 'where tofore-hond' as 'whereas' to resolve the conflict, but this translation misses the original's conflation of past and future in 'where tofore-hond þei schulden fully haue obeyed to hym.' The syntax conveys cause and effect, suggesting that Adam's punishments follow logically from his disobedience, but its conflation of time suggests that Adam's fall has always already happened.

What is perhaps, then, most remarkable about the existence of a text like *The Orchard of Syon* is what it tells us about the intellectual achievements of its intended audience, the nuns of Syon, whose task was, according to the translator, 'only to read and to sing [Our Lady's] service as her special servants and daughters' (1). This translation of Catherine of Siena's visions shows respect for the learning of its readers; the translator's only concession to their lesser education is to translate it into their mother tongue and divide it into parts, authority for which he, or she, might have found in many of the 41 Italian and Latin manuscripts of *Il Dialogo*. In all else the *Orcherd of Syon* preserves, as well as any translation can, the rationality, didacticism and difficulty of Catherine's text.

Though at first glance it seems about as far as it can get from the abstract and philosophizing bent of Catherine's *Il Dialogo*, the short fifteenth-century Middle English text known as *A Revelation Shown to a Holy Woman* displays an awareness of theological debate that might seem surprising for a pious laywoman. The text, which appears to be an actual letter written from a devout woman to her confessor, describes a series of three dreams the woman had in August of 1422 in which the soul of her late friend Margaret, a nun, appears to her and shows her the punishments of purgatory (Barratt, *Women's Writing* 163). It seems unlikely that the writer was a nun or an anchoress since she describes living alone with only a maidservant, and seems free to go on pilgrimages. At least one of the three extant fifteenth-century manuscripts (Oxford Bodleian MS Eng. Theol. c. 58), however, appears to have belonged to a religious institution since a rubric at the beginning addresses an audience of 'bretheryne and systryne' (f. 10).

The text itself appears deceptively simple, so much so that we might be tempted to dismiss it as an unsophisticated piece of popular piety. The narrative is a straightforward account of a series of fairly literal dream visions in which the narrator, like Dante, is ravished to purgatory where she sees the soul of her late friend Margaret. The prose consists almost exclusively of simple sentences beginning 'and then me thought'. The descriptions of the purgatorial punishments are vivid and quite lurid, focusing on horrific bodily torture, so much so it is difficult to resist quoting at great length. Describing, perhaps in an anti-clerical vein, the suffering of lecherous priests, for instance, she writes:

> Priests and their women were cast into deep pits full of strong fire. . . . And I thought that part of the pit was full of adders and snakes and of all wicked worms and there I thought they were so tormented that all the creatures in the world could not tell their pains. And then, dear father, I thought that they were taken out of that pit and cast into a strong deep water that I thought was so frozen that it seemed as cold as any and I thought the devils threw their flesh [in it] with strong hooks. And then, sir, I thought also [there were], lying on the water, many a strong light gibbet, such as men use to let down a bucket in a well to draw up water. . . . And I thought razors were put through the priests' throats and came out at their mouths. And it seemed to me they were plunged up and down in that stinking water as men plunge a bucket in a well and when they were taken down and brought out of that water, then suddenly they were cast into a strong fire and the devils cast oil and pitch on them and blew fast with strong bellows so that I could see nothing of them and soon after I thought the devil laid them upon anvils as smiths do when they burn iron and smite the priests with hammers. And then I thought they cried so horribly that all the world might not make so horrible a noise and so hideous a racket. And then I thought the devil took burning metal, I thought it was red gold, and put it into the priests' mouths and then it ran burning throughout their bodies. (Oxford Bodleian MS Eng. Theol. c. 58, f. 12v; translation mine)

It is certainly possible to see passages like this as the imaginings of a popular culture for which public torture and execution were a form of entertainment. This passage graphically displays the mentality Foucault describes in *Discipline and Punish* that invests the ruler (in this case God) with the power literally to inscribe the bodies of his subjects with punishments that proclaim their crimes (Dante's notion of *contrapasso*). Each of the punishments she describes is linked with a sin, usually one of the seven deadly sins (pride, envy, wrath, avarice, gluttony, sloth and lechery; the above tortures are punishments for lechery, gluttony and avarice).

Yet it would be a mistake to read this text only as a kind of admonition to an unsophisticated popular audience to amend their ways lest they suffer the same fate. It is important that this is not a description of the pains of hell, but of purgatory, that 'in-between' time and place – in-between heaven and hell, and in-between the individual's death and the general last judgement and resurrection of the body – where souls of individuals who have been saved but who have not yet expiated their sins are sent for punishment. *A Revelation Shown to a Holy Woman* displays an awareness of the complex theological controversies about the afterlife – and especially

143

about the status of purgatory – that had raged since the Second Council of Lyon in 1274 when purgatory as a liminal space for punishing the sins of those souls who will ultimately be saved was defined as doctrine (Bynum, *Resurrection* 280).

As Bynum points out, once articulated, the doctrine of purgatory came to play an increasingly important role in devotion and in social control. *A Revelation Shown to a Holy Woman* illustrates most of the complex contradictions and ambiguities of this doctrine. In the text, the horrors of purgatory serve as a warning to those still living to amend their ways. In her suffering, Margaret admonishes everybody to 'beware by me and, before he dies, do the penance that is given him by his spiritual father and forsake the lust of these wicked sins' (f. 11v). But the visions also serve as a reminder of the efficacy of prayers for the dead. In a long passage (ff. 11–11v), Margaret enumerates a series of masses (8 masses of the Requiem, 3 masses of St Peter, 2 masses of the Holy Ghost, etc.) and psalms and hymns (*Misere mei deus* and *Veni creator spiritus*)[34] that she wants said for her: 'I asked her why she desired this psalme *Misere* to be said so often for her and she said [it was] to have the mercy and the pity of God almighty, for, she said, as often as this psalm with the hymn [*Veni creator spiritus*] were said for her, she should be released from so many pains' (f. 11). For purgatory to serve as an effective form of social control it must offer hope that the souls of one's friends and relatives might continue to develop, and ultimately be saved, after death, while at the same time not allowing the living to become too complacent about their own salvation.

The doctrine of purgatory seems to challenge another central Church dogma about that afterlife – the resurrection of the body, the belief that after the Last Judgement body and soul will once again be united in either salvation or damnation. This doctrine suggests a view that the body – and psychosomatic unity – is essential to the self, that the soul is incomplete without the body (Bynum, *Resurrection* 8–13). The resurrection of the body would complete the process of salvation and the blessed soul would be admitted into the presence of God. Purgatory presents a view of the afterlife in which punishment for sins, as in the passage above, is strikingly somatic; the soul's ability to feel all the pains of the body would seem to render the resurrection of the body somewhat irrelevant for both saved and damned. This literalness occurs not only in the visions of a laywoman like the anonymous author of the *Revelation*, which we might be tempted to dismiss as unschooled; most preachers, poets, and theologians saw nothing fundamentally inconsistent in portraying the bodily punishment of disembodied spirits (Bynum, *Resurrection* 281). As the fourteenth-century *Gast of Gy* (*Ghost of Guy*), another popular visionary account of purgatory, suggests, the body is imagined as an instrument of the soul, which freely possesses all the body's powers to feel both pleasure and pain (Bartlett and Bestul, forthcoming). The Church militantly maintained both the doctrines of purgatory and the resurrection of the body against heretical teachings to the contrary.

In 1336 the Church proclaimed that the beatific vision could come to the saved before the resurrection of the body (Bynum, *Resurrection* 282). *A Revelation Shown to a Holy Woman* properly ends with a vision of Margaret's release from purgatory into heaven, where both the newly born soul and the narrator are granted a vision of God and the Virgin Mary. This *visio dei* was a matter of some controversy among fourteenth century theologians, and, while the controversy was largely settled by the fifteenth century, it does speak to the complexity of medieval views of the body; as Bynum argues, 'those who argued for a postponed *visio Dei* [until the resurrection of the body] spoke of the body as a garment or stole added at the end of time, those who supported immediate beatific vision spoke of the body as a manifestation or flowing out that appears almost timeless' (Bynum, *Resurrection* 283). The latter position prevailed, she argues, largely because medieval visionary and devotional literature imagined the beatific spirit as already possessed of, or expressed by, a body.

Devotional literature

Modern readers will doubtless have little sympathy for the kind of devotional prose that the Middle Ages produced and consumed in large quantities. It is hard for us to imagine why works that seem to us dull, repetitive and shapeless (at least on first reading) should have been so much more popular than the canonical poets – like Chaucer or the Gawain-poet, or even Marie de France – we still read and enjoy in the late twentieth century. The appeal of medieval devotional works has been lost to all but the handful of medieval scholars who study such texts because we have lost the context that gave these texts meaning. We lack the intimate familiarity with the texts, images and material culture which would have come as second nature to even the most uneducated laywoman of the fifteenth century immersed in the religious culture of the late Middle Ages. To illustrate how little prepared modern readers are to understand the culture that produced these texts, let me examine briefly how late medieval people read devotional texts. Two women who produced such texts included in their writing explicit instructions on how to read their work and these instructions provide a glimpse of a reading process that might help make sense of these texts' popularity.

In the prologue to her translation of the French *Meditation on the Seven Days of the Week*, Dame Eleanor Hull writes that her purpose is 'to inflame the heart and the courage of them that read it in the love of God and to make a man to know himself'. To this end, her meditations

> are not to be read in noise but in quiet, not lightly and quickly but little
> by little in great stillness and with great concentration. Those who read this
> should not set out to read them all over at once, but to take at one time
> only as much as they feel they can avail themselves of with the help of
> God to increase in them good will and devotion. . . . It is not necessary to
> begin every time at the beginning but [whoever reads this may begin]
> where ever he likes or has the most devotion to read. And for this reason
> they are marked by capital letters that they [readers] may begin where they
> like and leave when they like so that the reading will not begin to annoy
> them by being too long, but so the readers should gather and keep those
> things for which this book was made, that is for pity of heart, the love of
> God, and to know himself. (CUL MS Kk.1.6 f. 148; translation mine)

The anonymous author of the collection of meditative prayers called *The Faits and Passions of Our Lord Jesus Christ* adds 'I would you could get the sense without the book, for if you could you should feel much more comfort and union with God to see it so inwardly rather than to see it through writing' (Oxford Bodley MS Holkenham Misc. 41, f. 96; translation mine). This process of meditative reading, in which only a small part of the text is read, perhaps memorized, and then used for meditation, which allows readers to enter the text anywhere they like and leave off where ever they like, is foreign to late twentieth-century reading habits. We are much more likely to read a text sequentially even if we do not read it all in a sitting. Our reading habits spring from the belief that books are organically written so that readers must take in the whole in the order it was written. When we come to approach medieval devotional texts we often judge them, and find them lacking, by applying the same criteria, by looking for some kind of organic unity in them. But we search in vain for organic unity in devotional works like the anonymous *Faits and Passions of Our Lord Jesus Christ*, or the translations of Eleanor Hull. They draw on an entirely different, inorganic aesthetic which organizes the text extrinsically, according to the uses it expects readers to make of it – for instance *Meditations on the Seven Days of the Week* is organized with meditations for each day of the week – rather than according to some plan intrinsic to the content of the text.

The Faits and Passions of Our Lord Jesus Christ was most likely written sometime in the first half of the fifteenth century by an anonymous nun at the request of another sister. She begins, 'Religious sister, as much as you have desired and prayed me diverse times that I would write you the deeds and passions of Our Lord Jesus Christ, therefore now at this time, to satisfy your desire after my own simple knowledge, I will write them to you' (f. 2). And she begs her sister to pray for her to 'make me a good woman' (f. 3). It is entirely possible that this volume was produced by a nun of Syon for use there. Several references in the volume suggest such a provenance. In one passage the author thanks Christ for calling his 72 disciples (f. 35, see Barratt, *Women's Writing* 208). This reference to Christ's New Testament disciples may be a reference to *The Rule of St Saviour*, which governed Bridgettine convents (Syon was the only Bridgettine house in England), limiting its inhabitants to precisely 85 members (see above pp. 50–1): 60 sisters, 13 priests, 4 deacons and 8 lay brothers. The 13 priests represented the original apostles, while the 60 sisters, 4 deacons and 8 lay brothers symbolized the 72 New Testament disciples. Another possible indication that this text came from Syon is its inclusion of a prayer for the King:

> Oh mighty God, I especially pray you to keep and love, rule and counsel our King. Fill him with your Holy Ghost and give him good speed in all his works and make him withstand and avoid all that might in any way displease you. Holy God send him might and strength to have victory over all his spiritual and bodily enemies and give him a good life and a long one. (f. 15)

Syon was founded by Henry V and enjoyed continuous royal patronage up until the Dissolution of the Monasteries. It would be fitting for a work produced there to offer special prayers for its benefactor.

The text presents a series of prayers that meditate on Christ's life and especially on his passion and death. The prayers are conceived of as discrete entities, to be read not all at once, but 'as you have leisure and time' (f. 96). Characteristically, the prayer begins with a specific and often vivid image of Christ's life or death. The image is used not simply to move the reader to an emotional response. It also suggests an intellectual response; the reader is to use the image to examine the state of her own soul.

> You bore the heavy cross upon your sore bruised shoulders and wounded body. Lord sometimes the cross betokens penance and sometimes it signifies contemplation. O good God give grace that I may help to bear for your love all heavy burdens that fall to me. Also to do penance for your love as you did for me and grant me grace, blissful God, to be contemplative as my profession asks. (f. 65)

This passage moves from a contemplation of the image of Jesus carrying the cross to a perhaps predictable consideration of the heavy burdens the reader might need to bear. Less predictably it finishes by comparing that image with the contemplative life that was the almost exclusive province of those in religious orders. Similarly, consideration of the concrete image of Christ's garments being torn off his bleeding body leads the reader to contemplate union with God.

> O good Lord your clothes clung to your gracious body for the blood of your precious wounds was dried and congealed to them. And therefore in pulling them away, it pulled away both the skin and flesh of your blessed

back and sides. Have mercy and pity on all your people . . . and keep us
from all wickedness and knit us so fast to you with a love knot that the
knot be never unknit nor we separated from you. (f. 67)

Just as Christ's blood congeals his clothing to his skin, so God's people are
connected to him in a 'love knot' that cannot be untied.

The aesthetic principles on which literature of this type is based, then, is
quantitative. This aesthetic, which Jordan outlines in *Chaucer and the Shape
of Creation*, seems to me to fit this kind of devotional writing even better
than it does Chaucer. Such texts proceed by the rhetorical devices of
amplificatio and dilation. The translations of Dame Eleanor Hull perhaps
demonstrate this aesthetic most clearly. Hull (1394–1460), daughter and
wife of retainers of John of Gaunt (her husband was later a member of
Henry IV's household), was a devout laywoman, herself in the service of
Henry's second wife, Queen Joan. She was closely associated with the
abbey at St Albans (Barratt, *Women's Writing* 219). She translated from the
French an elaborate commentary on the seven penitential psalms (Psalms 6,
31, 37, 50, 101, 129 and 142) called *The Seven Psalms*, as well as a collection of prayers called *Meditations Upon the Seven Days of the Week*. In each
text, the organizational principle is external to the contents of the treatise:
the seven psalms organize the first, the seven days of the week, the second.
This principle is perhaps more obvious in the case of the *Meditations Upon
the Seven Days of the Week*, where, for instance, the story of Christ in the
Temple or particular saints' lives have no intrinsic connection with Wednes-
day or Thursday with the Last Judgement. The days of the week scheme
simply provides a convenient container for a series of meditative prayers.
The Seven Psalms consists of a series of glosses and commentaries on the
seven psalms that were considered appropriate for those who had confessed
their sins. In typical medieval fashion, the commentary glosses not the
whole of the psalm; instead it proceeds line by line, quoting a line of the
Latin text at the head of the commentary. For instance, glossing the line
from Psalm 37, 'Quoniam sagitte tuae infixae sunt mihi, Et confirmasti
super me manum tuam' ('For thine arrows stick fast in me, and thy hand
presseth sore'), the commentary says, 'These arrows are the vengeance of
God . . . that pierce through the body and the soul as the arrow of iron
pierces the flesh and sinews of the body of the man. And therefore he says
of the great mysteries of David that he felt the arrows of God fixed in him
so piercingly' (f. 54; translation mine). Though scriptural exegesis was, in
the Middle Ages, generally a preserve of the all-male universities, Hull's
translations, especially of *The Seven Psalms*, suggests that women did play
some role in the dissemination of scholarly texts.

Margaret Beaufort, Countess of Richmond and Derby, is perhaps more
interesting for who she was and the transitional position she occupies for us

as a woman writer than for the two devotional treatises she translated from French to English at the beginning of the sixteenth century. Great-grand-daughter of John of Gaunt, mother of the first Tudor king, Henry VII, and grandmother of Henry VIII, Beaufort, Janus-like, looks both backward to the period we have come to call the Middle Ages and forward to that period we call the Renaissance. She was renowned for her extraordinary piety, for her patronage of early printers like William Caxton and Wynkyn de Worde, and for her support of the humanist theologian John Fisher, who was her confessor (Barratt, *Women's Writing* 301). In 1503, Richard Pynson published her translation of Book IV of the *De Imitatione Christi* of Thomas à Kempis as part of a translation of the entire text of the popular *Imitation of Christ* by William Atkinson. It was followed in 1506 by *The Mirror of Gold*, another translation of a Latin treatise originally called *Speculum Aureum*. Beaufort sits on the cusp of several key developments in English culture occurring at the end of the fifteenth and the beginning of the sixteenth centuries. Her translations participated in the conversion from manuscript to print culture. She is the first English woman whose works circulated immediately in the new medium of print rather than initially in manuscript. In addition, Barratt argues that they point to changes in both religious and intellectual culture during this period, as well as the uneven-ness of those changes, even within individuals: 'the Lady Margaret's interest in *The Imitation of Christ* . . . indicates the humanist side of her piety. But her popularization of the *Mirror of Gold to the Sinful Soul*, a text firmly in the medieval tradition of contempt for the world, and her knowledge of French rather than Latin link her with the medieval tradition of learned women' (Barratt, *Women's Writing* 301). In *The Imitation*, she seems to embrace the spiritual movement known as *devotia moderna* (modern devo-tion), with its rejection of scholasticism and religious formalism, looking forward to humanistic models of devotion, while *The Mirror of Gold*, with its contempt for the world expressed in a vivid language of repulsion, looks backward to medieval forms of piety.

This very lack of intellectual consistency, however, even within a single individual like Margaret Beaufort, suggests that the Renaissance[35] represents less a decisive break with the medieval past, as modern scholars usually por-tray it, than a highly uneven development; if and when ruptures occur they do so in fits and starts. Recent work on medieval and reformation religion (Carpenter) is as concerned with the continuities between the two periods as previous historians had been with decisive breaks. The *Mirror of Gold*, 'now of late translated out of French into English by the right excellent princess Margaret, mother to our sovereign lord', with its focus on the 'misery and frailty of the World' (a. ii) perhaps seems medieval enough at first glance. Like Hull's *Meditations Upon the Seven Days of the Week*, it reveals an essentially inorganic architectonics; it is divided into 'vii chapters after the vii days of the week, so that the sinful soul soiled and befouled by sin may in every chapter have a new mirror wherein he may behold and consider the face of his soul' (a. ii; translation mine). It is full of vituperation in graphic language directed at all things non-spiritual.

> Certainly I am a sack full of sin and rottenness filled with stench and with blind horror, poor, naked and subject to all miserable necessities and tribulations, ignorant of my coming into and going out of the world, unknowing, miserable and deadly, of the which the day passeth suddenly and lightly as the shadow. And life wanes as the moon & as the green leaf on the tree that by a little heat of the sun is soon dry: & with a little wind is soon beaten down. (a. v)

However, is her conclusion that 'man is no other thing than a foul stinking froth and a sack full of rottenness and meat for worms' (a. v) really so different from Hamlet's observation that man is 'a foul and pestilent congregation of vapours' (II ii 311)? Even her invocation of the *ubi sunt* tradition which seems so characteristic of medieval meditations on death could find its echo in any religious age: 'tell me now, where are their laughings, where now are their joys, their diversions, their vanities, and organs. . . . Where are the kings, the princes, the emperors with the riches and powers of the world. They are as the shadow vanished' (a. v). Once again, *Hamlet*, that monument of Renaissance transcendence, could supply any number of witty variations on Margaret's theme: 'We fat all creatures to fat us, and we fat ourselves for maggots. Your fat king and your lean beggar is but variable service – two dishes, but to one table. That's the end' (IV iii 21–5). In fact, one might argue that the fire and brimstone of *The Mirror of Gold* seems a long way from the optimism expressed by a medieval religious writer like, say, Julian of Norwich, who seems confidently to embrace a loving God who wishes souls to be saved.

By the same token, *The Imitation of Christ*, with its Eucharistic devotion, does not seem all that far removed from the Eucharistic writings of a medieval mystic like Gertrude the Great. Even its rejection of medieval scholasticism, its call to submit reason to faith – 'All reason and natural inquisition ought to follow faith, without further reasoning' (Barratt, *Women's Writing* 304) – is not an alien idea in the Middle Ages; certainly the figure of Piers the Plowman in William Langland's fourteenth-century dream vision stands for much the same belief. Beaufort writes in *The Imitation* that 'It is enough to demand of you fast faith, a pure and clean life, and not the high and subtle profound mysteries of God; for if thou may not comprehend and understand that which is within thee, how mayst thou understand things that are above thee?' (Barratt, *Women's Writing* 303). Is she not demonstrating some of the power Foucault attributes to medieval devotional literature to hollow out a space of interiority, of subjectivity? Of course, it is important to bear in mind that Beaufort's translations finally tell us very little that is personal about the woman herself. They appear to be spiritual exercises, undertaken on the advice of her confessors as a means to pass her time industriously. Both tracts are highly impersonal; she rarely uses the first person and when she does she does not give the impression that she is necessarily speaking about herself. Reading these translations, we get nothing like the sense of highly individuated character that we get from reading the works of a St Bridget, a Margery Kempe or a Julian of Norwich. We get nothing even remotely like the lively dialogue between author and anonymous translator that we get in the Middle English version of *The Mirror of Simple Souls*. Margaret Beaufort's translations do not lead us to discover an essential woman writer beneath the veneer of the translator; however they do enable us to call into question the very boundaries of historical periodization. We might even want to see her as an early precursor of such rhetorical displays of interiority as the Shakespearean soliloquy, but, at the same time, we cannot deny that the disciplines by which her readers are to achieve this interiority are very much of the Middle Ages.

NOTES

1. John Benton argues that the group of texts attributed to the medieval physician Trotula used the name of this prominent woman physician to establish their credibility to discuss women's diseases (Benton 'Women's Problems' 47); a sixteenth-century marginal note in *The Boke of Noblesse*, a late fifteenth-century manuscript which includes portions of Christine de Pizan's *Faits d'Armes*, claims that Christine's signature indicates not that she was the writer of this text, but merely its patron.
2. A set of specific practices that organizes some aspect of social life. See Foucault, *Power/Knowledge* 194.
3. The titles of the poems are the inventions of their editors, not their authors.
4. However, that at least one scholar thought 'Wulf and Eadwacer' was a riddle because it preceded the *Exeter Book* riddles suggests that various textual and contextual cues will activate different assumptions about a text (Gordon, *Anglo-Saxon Poetry* 91).
5. Dolores Warwick Frese (1983) identifies the speaker as a mother mourning the death of her son (Wulf) in the tradition of Hildeburg's lament in *Beowulf*.
6. See Finke, *Feminist Theory* 29–74 for a more detailed discussion of these rhetorical strategies.
7. Bodley MS Rawlinson C. 86 ff. 155v–156; printed in Barratt, *Women's Writing* 275. I have not translated this lyric because modern English would obscure the metrical form, which I analyse here.

8. A 1933 MA thesis edited some of her poems; see Lloyd-Morgan 186–98 for a discussion of Gwerful Merchain.

9. Citations from *Floure and Leafe* and *Assembly of Ladies* will be from the edition by Derek Pearsall.

10. The term 'epicene' describes words that can indicate either sex with one grammatical form. I use it to indicate the ways in which textual clues in the poems suspend readers between male and female without ever resolving the uncertainty.

11. These two companies may represent real or fictional chivalric orders rather than the allegorical figures we expect from a love vision.

12. See Mehl, *Middle English Romances* 5; Crane, *Insular Romance* 179, R.F. Green, *Poets and Princepleasers* 13.

13. All citations from *Sir Launfal* are from the text in Garbáty.

14. All citations from Marie's *lais* are from the translation by Ferrante and Hanning.

15. The Auchinleck *Lay of Freine* is missing several pages at this point, breaking off with the arrival of Guroun's new bride.

16. Breeze 76–7; Breeze, 'Celtic Writer Princess', email, medfem@u.washington.edu, 7 June 1997.

17. Breeze, 'Celtic Writer Princess', email, medfem@u.washington.edu, 9 June 1997.

18. There has been speculation that the earliest native saint's life, the Anglo-Saxon Life of Pope Gregory, was composed at Whitby by a woman (Leyser, *Medieval Women* 28).

19. See Kamuf, *Fictions* 149 and McLeod, 'Wholly Guilty' 82 for a summary of this scholarship.

20. A translation of this letter may be found at the following web site: www.millersv.edu/~english/homepage/duncan/medfem/medfem.html.

21. The Plumpton correspondence, which contains only 2 letters by women before the sixteenth century, need not concern us here. The Paston women will be treated more fully in Chapter 4.

22. All references to the Stonor Letters are from the edition by Kingsford and are noted by letter number parenthetically in the text; translations are mine.

23. In 1194 the Emperor Henry IV sacked Salerno and during the thirteenth century Montpellier and Paris replaced it as the centre for medical education; see Benton, 'Trotula' 45–6.

24. The *Liber Trotuli* also suggests that women are loath to reveal the 'most prive place' of their bodies to men; they 'will not tell to the physician, for shame, the sickness that befalls them' (BL MS Additional 34111, f. 197).

25. Oxford Bodley MS Rawlinson poet 143, ff. 1–11 and Lambeth Palace MS 491B, ff. 287–94; see Barratt, *Women's Writing* 232.

26. 'Religious Instruction' 413; Anne Clark Bartlett and Thomas Bestul have tried to draw out the implications of this comparison in their introduction to *Cultures of Piety* (forthcoming).

27. She also recorded her own visions in the *Legatus Divinae Pietatis* or *Herald of God's Loving-Kindness*; see Petroff, *Visionary Literature* 222–30.

28. This text has been attributed by some to Bakhtin. For a discussion of the problems of authorship in the works of the Bakhtin Circle see Morson and Emerson, *Mikhail Bakhtin* 31–48.

29. Other candidates include Elizabeth of Thuringia (d. 1231), wife of the Count of Thuringia, who never became a nun but did become a Franciscan tertiary

(lay people who were not enclosed but instead lived a life of piety in the world) and Elizabeth of Schönau, a twelfth-century German Benedictine nun and mystic; see Barratt, *Women's Writing* 71.

30. This bridal imagery is used by other medieval mystics as well; it is picked up by Margery Kempe.

31. On Catherine of Siena see Barratt, *Women's Writing* 95–6 and Petroff, *Visionary Literature* 238–40.

32. Some have suggested that the treatise had some connection with Barking Abbey; see Hodgson and Liegey, *Orchard* vii.

33. There is no reason to assume the anonymous translator was necessarily a man. It might have just as easily been another of the sisters. The translator recommends to the sisters a Don James, who 'for the most part has laboured to the end of the ghostly orchard', but this evidence of a male collaborator does not preclude female authorship.

34. *Miseri mei deus* was one of the seven penitential psalms and *Veni creator spiritus* was a Pentecost hymn to the Holy Spirit.

35. Or, in more current parlance, the early modern. If the term Renaissance suggests that the sixteenth century saw a 'rebirth' of classical learning after the 'dark ages', the term 'early modern' is equally loaded, implying that modernity begins only with the sixteenth century. Once again it is important to note the ways in which our periodization and terminology reproduce the repression of the Middle Ages from our accounts of European civilization.

CHAPTER FOUR

Major Authors

In the previous chapter, I have tried to establish the extent to which women contributed to the development of both secular and religious culture in the Middle Ages. This analysis provides a context for the five 'major authors' I will examine in this chapter, suggesting that the medieval woman writer was not a lone genius – an exception to the rule – who rose above the limitations of her sex. The 'major authors' treated below belonged to communities of both men and women who wrote to sustain and enlarge their cultures. Two of the writers I will examine wrote in French. While this choice may seem out of place in a volume devoted to English women writers, as I argued earlier, feminist literary criticism cannot simply recover a tradition of women writers; it must also challenge the assumptions that have guided literary criticism in the past, in this case the belief that *English* literature is the expression of some kind of *English* national spirit. To do so is to buy into the very representations that excluded women in the first place. While the Norman Conquest of England is a major event in the medieval history of England, in literary history it barely merits recognition. The 'tradition' of English literature moves from *Beowulf* to Chaucer with barely a glance at the intervening centuries, when much 'high culture' and hence much of the culture that was committed to writing, was French, which continued to be a viable literary language in England well into the fifteenth century. Besides obscuring the general features of medieval literary culture in England from the twelfth to the fourteenth century, the limitation of *English* literature only to those authors who wrote in *English*, excludes from the canon of English literature the two greatest women writers of the period – Marie de France and Christine de Pizan. Both of these women wrote in French; yet both contributed enormously to the development of English literature as we understand it today. For this reason, this chapter will treat both along with women who wrote in the English language.

MARIE DE FRANCE

In the epilogue to her *Fables*, Marie de France gives her name 'pur remembrance' [for memory] (*Fables*, 256: l. 3), so that her authorship will be remembered and appropriately rewarded: 'My name is Marie; I am from France' (l. 4). The epilogue, which also names her patron, 'count William', seems almost another fable with its generic names – how many Maries and Williams were there in the French speaking world of the twelfth century? They tantalize us with the promise that these are historical personages associated with the Plantagenet court of Henry II.

The woman we know as Marie de France may have been the greatest writer of short fiction before Boccaccio and Chaucer and arguably her fiction rivals even theirs. It is important to remember, however, that her artistry did not emerge out of a void. Marie participated in a highly sophisticated Anglo-Norman aristocratic culture in which women played important roles as patrons and even as *auctores*, often setting the canons of taste both within the royal court and in the powerful English abbeys that enjoyed royal patronage. Three literary works are signed with Marie's name, although no one can demonstrate unequivocally that the signature in all three texts refers to the same woman. A collection of *lais* or short romances, a collection of fables and the hagiographic *St Patrick's Purgatory* were all written between 1160 and 1215, more than a century after the Norman Conquest of England (Ferrante and Hanning, *Lais* 1).[1] In the *Fables*, Marie says she is 'from France' meaning perhaps that she was born in France, although it is just as likely that she would have perceived the English court as a satellite of the Norman French court and so literally 'of France', and if, as some have suggested, she was in fact a member of the royal family, she is literally of the noble house of France. Scholars have suggested, at various times, that Marie was the Abbess of Reading or Shaftsbury, Henry II's half-sister, the daughter of Waleran II, Count of Meulan, or the daughter of Henry's predecessor, King Stephen.[2]

We can glean a few more facts about her from her writing. She was probably literate in English, Latin and her native French. She also shows some knowledge of classical literature, especially Ovid. There is nothing to indicate that she ever married or owned property. She may have been a nun, which would explain her exceptional education. We have already seen the kind of learning that characterized the Norman convent of Barking during the twelfth century (p. 107). There is no reason to believe that other wealthy houses like Reading and Shaftsbury would not have offered similar opportunities to aristocratic women. If Marie was a nun, it is not unlikely that she was an abbess who had been raised in the Norman court and was still capable of and interested in entertaining an audience of courtiers (*Fables* 5), as both the *lais* and fables suggest a courtly and secular audience. While today Marie is probably best known for her *lais*, judging from the numbers of extant manuscripts (23 of the *Fables* and 5 of the *Lais*), her collection of fables may have been the more popular text in the Middle Ages.

More than any medieval writer, male or female, that I know, Marie seems obsessed with establishing her claim to her writing as intellectual property. In each of her works she demonstrates an anxiety about authorship which is not an anxiety about being a *female* author, such as we see in Christine de Pizan's writing[3] or that of the anonymous nun of Barking who wrote the *vita* of Edward the Confessor (see above 107–8), but an attempt to define her writing as a form of possession and an attendant anxiety that this possession might be stolen or her rights forgotten.[4] She states these claims most succinctly in epilogue to the *Fables*:

> I am from France, my name's Marie.
> And it may hap that many a clerk
> Will claim as his what is my work.
> But such pronouncements I want not!
> It's folly to become forgot! (Spiegel 257)[5]

In the prologue to the *lai Guigemar*, she names herself as Marie, 'who in her time should not be forgotten'.[6] Finally in *St Patrick's Purgatory* she writes 'I, Marie, have recorded, in order to be remembered, the book of Purgatory' (*Fables* 4). These claims set Marie apart from many medieval women writers who use the humility topos to deprecate their authorship out of anxiety about their sex. Marie desires to be remembered as an author, an *auctores*.

How does Marie understand authorship or at least her own role as author? The evidence of the texts suggests that Marie sees herself primarily as a translator. *St Patrick's Purgatory* is a translation of a Latin *vita* into Norman French. The *lais* translate Breton tales that she has heard. Finally, in *The Fables* Marie states that she translated these 103 fables from Aesop by way of an English translation she says was made by King Alfred (*Fables* 257–9). However, she imagines the task of translation somewhat differently from the way we in the late twentieth century understand it. We understand translation as an attempt to 'carry over' the sense of a text from one language to another. We judge translations by their faithfulness to an original and hold the work of translation to be less original – and so less artistic – than that of composing. Like our understanding of authorship, our notions of translation are formed within an aesthetic that includes legal protection for intellectual property (copyright law) that gives precedence to originality and understands translation is always, in effect, a deformation of an original.[7]

Marie's secular translations are, in fact, translations without originals. In the fables, Marie claims to have translated from an English translation made by King Alfred. Marie's, however, is the earliest surviving vernacular collection of fables and, as Harriet Spiegel suggests, 'a lively and charming, wry and witty verse rendering of these tales, some in the Aesop tradition and some of which hers is the first recorded version' (*Fables*, 1). Similarly, there are very few recorded antecedents of Marie's *lais* so that if any originals existed (and there is good reason to doubt that they did), they are long since lost to us. For instance, although the *lai Chevrefoil* draws upon the familiar romance of *Tristan and Isolde*, the brief story it tells is not recorded anywhere else in the legend. Marie's invocation of King Alfred in the fables is also worth noting. No record of such a translation or any Anglo-Saxon or Middle English fables have survived. It is possible that Marie invokes a Celtic tradition of storytelling and an Anglo-Saxon king famous for his learning and translations as a means of establishing her credentials as a particular kind of translator, as a go-between, one who mediates between warring cultures, between a colonizer and the colonized.

It is worth noting that Marie claims her originals were written in the languages of the very cultures that the Normans had successfully colonized and hence marginalized: Breton (a Celtic language presumably brought to France by Celts escaping invaders) and English. We are familiar with the role that Native American women like Pocohontas, Sacajawea, or, in Mexico, La Malinche played in mediating relations between the colonizing Europeans and native populations. Women seem ideal for the purpose of translating cultures in colonial situations. They are not, unlike the men, involved in the actual fighting. Once hostilities cease, they are likely to be exchanged between the warring factions in marriages designed to lessen tensions. One outcome of the Norman Conquest of England was that it brought the French-speaking Normans into close and often conflicted proximity with two previously distinct cultures and languages – the Celtic and the Anglo-Saxon. Henry II's grandfather, Henry I, took a Scottish queen (Matilda) who had been educated in Anglo-Saxon convents for his bride and even three generations after the conquest her grandson, Henry II, was still fighting the Welsh, and uneasily coexisting with his English subjects while maintaining a French-speaking court.

Marie's secular works suggest the intellectual labour required to mediate between these different and often hostile cultures. In the *lais*, she keeps before her audience the heteroglossia that characterizes the political status quo. In the opening of *Laustic*, for instance, she writes

I shall tell you an adventure
about which the Bretons made a *lai*.
Laustic was the name, I think,
they gave it in their land.

In French it is *rossignol*,
and *nightingale* in proper English. (*Lais* 155)

She provides similar glosses in *Bisclavret*, noting that *bisclavret* is the Breton word for werewolf, while in Norman the word would be *garwaf*, and in *Chevrefoil* she states that what the French call *chevrefoil*, the English call *goatleaf*. It seems unlikely that Marie felt the need to gloss the titles of these *lais* because she is writing in a multilingual environment. Her audiences were fluent primarily, if not solely, in French. It seems more likely that her goal was to keep before her audiences the heteroglossia of the larger environment outside of the rarefied atmosphere of the court, to remind them of the several languages that were spoken throughout the domains Henry ruled. Like the reference to the English king Alfred in the *Fables*, these glosses identify Marie as the translator, the one who mediates cultural differences and inequalities.

Marie's self-assumed role as cultural translator suggests political readings of the *Fables* as well. It would be a mistake to dismiss these tales as mere children's literature. Unlike the glib, rather abstract and general moralism of the tales we associate with Aesop today, Marie's fables are filled with fairly caustic observations of Norman court life, often criticizing specific abuses of power in what seems like political satire. In the fable of 'The Sun who Wished to Wed', Marie describes how the Sun informs the creatures of the earth that he wishes to take a wife. The animals go to Destiny for help, complaining that the Sun is already too powerful, that it parches the earth in summer so that 'no trees can blossom or bear fruit' (*Fables*, 45). If the Sun acquires a partner, they complain, he will be even stronger. Destiny agrees, decreeing that 'I won't allow his strength to grow'. Marie draws the following moral from the tale.

> Thus everyone should cautioned be
> When under evil sovereignty
> Their lord must not grow mightier
> Nor join with one superior
> To them in intellect or riches
> They must do all they can to thwart this.
> Stronger the lord, the worse their fate:
> His ambush always lies in wait. (*Fables* 47, ll. 25–32)

In this fable, and in many others like it, Marie seems most interested in highlighting the abuses of power that the wealthy and powerful (and in England in the twelfth century that meant the Norman aristocracy) perpetrate against the weak. She seems specifically to target the kind of feudalism the Normans imposed on England after the Conquest. I have already noted that the Norman kings attempted to concentrate their power and curb that of the barons by holding their feudal prerogatives more closely than their

French counterparts. They also, as this tale suggests, attempted to consolidate their position further through strategic marriages, as Henry's marriage in 1152 to the powerful Eleanor of Aquitaine suggests. In Marie's original French, the criticism of Norman imperialism is perhaps more specific than Speigel's generalized vocabulary suggests. The abstract noun 'evil sovereignty' of l. 26 translates a more concrete reference to 'Qui sur eus unt les maus seignurs', literally those who suffer under 'evil seigneurs' or feudal lords, suggesting that Norman rule was not simply an abstract or impersonal system of government, but a set of very personal relationships. The verb 'esforcier' in l. 27, referring to the might of these lords, in Old French carries suggestions of rape and plunder as well. Marie seems, at times, cynical and even bitter about the abuses of the powerful. In the fable of the 'Dog and the Ewe' she concludes

This example serves to tell
What's true for many men as well:
By lies and trickery, in short,
They'll force the poor to go to court.
False witnesses they'll bring
And pay them with the poor folks' things.
What's left the poor? The rich don't care
As long as they all get their share. (*Fables* 43, ll. 35–42)

Marie's fables speak to the reality of the twelfth-century Norman court of Henry II. It was a witty and sophisticated place where arts and letters served a purpose in legitimating Plantagenet monarchical ambitions, but the glittering inhabitants of Henry's court were ruthless, rapacious and grasping when it suited their purposes. Success depended on political acumen and a willingness, when necessary, to resort to violence and force. Marie's fables sympathize with the perspective of those who were the victims of Norman aggression.

Marie's role as cultural mediator is much subtler in the *lais*, which seem much less political satire than pure fantasy. In her prologue, Marie says very little about the sources for her tales except that she had thought about translating some stories from Latin, but decided 'that was not to bring me fame' (*Lais* l. 31); 'Then I thought of the *lais* I'd heard' (l. 33). In the opening lines of *Guigemar* she refers to 'The tales – and I know they're true – from which the Bretons made their *lais*' (ll. 19–20). Marie draws on Celtic lore for her *lais*; translating these stories enables her to make at least slightly more accessible to her courtly audience the strangest and most alien of all the cultures within the Norman empire (which during the twelfth century stretched from Scotland to the Pyrennees). I would argue that Marie's *lais* draw upon the symbolic power – a power that is often characterized as magic – attributed to the group which is the most marginal of all

159

to explore the situations of those marginalized members of the Norman aristocracy, specifically women and bachelor knights, those younger sons dispossessed by the system of primogeniture by which the ruling class perpetuated itself. Under the Norman system of primogeniture, only the first-born son could inherit a family's property. All other children were effectively disinherited. To take advantage of this system, an aristocratic family would try to marry off all of its daughters in ways that would enhance the family's fortune and influence rather than the daughter's happiness, while younger sons were left dependent on the patronage of more well-endowed (landed) lords, serving as members of their household or *mesnie*. While Glyn Burgess argues that Marie's heroes are predominantly from the class of 'young, active well-connected knights in search of personal happiness', lords or potential lords ('Social Status' 73), many of Marie's *lais*, in fact, focus on the hero's (Milun, Lanval, Tristan, Eliduc) initial distance from the centres of economic, political and sexual power.

Two prominent themes in Marie's *lais* explore the situation of women in unhappy arranged marriages (for example *Guigemar* and *Yonec*) and that of bachelor knights in search of their fortune, or *aventure*.[8] At their simplest level, the *lais* offer women the fantasy of romantic love triumphing over marriages arranged for economic or political gain[9] and impoverished bachelor knights the fantasy of acquiring through adventure the land, women and wealth they lacked. It would be easy to dismiss these tales as so much escapism, pleasurable but a dangerous retreat from the demands of reality. This would be our common-sensical reading of fantasy: 'reality is a given, and pleasure is not itself a way of knowing or shaping reality; pleasure blocks, rather than results from, maturation; pleasure, not reality, can be dangerous' (Fradenburg, 'Social Meaning' 216). Louise Fradenburg, in an insightful essay on the social meanings of fantasy in the Wife of Bath's Prologue and Tale, however, proposes that fantasy does not necessarily separate us from reality. She considers fantasy as a means of knowing or shaping reality, of remaking social reality. What if, as Fradenburg suggests, both the preservation of power and its transformation depend upon 'the fantastic pleasure of imagining the world otherwise' (Fradenburg, 'Social Meaning' 220)?

A reading of Marie's *lais* that attempts to explore rather than dismiss its fantasy elements must begin with a view of artistic representation that goes beyond a reflective theory of art. Marie's *lais* do not simply attempt to reflect what life among the twelfth-century Norman aristocracy was like. Like any other ideological texts, the *lais* existed in a complex relationship both to other texts and to the social conditions of their creation. They reflect and refract, at the same time they attempt to shape, lived realities. That romance texts like the *lais* could appeal to the fantasies both of aristocratic women and bachelor knights is a testament to the contradictions inherent in the ideology of courtly love. While the fantasy on which the romance genre is based might seem to involve the relations between men and women, closer analysis reveals that the homosocial bonds by which men established relations with one another, using women as tokens of exchange, are central to courtly ideology. Within this homosocial system, women are defined solely in terms of their sexuality, which becomes the reward for competition and the grounds for co-operation between men. Within this ideology, sexual conflicts become the grounds for disputing other social, political and economic conflicts.

Marie's fictional bachelor knights replicate the hierarchical relations among men in the Norman court. At the same time they also attempt to reshape those relationships by manipulating the patronage networks that mediated relationships among aristocratic men to enhance their positions. The *lai Milun*, for instance, offers a cautionary fantasy that corresponds with at least some things that we know about the social and economic mobility of the lower Norman aristocracy. Marie describes Milun as a knight of indeterminate origin who is 'generous and strong, courteous and proud' (l. 14).[10] He is beloved and honoured by many princes, but a bachelor knight in the position of client to more powerful patrons. He falls in love with the daughter of a baron, and she becomes pregnant with his illegitimate child. Despite his many virtues, however, Milun is not seen as an eligible match for the woman he loves, most likely because he does not hold any land of his own. His lover is 'given' by her father to 'a rich lord of the region, / a powerful man of great repute' (ll. 125–6), and the illegitimate child is secretly sent to Northumbria to be raised by Milun's sister. Georges Duby argues that the division in twelfth-century Norman England between married and unmarried men constituted a class division, a nearly insurmountable divide between men who had land and wives to produce heirs for them and those unmarried men who attached themselves as clients to more powerful men who bore the cost of their upkeep as part of their household or *mesnie* (Duby, *William Marshal* 64–79).

Milun's career bears a strong resemblance to that of William Marshal, the Earl of Pembroke and marshal of England under Henry II. Georges Duby recounts the life of William Marshal based on the *vita* of an anonymous chronicler named Jean (Duby, *William Marshal* 1985). He was the fourth son of a minor Norman nobleman and, in a world in which inheritance was governed by the principles of primogeniture and non-partition, a man with no prospects. Yet he eventually rose to become the marshal of England, regent for Henry's eldest son and heir and one of the richest and most powerful men in the realm. He accomplished this by securing the 'love' of increasingly more powerful patrons, including that of Henry II and his son, until he could acquire for himself land, a wife, title and the position of a powerful patron. Neither William Marshal, as a younger son, nor Milun, whose class status is left unarticulated, are powerful enough to marry or to hold land – at least initially. Both seek their fortune by attaching themselves as bachelor knights to the households of increasingly powerful patrons. Their success is measured primarily by success in tournaments which is heavily rewarded by their patrons, often so much that they are themselves able to support clients of their own, bachelor knights less fortunate than themselves. In the case of Milun's son, who, like his father, begins his adventures as a bachelor knight, success in tournaments is so great that he is eventually able, without consulting anyone, to give his now-widowed mother to his father; he is able to act the part of the powerful patron, just as eventually Marshal was rewarded by the 'gift' of a wife and, with her, the lands that would make him Earl of Pembroke.

Marshal's well-chronicled life helps us to understand Marie's interest in the *Lais* in the ways young men of uncertain status negotiated the patronage networks in which they were entangled; it helps us to understand the fantasy of social mobility that drives her tales. The complexity of these social networks is hinted at when Marie describes Milun's son's successes in Brittany:

> There he spent lavishly and tourneyed
> and became acquainted with rich men.
> In every joust he entered,
> he was judged the best combatant.
> He loved poor knights;
> what he gained from rich ones
> he gave to them and thus retained them in his service;
> he was generous in all his spending. (ll. 321–8)

In the passage above, Milun's son gives to the poor knights who are his clients what he receives from rich ones who are his patrons. This economy of expenditure that structures many of the *lais* requires that gifts must continually circulate; they cannot be hoarded. It is this circulation that provides the energy that fuels this social system. One kind of gift that must continually circulate within this system is the gift of women, whose distribution is closely linked with the distribution of land, the primary economic resource.

Women's position within the ideal fantasized by courtly love is marked by massive contradiction. The demands of primogeniture and lineage required the strict control of women's sexuality. An aristocratic woman's primary function was to guarantee the continuity of her husband's patrimony by producing an heir. To ensure the heir's legitimacy, she must have no other sexual partner than her husband. The *lai Yonec* imagines the strictest possible control of women's sexuality.

> There once lived in Brittany
> a rich man, old and ancient. . . .
> The man was very far along in years
> but because he possessed a large fortune
> he took a wife in order to have children,
> who would come after him and be his heirs.
> The girl who was given to the rich man
> came from a good family; . . .
> Because she was beautiful and noble
> he made every effort to guard her.
> He locked her inside his tower
> in a great paved chamber. (ll. 11–28)

The unnamed lady is kept imprisoned in the tower for seven years, though the couple produces no children during this time. The old lord of Caerwent hoards his wife; he takes her out of circulation. He has understood only half of the role women play in the circulation of aristocratic wealth.

The organization of the aristocratic household required *both* the control and the display of female sexuality. If women's sexuality had to be controlled in order to ensure the production of legitimate heirs, the system of patronage that bound together groups of unmarried men in the households of more powerful (and married) lords required the circulation of some species of 'symbolic capital' capable of reconfiguring what were primarily economic transactions as forms of generosity and gift-giving. Women's sexuality was ideally suited for this function, and literary conventions like courtly love were ideally suited for the covert display of female sexuality. Literary artifacts like the poetry and romances that were carriers of the ideology of *fin' amor*, because of their metaphoric dimension – their abilities to transmute, to substitute, to supplement – would not simply reflect life at court, they would reproduce, sustain and even transform the patronage relationships that constituted life at court. One way for bachelor knights to disguise their appeals for patronage to their lord was through erotic fictions involving the lord's wife. William Marshal, according to one story, was exiled from young Henry's court and nearly ruined because of rumours of an adulterous relationship with Henry's wife, Margaret (Duby, *William Marshal* 47–54, 119–20). Yet the competition for the favours of the lady of the castle, favours which were seen as conduits for the patron's favour, must have been just as keen among all the knights as the martial competition of tournaments.

The *lai* Marie calls *Eliduc* illustrates the instabilities and uncertainties of this system of homosocial bonding that uses women as the social glue: 'the love of a lord', Marie writes in this *lai*, 'is not a fief' (l. 63). Like William, Eliduc is banished from the court of his lord because of the envy of his fellow knights. He seeks service elsewhere, leaving his own wife behind at home. Crossing the sea, he enters the service of another king who has no male heir, but only a daughter 'of marriageable age'. The extent to which the more mercenary aspects of patronage relations had to be disguised is indicated by Eliduc's command to his own men that they may not accept 'any gifts or money' for forty days (ll. 141–4). What is interesting in this *lai*, however, is the inevitability that the nubile Guilliadun, the king's daughter, is dangled in front of the already married Eliduc as both a reward for his loyal service and a test of that loyalty. Everyone in the *lai* seems aware of the extent to which the exchange of gifts dominates all transactions. Even Guilliadun, pondering what kind of gift to send Eliduc as a sign of her love, recognizes the rules of this game:

> I've never seen a knight
> who had to be begged –
> whether he loved or hated –
> who would not willingly take
> a present that was offered to him. (ll. 369–73)

In *Eliduc* Marie creates an impossible situation, playing on all of the contradictions inherent in a system that must both control and exhibit female sexuality, pushing that situation to its very limits. To fulfil the role of grateful client and king's champion, Eliduc must betray both his own wife and the lord he supposedly serves. And yet the tale does not condemn Eliduc's actions as either mercenary or dishonourable.[11] Eliduc is rewarded for his actions when his wife retreats to a convent, allowing Eliduc to marry his paramour. We might wonder why Eliduc is rewarded for his adultery when a character like Equitain in the *lai* of that name is so unequivocally punished for his. I suspect that the differences in evaluation of the two situations lies in the class status of the adulterers. Equitain is a man of high rank, a king, who becomes involved in an adulterous relationship with the wife of a subject. Courtly literature clearly condemns love between a woman and a man of higher rank. The *trobairitz* Azalais de Porcairages, for instance, writes in her *canso*:

> A lady's love is badly placed
> who argues with a wealthy man,
> one above the rank of vassal:
> she who does it is a fool. . . .
> love and money do not mix,
> and the woman money chooses
> they say has lost her honor. (Bogin, *Women Troubadours* 94–5)

While women frequently *married* men of higher rank, this situation fell outside of the ideology of courtly love, an ideology designed to display, not to control, female sexuality. To bestow her love on someone of higher rank would take a woman out of the circulation of symbolic capital that fuelled the patronage relationship between overlord and knight. It is not the man at the apex of the feudal system who required the status that is conferred by the lady of high rank; it is the bachelor knight of uncertain status. Technically, of course, the arrangement with which Marie ends *Eliduc* would never have been sanctioned by the Church. The ending of *Equitain* is perhaps more 'realistic' in warning its readers of the dangers of indulging in pleasure. There are no grounds for a divorce or annulment of Eliduc's first, legally binding marriage. Yet Marie's fantasy ending tests the limits of the social reality of Norman court life – and especially the relations between love, marriage and wealth – exposing, perhaps more effectively than the most realist ending, the contradictions that sustain that social reality.

Throughout the *lais*, the contradiction between the desire to control female sexuality and the need to display it generates a surplus that figures female sexuality, freed of the restraints of male control, as a powerfully transformative energy. Of course, such a subversive energy cannot be figured directly and so it takes the form of magic – the bird lover in *Yonec* who appears as the answer to the imprisoned wife's lament, the fairy mistress who appears out of nowhere to sustain the impoverished Lanval in the *lai* of that name, the mysterious fawn that wounds and is fatally wounded by the hero in *Guigemar* and the boat that appears suddenly to take the hero to the imprisoned lover who will heal him. Marie's use of fantasy elements in the *lais* offers some imaginative shape to the social reality which Lacan says can never be represented – woman's pleasure.

JULIAN OF NORWICH

In her 1984 collection, *Breathing the Water*, the contemporary poet Denise Levertov, calling upon Julian's most famous image, explains why so many nineteenth- and twentieth-century writers have been attracted to the religious visions of the late fourteenth-century English mystic, Julian of Norwich:

> . . . you ask us to turn our gaze
> inside out, and see
> *a little thing, the size of a hazelnut*, and believe
> it is our world? (75)

One can only speculate that this power to turn our gazes inside out, as well as the ability to condense so much meaning into such homely images, is what also fascinated William Butler Yeats, Charles Williams, Aldous Huxley, T. S. Eliot and Thomas Merton about Julian's writing (Birrell 223–4 and 227, Crampton, *Shewings* 16, 172–3).

Almost everything we know about Julian of Norwich comes to us from her account of the visions she experienced on the eighth of May of 1373. Some time earlier, she tells her readers, she had asked God for three gifts: '(i) to understand his passion; (ii) to suffer physically while still a young woman of thirty; and (iii) to have as God's gift three wounds' (*Revelations* 63).[12] Midway through her thirty-first year, this woman, who proclaims herself 'a simple and uneducated creature' (63) (actually in the Middle English, 'a simple creature that cowde [knew] no letter'), was afflicted with an illness that lasted seven days and nights during which she had what can only be described as a near-death experience.

> Then my sight began to fail, and the room became dark about me, as if it were night, except for the image of the cross which somehow was lighted up; . . . Then the rest of my body began to die, and I could hardly feel a thing. As my breathing became shorter and shorter I knew for certain that I was passing away. (65)

In the midst of this crisis, she was granted fifteen 'shewings', which were confirmed the following night in a sixteenth. These visions included visual images, mostly relating the events of Christ's passion, words which, 'without voice and speech, [God] framed in my soul' (83), and other events whose spiritual significance required further contemplation, as the justly famous image of the hazelnut: 'And he showed me more, a little thing, the size of a hazelnut, on the palm of my hand, round like a ball. I looked at it thoughtfully and wondered, "What is this?" And the answer came, "It is all that is made"' (68). While her method, and particularly her quite medieval compulsion to provide allegorizing interpretations of every event and image may seem alien to modern readers more comfortable with the imagist poetry of a T. S. Eliot, Julian recounts her visions in a prose that is remarkably lively and engagingly homely. Her style is admirably suited to the process of twenty years' contemplation on a single experience. The result is a text that seems at once childishly simple and dauntingly complex, straightforward and elusive, reasoned and passionate, strikingly immediate and carefully reflective.

Julian recorded her visions in two separate accounts. We can only speculate that the first, shorter version which survives in a single manuscript (BM MS Additional 37790; the manuscript which also contains a copy of Marguerite Porete's *Mirror of Simple Souls*) was written immediately after her illness while the experience was still fresh. The second much longer version, because it contains more exposition of the visions, may have been written years later after Julian had had time to contemplate her experiences: 'It was more than fifteen years after that I was answered in my spirit's understanding' (211). However, this longer account survives only in a few seventeenth-century manuscripts owned by English Benedictine nuns in exile in continental convents (Crampton, *Shewings* 15).[13]

If Julian experienced her visions in 1373 at the age of thirty she would have been born around 1342. The only authority for the tradition that Julian was an anchoress living at St Julian's church in Norwich is a manuscript rubric that opens the unique copy of the short version of her 'showings'.[14] 'Here is a vision showed by the goodness of God to a devout woman and her name is Julian, who is a recluse at Norwich and is still alive, the year of our Lord 1413' (DM Add. 37790, f. 97, translation mine). The tradition is certainly plausible. This heading also demonstrates that Julian was still alive as late as 1413. Additional external clues about her biography include a bequest to 'Julian, recluse at Norwich' in the 1416 will of Isabel Ufford, Countess of Suffolk and bequests to an unnamed recluse of Norwich as late as 1429 (Crampton, *Shewings* 7). These tantalizing fragments suggest she may even have still been alive in 1429 at the age of advanced age of 89.

It is next to impossible to ascertain what Julian meant when she called herself a simple creature who knew no letters. It seems extremely unlikely that this anchoress of Norwich was completely uneducated and illiterate. The sophistication of her theological speculations would seem to suggest that even if she was illiterate, she must have possessed considerable learning. It is also possible that she was literate in English but not in Latin, since, as I noted in Chapter 2, literacy in the Middle Ages most often meant Latin literacy. Alternately, it may mean, as Crampton suggests, that Julian was 'unlettered' when she experienced her visions, but later in life became literate enough to commit them to writing (4). After all, the purpose of living the enclosed life of an anchoress was to create the leisure time for contemplation of the higher mysteries of divinity, an occupation that would require some literacy. Edmund College and James Walsh, the editors of the standard edition of the 'Showings', believe that Julian may have made her own translations from the Latin Vulgate Bible, which would suggest at least rudimentary knowledge of Latin (Crampton, *Shewings* 167–8). The statement that she is a 'simple creature' may be more than a nod to literary convention, yet another example of the medieval humility topos. In the short version of the revelations, Julian does express some anxiety about her status as a woman writing, an activity which might too easily be associated with preaching or teaching:

> But God forbid that you should say or take it that I am a teacher, for I do not mean that, no I never meant so. For I am a woman, ignorant, feeble, and frail. But know well, this that I say; I have it of the showing of Him who is the sovereign teacher. But truly charity stirs me to tell you of it. For I would that God were known and my fellow Christians sped, as I would be myself, to hate sin more and love God more. Because I am a

woman, should I therefore believe that I should not tell you the goodness of God, since I saw in that same time that it is His will that it be known? And that you shall see well in what follows, if it is well and truly understood. Then you shall soon forget me, a wretch; and do this so that I do not hamper you – and behold Jesus, who is the teacher of all. (BL MS Additional 37790 f. 100ᵛ; see Crampton, *Shewings* 208)

Perhaps Julian felt the need to present herself as unthreatening, as a simple, unlearned creature as well as a woman 'ignorant, feeble, and frail'. She often makes fairly bold claims and ventures opinions on issues that, in the four-teenth century, were controversial – the nature of the Trinity, the relation of the individual soul to God, salvation and damnation, the nature of sin, and the role of grace. Such assertions of her status temper her more auda-cious claims. The late medieval Church strictly forbade women to serve any ministerial or sacerdotal function, so they were not allowed to preach or to instruct, which is exactly what Julian fears others may think she is doing. Although no evidence survives to suggests how Julian's account of her visions was received by Church authorities, there is nothing to indicate that Julian's work was ever considered anything but orthodox. Yet this passage suggests Julian's fears that she might be misunderstood – or perhaps more accurately, that she might be understood all too well. For the passage both asserts and denies her right to preach and instruct her 'even Christian'. Like most of the female mystics, Julian denies her role as a teacher, arguing that she is not speaking at all; rather God is speaking through her. At the same time she asks if, just because she is a woman, she should keep silent in the face of God's command that she speak.

An analysis of the *Shewings of Julian of Norwich* provides an occasion to examine the nature of the mystical vision as it was understood in the Middle Ages. The modern reader might be tempted to conceive of a vision as a spontaneous and essentially private experience brought on by heightened affective or psychological states, in Julian's case by her near-death experience. In the Middle Ages, however, mysticism was a public discourse – communal, active and dialogic. It involved not only dialogue between the mystic and the divine, but also between the mystic and her public. Julian's visions are, perhaps, never quite as public as those of, say, Mechtild of Hackeborn who often had visions during the performance of the mass, but she does experi-ence her visions in the presence of her mother, her priest, a curate, and other unnamed bystanders in the sickroom and, unlike Mechtild, willingly commits her visions to writing for the purpose of instructing others. Mys-tical discourse, as Karma Lochrie has argued, is not a constative language, but a performative one.[15] The mystic produces utterance rather than state-ments of 'truth' or objects of knowledge (Lochrie, *Margery Kempe* 62). The process through which the mystic produces her utterance is neither haphazard nor spontaneous. Mystical visions were the anticipated result of a programme of spiritual exercises. 'The mystic who wishes to make a place of herself for the divine will to speak enters upon a struggle with language itself, the "trouble" from which mystical texts are born.' If the mystical experience begins with a 'void that the communication-to-come will fill' (Lochrie, *Margery Kempe* 62), the means of achieving that void was a highly structured discipline. The exercises of desire, to paraphrase Lochrie (33), favoured by medieval mystics might include meditation, mantric prayer, flagellation, fasting and vigils, all designed in *imitatio Christi*, in imitation of Christ's life and suffering, to produce the 'emptied out space of the self' that will be filled by the mystical revelation. Julian offers little information about her spiritual activities, but she fits the pattern generally when she informs the reader that she had petitioned God in advance for an understanding of his passion and great physical suffering. Julian's illness, for her, is not a chance event; rather it is an opportunity for *imitatio Christi* allowing her to explore more fully the meanings of Christ's passion, and a mechanism for emptying out the self and preparing a place for the mystical dialogue.

The performative, however, always implies an audience toward whom the performance is directed. Lochrie's important analysis of how to read mystical texts focuses on describing the nature of the mystic's dialogue with God; she touches only briefly on the third term which must always intervene in that relationship and reshape it – the mystic's human audience. If, as Michel de Certeau has argued, the mystical text is always destabilized because the written text, which presents the evidence for this relationship, 'is ultimately incapable of manifesting the divine utterance that founds it' (Lochrie, *Margery Kempe* 68), the only reason for the written text's existence is the mystic's human audience. The presence of this audience raises thorny questions about how mystical discourse will be authorized. How is the reader of a mystical text supposed to know if the vision is a true or false one? The answer de Certeau gives, that the mystical text's authority depends on its being 'in the very place at which the Speaker speaks', as Lochrie points out, leaves quite a bit of room for doubt, both on the part of the mystic and that of the Church officials who controlled the power to authorize mystical speech (Lochrie, *Margery Kempe* 63).[16] The mystic's discourse may have stood outside of official pronouncements about doctrine but it nonetheless was constantly scrutinized for its doctrinal correctness. Julian's anxieties about her authority to speak even though she is a woman, expressed in the short version of her revelations, speak to the difficulty of the mystic's position as she claims divine authority, sometimes flying in the face of Church authority. We also see Julian's consciousness of the difficulty of her position in her constant assertions of her orthodoxy and the care with which she describes the modes by which she perceived her visions: 'All this

was shown to me in three ways, in actual vision, in imaginative understanding, and in spiritual sight' (76). Julian insists that her visions are *both*
external and internal, corporeal and spiritual; they involve both body and
the imaginative faculties.

If we understand both the public and disciplined nature of the medieval
mystical vision, we are, I think, in a much better position to understand
and appreciate those passages in the *Shewings* that initially seem to modern
readers idiosyncratic, bizarre, even alienating. Julian understands all too well
the belatedness of the visionary experience. There is always a gap between
the experience of the vision and its writing. Julian frequently fills these gaps
with homely images drawn from her surroundings, a practice that contributes
to the uniqueness of her style. For instance, in a vision of Christ's suffering
during the crown with thorns, she writes:

> I still seemed to see with my actual eyes the continual bleeding of the head.
> Great drops of blood rolled down from the garland like beads [pellots],
> seemingly from the veins; and they came down a brownish red color – for
> the blood was thick – and as they spread out they became bright red, and
> when they reached his eyebrows they vanished. . . . They were as fresh and
> living as though they were real: their abundance like the drops of water
> that fall from the eaves after a heavy shower, falling so thickly that no one
> can possibly count them; their roundness as they spread out on the forehead
> were like the scales of herring. I was reminded of these three things at the
> time: round beads as the blood flowed, round herring scales as it spread
> out, and raindrops from the eaves for their abundance. (71–2)

In this passage, the copiousness of Christ's blood – its palpable physical
presence – becomes a metonymy responsible for conveying the horror of
Christ's suffering (once again reminding the reader of the importance of
the affective experience of the *imitatio Christi* for mystical writing). But
what perhaps most immediately stands out on a first reading are the homely
images of the pellets (beads), the rainfall on the eaves, and especially the herring scales she uses to describe the blood. The images tend to work against
the goal of identification with Christ's suffering; they seem too artificial,
especially the rather unlovely image of the herring scales. It is possible, as
Crampton suggests, that the image of herring scales may have suggested
itself because herring was one of Norwich's sources of wealth. This seems
a plausible reading, but it doesn't explain why Julian finds this an apt image
to describe Christ's suffering. As Julian traces the path of the blood down
Christ's face, as it changes colour from brown to bright red, other images
suggest themselves that transform this suffering into something else, a representation that seems self-conscious in its artifice. I have to disagree that the
imagery of this passage is an 'effort to communicate, to get the vision down
exactly as remembered' (Crampton, *Shewings* 163). I feel that the imagery
functions instead as a reminder of language's failure to communicate the

vision effectively. The tableau conveys the same artifice one might find in an illumination in a Book of Hours, a station of the cross, or some other church picture that Julian might have seen. It is almost as if, in meditating on the vision as one would a painting or illumination, the whole picture – the gestalt – disappears and Julian is left contemplating brushstrokes that remind her of pellets or herring scales (Finke, *Feminist Theory* 97).

Julian's best writing uses the kind of artifice that grows out of its own excessiveness to transform the signs of Christ's physical suffering into symbols of divine power. In Chapter 12, for instance, she uses this technique to good exegetical effect to move her vision from a literal account of Christ's passion to an allegorical interpretation. She begins by describing the scene of Christ's scourging in literal terms, which quickly become almost surreal as the scene becomes awash in blood:

> So copious was the hot flow that neither skin nor wound could be seen: it was all blood. . . . To me it seemed so copious that had it been real the whole bed and more would have been soaked with blood. (82)

In explicating the meaning of this vision, Julian moves effortlessly between the tropological and anagogical levels of exegesis. First she describes the blood's effect on the individual soul (tropological): 'And I recalled the truth that though God through his compassionate love has made an abundant supply of water on earth for our use and comfort, he wishes us to use quite simply his blessed blood to wash ourselves clean of sin' (82). Then she elucidates its implication for salvation history (anagogical): 'The costly and copious flood of his most precious blood streamed down into hell, and burst the chains, and freed all there who belonged to the Court of Heaven' (82–3). Finally, she returns to the salvation of the individual, reminding her readers that Christ's blood 'is available to wash all creatures (if they are willing) from their sin' (83). In this chapter the blood ceases to be a metonymy for Christ's suffering and comes to stand in for his divine power to redeem human sin.

Perhaps the most striking feature of Julian's *Shewings* is her development of the theme of Jesus as Mother, a theme which one commentator argues she handles with 'delicacy and skill' (Wolters, *Revelations* 34). 'The mother's is the most intimate, willing and dependable of all services because it is the truest of all. None has been able to fulfill it properly but Christ, and he alone can. We know that our own mother's bearing of us was a bearing to pain and death, but what does Jesus, our true Mother, do? Why, he, All-love, bears us to joy and eternal life! . . . Thus he carries us within himself in love. And he is in labour until the time has fully come for him to suffer the sharpest pangs and most appalling pain possible – and in the end he dies' (169). To be sure, this theme is not unique to Julian, nor is it characteristic only of religious women; it had been developed much earlier by other writers, especially those of the Cistercian revival (see Bynum, *Jesus as Mother*). However, Julian's insistence on the motherhood of God and her extensive development of this maternal theme (the theme of Jesus as mother is given its most intensive treatment in Chapters 57–63) are surprising in so orthodox an adherent of an essentially patriarchal religion. Do we read these chapters as an appropriation of the female to serve patriarchal and conservative ends, reinforcing gender hierarchies and asserting the superiority of the male by showing that male maternity simply subsumes female motherhood? Or do we understand Julian to be engaged in these chapters in some subversive gender-bending?[17] Perhaps it is counterproductive to attempt to answer these questions definitively; there may be elements of truth in both readings. What seems important about Julian's use of the theme of Jesus as Mother is her insistence that the divine is inclusive of both male and female. In explicating her vision of the Trinity she writes, 'I saw the blessed Trinity working. I saw that there were these three attributes: fatherhood, motherhood, and lordship – all in one God' (165). Instead of the usual Trinity – God the Father, God the Son and God the Holy Spirit – she gives us God the Father, God the Mother and God the Holy Spirit. And it is the maternity of God, not the paternity or the lordship that she singles out for extensive commentary. Julian seems ahead of her time – indeed she seems to anticipate developments in late twentieth-century feminist theology – in her insistence that the Godhead must include the feminine as a significant attribute of divinity.

In her development of Christ's motherhood, Julian once again uses the image of Christ's blood, transforming this symbol of his suffering into a symbol of Eucharistic transcendence, but she does so in terms that the comparison makes uncomfortably literal. 'The human mother may put her child tenderly to her breast, but our tender Mother Jesus simply leads us into his blessed breast through his open side, and there gives us a glimpse of the Godhead and heavenly joy – the inner certainty of eternal bliss' (170). Julian's Jesus invites the reader to violate the intact boundaries of his body by penetrating his 'sweet open side'. The blood which he shed during his Passion now feeds the world. The arresting image of a lactating Christ, nursing actual individuals, not an abstract humanity, with the blood flowing from the wound in his side may have been influenced by iconography in late medieval religious art that depicts Christ's wounded side in ways that visually parallel representations of the Virgin Mary nursing the infant Christ (Bynum, *Holy Feast*, see esp. plates 12–30 pp. 270–6).[18] The literalness of this image is somewhat disturbing. In its violation of the intact body the image of a lactating Christ recalls the process Julia Kristeva calls 'abjection', the process whereby the limits of the self, the border between self and other, inside and outside, are revealed as the fictions they usually are, typically with horrifying results, since abjection is almost always bound up with taboos (*Powers of Horror* 4). Julian seeks revelation not in the intact classical body of traditional religious discourse, but in the ruptures of the leaky grotesque body, in the transgression of medieval taboos against bodily pollution. This rupture is, for Julian, the first step in a process that leads from rupture to compassion through *imitatio*, to heightened consciousness, and eventually to transcendence (Lochrie, *Margery Kempe* 41).

The centrality in Julian's writing of this image of Christ as Mother perhaps leads to the optimism that pervades Julian's theology. Julian's God is a loving, nurturing God who desires only eternal life for his children. 'A mother may allow her child sometimes to fall, and to learn the hard way, for its own good. But because she loves the child she will never allow the situation to become dangerous. Admittedly, earthly mothers have been known to let their children die, but our heavenly Mother, Jesus, will never let us, his children, die' (172). Despite her protests of orthodoxy, Julian seems virtually unable to imagine damnation. God reassures Julian that 'Everything is going to be all right' (109). This is the theme of Chapter 32, which repeats the phrase 'all will be well' almost as a mantric chant. Of course, Julian understands that damnation is an article of faith: 'Another part of our same belief is that many creatures will be damned; for example, the angels who fell from heaven through pride, and are now fiends; and those men on earth who die apart from the Faith of Holy Church, namely, the heathen; and those too, who are christened but live unchristian lives, and so die out of love – all these shall be condemned to hell everlastingly, as Holy Church teaches me to believe' (110–11). However, she cannot imagine how this eternal damnation could be reconciled with God's promise that 'all will be well'. She prays for a vision of hell and purgatory so that she can better understand, but 'for all my desire I saw absolutely nothing' (111). In the end, she can only resort to faith to explain the paradox: 'I thought it quite impossible that everything should turn out well, as our Lord was now showing me. But I had no answer to this revelation save this: "What is impossible to you is not impossible to me. I shall honour my word in every respect and I will make everything turn out for the best." Thus was I taught by God's grace to hold steadfastly to the faith I had already learned, and at the same time to believe quite seriously that everything *would* turn out all right, as our Lord was showing. . . . How this will be no one less than Christ can know – not until the deed is done' (110–11). Julian never finds an answer to her question; it is simply postponed in the aporia of faith. Julian can never reconcile the conflict between God's assertion that 'all will be well' and the fate of the damned. She simply cannot imagine a wrathful God because she cannot imagine a wrathful mother.

Julian's belief in the essential goodness of God's maternity – and its ability to make all things right – creates similar problems for her when she considers the doctrine of sin. She has a very difficult time reconciling the reality of sin with her visions of Christ's beneficence. Initially, when Christ tries to remind her that she will sin, she is 'so enjoying looking at him' that she simply cannot pay attention (117). But the anxiety aroused by her attempts to understand sin is evident in her repeated assertions that, despite her refusal to deal adequately with the existence of evil, she is orthodox in her theology. She is adamant on this point: 'For though the revelation was one of goodness, with very little reference to evil, I was not drawn thereby from any article of the Faith in which Holy Church teaches me to believe' (112). Julian's questions about the existence of evil place her firmly in the tradition of medieval philosophy: 'In my foolish way I had often wondered why the foreseeing wisdom of God could not have prevented the beginning of sin, for then, thought I, all would have been well' (103). If God is so powerful and wise, why does he not simply do away altogether with sin? In her vision God's answer is the same: 'Sin was necessary – but it is all going to be all right; it is all going to be all right; everything is going to be all right' (103). This answer, of course, does not end the debate. Julian cannot leave the question alone. She circles around it again and again in subsequent chapters. Despite her recitation of all the orthodox doctrines of sin – sin is nothing, it has no substantive being (Chapter 27), all men and women sin and suffer for their sins (Chapters 37, 39 and 40), God is able to overcome such failings (Chapter 38), the inadequacy of the answers leads her to tread dangerously close to heterodoxy when she finally states that 'In every soul to be saved is a godly will that never consented to sin, in the past or in the future' (118). Julian's optimism patently does not represent the Catholic doctrine of original sin,[19] but it is a logical outcome of the visions she reports, especially of the constant iteration that all shall be well.

Julian's solution to her doubts, the answer that she seeks to reconcile the existence of sin with her vision that tells her 'all shall be well', comes in Chapter 51 in the form of a parable about a lord and his servant. This parable is so 'mistily' shown that it takes Julian nearly twenty years of contemplation to begin to unravel it. The chapter, which is the longest chapter in the *Shewings*, is mostly taken up with Julian's exegesis which seeks to discern several layers of meaning within this deceptively simple parable. Her vision begins by showing a lord sitting solemnly 'in rest and in peace' (141). At his side is a servant ready to do his bidding. The lord sends the servant on an errand to a certain place. 'Not only does that servant go, but he starts off at once, running with all speed, in his love to do what his master wanted. And without warning he falls headlong into a deep ditch, and injures himself very badly. And though he groans and moans and cries and struggles he is quite unable to get up or help himself in any way' (141). The parable seems a clever attempt to elucidate Julian's position that every saved soul is incapable of assenting to sin. The servant clearly does fall and, as a result of his fall, fails to complete his lord's errand. And yet equally clearly the servant is not really to blame for his failure: 'I sought most carefully to find some fault in him, and to know if his lord regarded him as blameworthy. And, in truth, I could see neither' (142). The parable seems on one level to suggest that the saved soul may well stumble as it attempts to do God's will, but, even in the face of grievous harm, its will is kept whole in God's sight.

Yet the parable is not so easily grasped nor so one-dimensional. It must be understood on several levels. The lord, of course, represents God. He is sitting as a sign of his Godhead, for in Godhead there is no activity (149). The servant who is standing is active, and his standing on the lord's left side is a sign of his inequality. The servant can be understood to represent Adam on one level, the individual soul in its relation to God on another, and Jesus Christ on yet another. 'In the *servant* is represented the second Person of the Trinity, and in the *servant* again Adam, or in other words, everyman' (147). These various interpretations interact with, and occasionally even contradict, one another. For instance, a detail like the proximity of the servant to the lord can only represent God the Son who shares God the Father's divinity, while the detail describing the servant standing on the left side can only point to Adam (by which Julian understands 'everyman') because he can never be equal to God. As Julian's exposition of the parable continues it shifts from an attempt to write sin out of existence to an allegory of the Incarnation: 'In this way we can see how our good Lord Jesus has taken upon himself all our blame, and that, as a result, our Father cannot and will not blame us more than his own dear Son, Jesus Christ. So the servant, before he came to this world *stood before* his Father, ready for his will and against the time he should be *sent* to do that most worthy deed by which mankind was brought back to heaven. . . . He started off with all eagerness at his Father's will, and at once he fell low, into the Virgin's womb' (148). Julian's exposition of this parable demonstrates her considerable skill in the medieval art of exegesis, a skill that belies her claim to be a simple unlettered creature. Her contemplation of this vision moves fluidly between several levels of interpretation, building from a simple parable a complex theological commentary on sin and redemption.

Because Julian's theological speculations may seem far removed from the concerns of English literary studies it is useful to remember that she is dealing with almost exactly the same set of questions that troubled her contemporary William Langland in *Piers Plowman*, a text that also exists in several versions, a testament to its author's struggle to convey an elusive vision in ordinary language. Both texts grapple with the inadequacy of language to capture mystical experiences; both express the frustration of trying to find in a fallen language approximate analogies for the sublime. It is in that struggle and that failure that Julian's power to 'turn our gaze inside out' inspired some of the greatest poets of the twentieth century, though she herself has languished nearly forgotten.

MARGERY KEMPE

Not more than forty miles from Norwich, the medieval port town of Bishop's Lynn produced yet another remarkable spiritual work by a woman. *The Book of Margery Kempe*, written in 1436 according to a manuscript rubric, lays claim to being the oldest surviving autobiographical writing in English. It documents the life and spiritual quests of Margery Kempe, a member of the fifteenth-century bourgeoisie of the town and a woman, according to one commentator, 'of unforgettable character, undeniable courage, and unparalleled experience' (*The Book of Margery Kempe* 10). Julian and Margery were not only close geographical neighbours in Norfolk. They knew each other and Margery's spirituality was, at least in some small degree, shaped by a visit she made to her older contemporary. In Chapter 18 of her book, she describes how God instructed her to 'go to an anchoress in the same city [Norwich] who was called Dame Julian . . . to find out if there were any deception' in her visions. The two had 'holy conversation . . . through talking about the love of our Lord Jesus Christ for the many days that they were together' (Kempe 77–9).[20]

However, in personality the two women could not be more different. There is no evidence that Julian ever left Norwich and good reason to think that she lived most of her adult life enclosed within the four walls of an anchorhold. Kempe, on the other hand, travelled widely not only in England, but throughout Europe and the Holy Land. She went on pilgrimages to Jerusalem, Rome and Santiago de Compostella, the three most popular pilgrimage sites in the Middle Ages.[21] In her sixties, she accompanied her daughter-in-law across the channel to Germany. We have no records of Julian meeting with anyone other than Kempe, while Margery's book documents her meetings with such historically identifiable dignitaries as the Archbishops of Canterbury and York and the Bishop of Lincoln. Julian's *Shewings* suggest a contemplative mind. She gives her readers very little information about herself or her life, preferring to focus in her writing on the visions themselves and her understanding of them. Kempe's book suggests a forceful, even eccentric personality. She is garrulous, assertive, and at times downright annoying. In short, her autobiography is thoroughly entertaining. *The Book of Margery Kempe* presents a mélange of medieval genres. It is part hagiography, part mystical revelations, part confession, part travelogue. Sheila Delany has compared her to Chaucer's fictional Wife of Bath: both are independent businesswomen and members of the late medieval bourgeoisie, married and obsessed with sexuality; both like to travel and are inclined to talk about themselves – at great length; both dress ostentatiously (Delany, *Writing Woman* 76–7).

The Book of Margery Kempe, which records almost everything we know about this remarkable woman, has survived in a single manuscript, the Butler-Bowden manuscript (BL MS Additional 61823). This fifteenth-century manuscript at one time belonged to, and was annotated by, monks in the Carthusian monastery of Mount Grace in Yorkshire (see Lochrie, *Margery Kempe* 203–28). Until 1934, when this manuscript was discovered in the possession of the Butler-Bowden family, Kempe's book was known only through a seven-page pamphlet of extracts printed at the beginning of the sixteenth century by Wynkyn de Worde and reprinted in 1521 by Henry Pepwell (see *Book of Margery Kempe* 9 and Atkinson, *Mystic and Pilgrim* 19).

Kempe was probably born in 1373, the same year in which Julian experienced her revelations. Her father, John Burnham, according to extant records, was fives times mayor of Lynn (1370, 1377, 1378, 1385, 1391) and one of the town's members of parliament (*Book of Margery Kempe* 10). When she was twenty (1493), she married John Kempe, whose family is also mentioned in Lynn records, but who seems not to have achieved the prominence of Margery's father, as Margery reminds him when her husband rebukes her for her pride. She puts him in his place by reminding him that 'she was come of worthy kindred – he should never have married her' (Kempe 44). Nonetheless she bore him fourteen children (Kempe 153), though except for a brief episode involving one of her sons who eventually dies, none of these children is mentioned in the book. After the birth of her first child, she seems to have suffered some kind of postpartum breakdown and is so tormented by visions of devils that she 'was tied up and forcibly restrained both day and night' until a vision of Christ cures her (Kempe 41–2). Her book also relates the failures of the brewing and milling businesses that she began. But most of the book is taken up with her spiritual quests: her visions, her attempts to convince her husband to take a vow of chastity, her various pilgrimages, and her several defences against charges of heresy. Around 1431, her husband, with whom she had not lived for many years, suffered a fall and Margery moved in and nursed him until he died shortly thereafter. She probably died sometime after 1438, when a ten-chapter supplement was added to the book, but characteristic-ally her autobiography offers no neat ending. It simply stops.

Kempe's tendency to scream and cry led many of her contemporary critics to charge that she was possessed by demons; her visions, religious excesses, and especially her aversion to sexuality have led many twentieth-century critics to the more modern conclusion that she was deranged. One critic writes on her recovery from her first postpartum illness that 'it is just as obvious that she never recovered normality, and remained throughout her life profoundly psychopathic' (cited in Stone 31). Critics sometimes point to the scene in which she says that she would rather see her husband slain than have sex with him as evidence of her sexual hysteria. Yet after bearing fourteen children – apparently at considerable cost to her health – her attempts to convince her husband to take a vow of chastity might as easily be considered a sign of mental health!

Contemporary critics have also been somewhat loath to credit Kempe with the authorship of her story. Kempe claims to be illiterate and many have been all too willing to credit her amanuensis, the priest to whom she dictated her story, with whatever artistic felicities the book might possess: 'the texture of the written English and the overall organization of the material may not be so entirely Margery's responsibility as it would have been had she been capable of putting pen to paper herself' (*Book of Margery Kempe* 10). Recently, however, feminist critics have begun to dispute both the certainty of Kempe's illiteracy and the myth of scribal authorship. In one passage which raises doubt about Kempe's complete illiteracy, Christ says to her, 'I have often said to you that whether you pray with your mouth, or think with your heart, whether you read or hear things read, I will be pleased with you' (Kempe 259). Karma Lochrie asks why the writer would make such a distinction between reading and being read to unless Kempe could read (126). Lynn Staley, while not disputing the scribe's existence, argues that Kempe's illiteracy and her use of an amanuensis are 'carefully contrived strategies' designed to ensure the authority of her story (Staley, *Dissenting Fictions* 11). Even if the scribe had not existed, she would have been required to invent one to enhance the authority of her words, giving it the official authorization of the priesthood. 'Lacking a scribe, we would be left with one woman of forty-something (that age, thought of as postmenopausal and thus less "female," in which so many medieval women say they began to write), who sits down to record a series of visions and adventures that occurred some years before' (Staley, *Dissenting Fictions* 36).

The scene of writing described in the Proem to *The Book of Margery Kempe* deserves close scrutiny for its challenges to the assumptions about authorship that are foundational to modern literary studies.[22] In it we can glimpse the ways in which medieval texts establish the credentials of their '*auctores*', a process that is somewhat complicated by Kempe's sex. As Karma Lochrie points out, reading in the Middle Ages was more often linked with hearing or listening than it was with seeing; the written word was often viewed as an extension of the spoken word (102). While contemporary literary studies tend to give authorial credit to the person who does the actual writing, in the Middle Ages dictation was a much more common practice, even among those who could write. It is within this view of reading and literacy that we must understand the Proem's attempt to establish Kempe's as the controlling voice of the text, its authoring presence. Kempe dominates this brief preface, dictating the terms on which the writing will take place. The explanation of her autobiography's failure to keep to chronological sequence is just one example of the book's claim to 'orality', to a successful representation of the speaking voice and its guarantee of the author's presence: 'This book is not written in order, everything after the other as it was done, but just as the matter came to this creature's mind when it was to be written down, for it was so long before it was written down that she had forgotten the time and the order when things occurred' (Kempe 36). Memory, the organizing principle of any oral culture, is the structuring principle of Kempe's memoirs. The possibility that writing holds out for shaping her experiences according to some preconceived plan is both proffered and withheld because of the dangers inherent in such a possibility: such revision might call into doubt the authenticity of Kempe's voice – and hence its truth – by deforming it into something self-consciously literary. This is not to say that the book has not been consciously and artistically shaped, only that it must appear not to be.[23]

The proem suggests deep misgivings about writing as a technology that alienates the devout from God's word. Writing deforms Kempe's story, creating barriers between the reader and Kempe's mystical experiences. The proem repeatedly calls attention to the difficulties involved in recording her story. Twenty years pass between Kempe's first visionary experiences and her decision to write about them. When she finally finds someone to write for her, it is a man 'dwelling in Germany who was an Englishman by birth and afterwards married in Germany' (Kempe 35). He dies before he can complete the project and Kempe takes his work to a priest and asks him to read it. 'The book was so ill-written that he could make little sense of it, for it was neither good English nor good German nor were the letters formed or shaped as other letters are' (35). The priest promises to try. When a scandal erupts around Kempe, the priest, 'for cowardice', refuses to speak to her and refused to work on the book for four years. Finally he tells her he cannot read the book. He advises her to take the book to another man who had known the original scribe. This man tries his hand, but is unsuccessful. Finally the first priest agrees to try and finish the book. 'Trusting in her prayers', the priest finds he is miraculously able to understand it. 'So he read it over before this creature every word, and she sometime helping where there was any difficulty' (35).

It is Kempe who enables the text's writing, and not her three scribes. Her demonstration of God's power is the enabling condition of the narrative. Nothing short of a miracle performed through Kempe's intercession will allow the book to be completed:

> When the priest first began to write this book, his eyes failed, so that he could not see to form his letters and could not see to mend his pen. All other things he could see well enough. He set a pair of spectacles on his nose, and then it was much worse than it was before. He complained to the creature about his troubles. She said his enemy was envious of his good deed and would hinder him if he might, and she bade him do as well as God would give him grace and not give up. When he came back to his book again, he could see as well, he thought, as ever he did before both by daylight and candlelight. (Kempe, 37)

Kempe attempts through this miracle (which has its humorous side, as many of Kempe's adventures do) to ensure the absolute authority of her own claims by locating the written text within an authoritative Logos that is spoken through her. The text consciously strives to overcome the differences that writing necessarily preserves – its openness to transformation and deformation – by insisting on the spoken word as the guarantor of logocentric truth.[24]

Yet such attempts to authorize her voice by linking it with a divine Logos remain throughout *The Book of Margery Kempe* open to questions and doubts. Indeed, what I find most fascinating about this text – and what I believe sets it apart from others of its kind by mystics like Julian, St Bridget and St Catherine – is its presentation of the politics of sanctity, something which few medieval religious genres ever display as blatantly. What I mean by this phrase is that in Kempe's account of her life we see not the results of an individual's sanctification, but the messiness of the process – the conflict, opposition, persecution, ridicule and danger that followed in the wake of audacious claims to sanctity like Kempe's. If Kempe models her life on those of continental mystics like St Bridget and St Catherine, she is not nearly as successful in convincing others of the truth of her claims and her lack of success exposes the very worldly political conflicts that often lie just beneath the serene surface of otherworldly piety. To be sure, most hagiography, as Staley argues, represents the saint's value as continually in conflict with the values of the community in which she finds herself (Staley, *Dissenting Fictions* 40–7). And writings by and about medieval saints may recount their tormenting by devils or their persecution by non-believers. However, the end result – their sanctification – is never in doubt; it has, in effect, already happened. They are not the objects of ridicule and scorn, they are rarely depicted as annoying, and they never have to prove the orthodoxy of their beliefs in public trials.[25]

Kempe's text is compelling because it demonstrates why it was dangerous to be a woman writer, especially a woman writing about religious issues during a time of religious controversy. Kempe's very public career coincided with the religious and secular persecution in England during the early fifteenth century of those followers of John Wycliff who became known as Lollards. On no less than seven occasions in the *Book of Margery Kempe*, Kempe is either imprisoned or interrogated because of questions about the orthodoxy of her beliefs and actions. Once she is even arrested by the king's own guard (*Kempe* 167–8). Many of the clerics who interrogate her are best known for their persecution of Lollards, including Thomas Arundel, Archbishop of Canterbury (*Kempe* 307); Phillip Repyngdon, Bishop of Lincoln (*Kempe* 307); William of Alnwick, Bishop of Norwich (*Kempe* 311); Thomas Peverel, Bishop of Worcester (*Kempe* 318); and Henry Bowet, Archbishop of York (*Kempe* 320). We can begin to understand the hostility Kempe encounters in her life and the dangers that hostility posed for her only by placing her claims within the context of the Lollard heresy and the religious persecution that it prompted. As Clarissa Atkinson has written, 'The ecclesiastical disturbances of the early fifteenth century made it necessary for Margery to define and pursue her peculiar vocation against a background of both heresy and oppression' (*Mystic and Pilgrim* 105).[26]

The set of beliefs associated with Lollard heresy emerged in the 1370s and 1380s from the Oxford circle of John Wycliff. But what began as an intellectual movement was quickly spread throughout England by itinerant preachers, becoming as much a social movement against the political power of the institutional Church as a religious one. By the beginning of the fifteenth century, it had established itself as a loosely organized movement with some support from the gentry and a larger following among artisanal groups and the bourgeoisie (McSheffrey, *Gender and Heresy* 8). Lollard dissent from orthodoxy was as much a social rebellion as a doctrinal one. It challenged the stranglehold of the institutional Church – and especially the clergy – on devotional practices. Lollards denied that ordination conferred any special powers upon priests, and attacked especially the elite clergy for its wealth and avarice. They attacked such Catholic practices as pilgrimages, the adoration of images, saints and relics, holy days, fasting, prayers for the dead and transubstantiation (the miracle by which the communion host becomes literally the body of Christ) as idolatrous. Confession to a priest was unnecessary for salvation. Instead Lollards stressed the direct relationship between God and the Christian soul which required not the intercession of the clergy, but a thorough knowledge of scriptures (McSheffrey, *Gender and Heresy* 7–10; Atkinson, *Mystic and Pilgrim* 104–5). Lollards promoted the translation of the Bible into the vernacular so it could be directly available to lay readers. The response of both religious and secular authority to the Lollard heresy was swift and brutal. In 1401, *De haeretico comburendo*, which allowed the state to execute heretics, was passed by parliament. Kempe would have had first-hand knowledge of Lollardy and its repression. In 1401, the first heretic to be burned at the stake was William Sawtrey, a parish priest at St Margaret's in Lynn, the church Kempe frequently mentions in her book as the site of her devotions. In the early fifteenth century, Norwich was a centre of Lollard activity and persecution; records show that, between 1428 and 1431, at least sixty men and women were tried for heresy by its episcopal court (Atkinson, *Mystic and Pilgrim* 103–4).

There is no reason to believe that Kempe was herself a Lollard and much evidence against such a conclusion. Her regular participation in such practices as pilgrimage and fasting, her fascination with relics, her worship of the saints, and her participation in the rituals of the Eucharist all testify to her orthodoxy. Yet she shares with the Lollards a contempt for the worldliness of the clergy, an abhorrence of swearing, and a claim to enjoy a direct relationship with God unmediated by the clergy. But more than any one specific practice or belief, the anxiety and the backlash Kempe evokes result from the claims she makes to enjoying an unmediated relationship with God and the audacity with which she preaches her claims. That anxiety only makes sense within the context of a more widespread social movement that was empowering the laity at the expense of the clergy.

Kempe's first encounter with charges of heresy occurs in Chapter 13 when she is in Canterbury. There a monk, described as 'a powerful man and greatly feared by many people', challenges her right to speak, asking 'What can you say of God?' Kempe replies, 'I will both speak of him and hear of him', and proceeds to tell a story from scriptures (Kempe 63). Her knowledge of scriptures instantly raises suspicion, presumably because, unless they had access to heretical vernacular translations, laypersons were not supposed to have an intimate familiarity with the Bible. This suspicion is expressed by another monk, 'Either you have the Holy Ghost or else you have a devil within you, for what you are speaking here to us is Holy Writ, and that you do not have of yourself' (63). Kempe responds with an exemplum, a stock device of the preacher (Lochrie, *Margery Kempe* 141–4). Though her audience in this episode is small and, of course, not institutionally sanctioned, she does call upon the rhetorical devices of the preacher to defend herself and she asserts her right to speak about God. The first monk expresses his horror at her audacity by wishing her 'enclosed in a house of stone, so that no one should speak with you' (63). In other words, he wishes that, like Julian, she would restrict her religious devotion to the more acceptable role of anchoress, that she would limit herself to the non speaking occupation of invisible example. The other monks are much less charitable: 'You shall be burnt, you false Lollard! Here is a cartful of thorns ready for you and a barrel to burn you with' (64). On another occasion when Margery is in London seeking an audience with the Archbishop of Canterbury, she rebukes a group of the Archbishop's men for swearing (71). If we remember that swearing was one of the practices the Lollards especially condemned, the remark of a townswoman that follows makes more sense. She says, 'I wish you were in Smithfield[27] and I would bring a bundle of sticks to burn you with it is a pity you are alive' (72).

Kempe is called upon again and again to prove the orthodoxy of her religious practices. Chapters 46 to 55 document a whole series of accusations, imprisonments, arraignments and interrogations that Kempe must endure. In Leicester, she is ordered to appear before the mayor who calls her 'a false strumpet, a false Lollard, and a false deceiver of the people' (149). He wants to send her to prison. Instead she is put under house arrest in the jailer's own house, so that she would not have to be jailed with men. While she is in custody, the Steward of Leicester attempts to rape her (150). Only a terrible storm compels the townspeople to question Kempe's travelling companions, who had also been imprisoned, to discern if she were 'a woman of true faith', and subsequently release all three of them.

She is still required to appear in the church in Leicester before a panel of clerical judges, where she is examined on the Articles of Faith. They especially question her closely about her beliefs in the sacrament of the Eucharist. Her affirmation of the doctrine of transubstantiation absolves her of any charge of Lollardy: 'I believe in the sacrament of the altar in this way: that whatever man has taken the order of priesthood be he never so wicked a man in his manner of life, if he duly says those words over the bread that our Lord Jesus Christ said when he celebrated the Last Supper sitting among his disciples, I believe that it is his very flesh and his blood, and no material bread' (152–3). Though the clerics who examine her are satisfied with her response, the Mayor of Leicester is not and he requires her to get a letter from the Bishop of Lincoln, testifying to her orthodoxy.

Travelling to York, she is once again imprisoned and required to appear before the Archbishop of York to answer accusations there that she is a Lollard. The details of the text convey the seriousness of her situation: 'her flesh trembled and quaked amazingly, so that she was glad to put her hands under her clothes so that it should not be noticed' (162). However, her fear does not prevent her from responding to the Archbishop's charge that she is a wicked woman with a counter-accusation: 'I also hear it said that you are a wicked man. And if you are as wicked as people say, you will never get to heaven' (163). The Archbishop of York examines her closely to determine if she has violated the Church's prohibition against women preaching.

He requires her to swear that she will 'not teach people or call them to account in my diocese'. Kempe refuses, arguing that 'the Gospel gives me leave to speak of God' (164). Her citation of scriptures leaves her open to further charges of Lollardy, as her accusers are quick to note. They also quote the Pauline injunction that was the basis of the Church's prohibition: 'But I suffer not a woman to teach, nor to use authority over the man: but to be in silence. For Adam was first formed; then Eve. And Adam was not seduced, but woman being seduced, was in the transgression' (1 Tim. 2:12–14). Kempe denies that she is preaching; she claims no institutional authority: 'I do not preach, sir; I do not go into any pulpit. I use only conversation and good words, and that I will do while I live' (164). However, as both Lochrie and Staley have noted in their analyses of this scene, Kempe's replies to her accusers are much more subtle and ambiguous than they might at first appear (Lochrie, *Margery Kempe* 106–12; Staley, *Dissenting Fictions* 5–11). She preaches at the same time she denies she is doing it, following her disclaimer by preaching a parable condemning the wickedness of the clergy to those assembled. When one of the examining priests complains, her reply obliquely suggests an analogy between preaching and the story she has just told: 'in the place where I mostly live is a worthy cleric, a good preacher, who boldly speaks out against the misconduct of the people and will flatter no one. He says many times in the pulpit: "If anyone is displeased by my preaching, note him well, for he is guilty." And just so, sir . . . do you behave with me' (166). Her reply silences the priest and, even though the Archbishop's assembly finds her innocent of any heresy, the trial is inconclusive. In a later chapter she finds herself once again up before the Archbishop of York on charges of heresy, presumably at the prompting of the Duke of Bedford, the king's brother. This time she asks for written proof of her vindication: 'My lord, I pray you, let me have your letter and your seal as a record that I have vindicated myself against my enemies, and that nothing admissible is charged against me, neither error nor heresy that may be proved against me' (173).

What I am calling the *Book of Margery Kempe*'s politics of sanctity – the struggles that surround Kempe's claims to divine favour – emerge not only in her public heresy trials but also in her private interactions with others in the communities of which she is a member. Her piety is manifested through a series of external religious practices that continually annoy and alienate those around her. Even though she is imitating the religious practices of holy men and women she has heard about, it is rare to see anywhere in medieval devotional literature a religious figure so disliked and so unlikable as Margery Kempe. Everywhere she goes she is ostracized by others; at one point, even her husband deserts her: 'she was greatly despised and reproved because she wept so much – both by the monks and priests, and by secular men, nearly all day, both morning and afternoon – and so much so that her husband went away from her as if he did not know her, and left her alone among them, choose how she might, for no further comfort did she have from him that day' (63). The community's censure results primarily from practices regarding food, dress and crying, all of which show Kempe to be significantly at odds with the values of the communities in which she finds herself.

Curiously Kempe's eating practices are never as extreme as those re-corded in hagiographies of many medieval saints, such as those of Catherine of Siena who starved herself to death at the age of thirty-two. Yet they arouse a great deal of animosity in her travelling companions during her pilgrimage to Jerusalem. They are annoyed with her because she refuses to eat meat, which they take as a refusal to participate in the communal rituals of the group (Staley, *Dissenting Fictions* 49–52). Among a group of pilgrims who, like Chaucer's Canterbury pilgrims, are as interested in entertainment and merry-making as they are in repentance, Kempe's piety is a constant irritant and she becomes an object of ridicule for the other pilgrims: 'They cut her gown so short that it only came a little below her knee, and made her put on some white canvas in a kind of sacking apron, so that she would be taken for a fool, and people would not make much of her or hold her in any repute' (98). Because she will not join the pilgrims' merry-making, she becomes a source of entertainment for them.

Kempe's habit of shedding tears and crying aloud when she thinks about the Passion of Christ also earns for her the contempt of those around her. Kempe's tears begin early in her career. She represents them as an involuntary gift from God: 'through the gift of which graces she wept, sobbed, and cried very bitterly against her will – she might not choose, for she would rather have wept softly and privately than openly, if it had been in her power' (193). During her pilgrimage to Jerusalem she has 'such great compassion and such great pain to see our Lord's pain', she adds to the tears an involuntary crying: 'she could not keep herself from crying and roaring though she should have died for it' (104). Her histrionics in church are so distracting to those around her that at one point, an itinerant friar bans her from any church in which he is preaching (190). Interestingly, the friar, who becomes Kempe's implacable enemy, is willing to allow her to return to church and hear him preach if she is willing to admit that her crying fits are the result of a disease, a 'natural illness' (190). Among those who take offence at Kempe's 'gifts' of crying and weeping is the priest who served as her scribe. As a result of the friar's preaching against Kempe, this priest resolves never to believe her feelings again. He is only convinced of the sincerity of her devotion when he reads the *vita* of Marie d'Oignes, the thirteenth century beguine 'who could not endure to look upon the cross, nor hear our Lord's Passion, without dissolving into tears of pity and compassion' (192). Only the authorizing discourse of Jacques de Vitry's Latin *vita* provides the priest a suitable model for understanding Kempe's devotional practices.

Finally, there is conflict throughout the *Book of Margery Kempe* over Kempe's dress. Early on, in Chapter 2, the narrative describing her pride and her 'showy manner of dressing' before her conversion gives us some sense of the importance both Kempe and her culture attach to dress: 'she wore gold pipes on her head and her hoods with the tippets were fashionably slashed. Her cloaks were also modishly slashed and underlaid with various colours between the slashes' (43). In a culture in which sumputary laws at least attempted to regulate how groups of people dressed, clothing carries significant cultural meaning and may be the site of serious cultural conflicts. Kempe seems to dress lavishly not so much because of an inordinate love of beauty, but 'so that she would be all the more stared at, and all the more esteemed' (43). Like the *Canterbury Tales'* portrait of the Wife of Bath, *The Book of Margery Kempe* suggests that her clothing is a sign of her elevated social status and wealth. After her conversion to a life of devotion, Kempe continues to use clothing as a means of signalling status – this time her status as a holy woman. When Christ tells Kempe that she is to wear white clothes, she initially expresses doubt: 'if I go around dressed differently from how other chaste women dress, I fear people will slander me. They will say I am a hypocrite and ridicule me' (68). The white clothing most probably was meant as an external sign of virginity or chastity, a state to which Kempe obviously has no claim, but which she just as obviously desires. On several occasions she expresses her anxiety and regret that she is not a virgin, a fear that she will not dance as merrily in heaven as those whose virginity is still intact (see, for instance, p. 86). The white clothing that Christ demands Kempe wear is God's (or Kempe's) way of establishing a distinction between technical physical virginity (the state of never having had sex) and an inner moral state of chastity that has nothing to do with the use of the body and to which Kempe may make some claim. This distinction was a common one throughout the Middle Ages, though it does tend to reduce to nonsense the argument for virginity's superiority. That those around Kempe had difficulty with this distinction is obvious from their shocked and hostile reactions to what the Bishop of Lincoln calls her 'singular clothing' (70). They read the signs of her clothing as staking out a claim to virginity and special holiness which she had long ago forfeited.

Kempe seems to alienate not only strangers but those to whom she should be the closest as well. Her son is so exasperated that 'he fled her company, and would not gladly meet her' (265). After her son dies and she escorts her daughter in law back to Germany, 'there was no one so much against her as was her daughter-in-law, who ought to have been most on her side' (272). Once they take their vow of chastity, Kempe and her husband live in separate residences until John is fatally injured and she must move in to take care of him, though of all those who people her life, he seems the most consistently loyal. Of him she writes, 'And always, her husband was ready when everybody else let her down, and he went with her where our Lord would send her, always believing that all was for the best, and would end well when God willed' (69). *The Book of Margery Kempe* exposes, in each of Kempe's encounters, both public and private, a politics of sanctity in which judgements of a woman's holiness are as much about accumulating allies, patrons and supporters as protection from those threatened by her devotion as they are about the quality of the life she lived.

THE PASTON WOMEN

In the second half of the fifteenth century, Norfolk produced yet another significant collection of women's writing in the Paston Letters, a collection of some 930 letters to and from various members of the Paston family between 1425 and the early sixteenth century. Of these, 174 were from women. The more than one hundred letters contributed by Margaret Paston, wife of John Paston I and the most prolific Paston correspondent, alone constitute the largest volume of personal writing by an Englishwoman during the Middle Ages. It may seem odd to classify the authors of letters as major authors, but in an age in which the letter was often elevated to an art form (see above pp. 111–17) we should be wary of dismissing the letters of the Paston women as mere ephemera or of interest only to social historians. To be sure, the letters contain little in the way of self-reflection and they are not self-conscious literary artifacts; they were probably saved as evidence for the many legal disputes in which the Pastons were involved (Watt, 'No Writing' 123). As Virginia Woolf noted of the letters, 'in all this there is no writing for writing's sake; no use of the pen to convey pleasure or amusement or any of the million shades of endearment and intimacy which have filled so many English letters since' (cited in Watt, 'No Writing' 123). The Paston Letters, however, are a significant cultural event for several reasons. These letters have much to tell us about the development of English prose in the fifteenth century. Furthermore, the letters by women provide significant insight into women's day-to-day lives in the late Middle Ages. They tell us much about the ways in which women inhabited the roles they were allotted by the culture and the ways they turned their limitations to their advantage, 'poaching' on the very culture that restricted their lives.

The Pastons were a Norfolk family of landowners and lawyers. Although John Paston II, after the death of his father, John Paston I, was able to convince King Edward IV to issue a statement that he and his uncles William and Clement were 'gentlemen descended lineally of worshipful blood sithen the Conquest hither' (Davis xlii), the family seems to have risen to prominence no earlier than the end of the fourteenth century. In fact, if the genealogy proposed by one fifteenth-century Norfolk document, written by someone hostile to the family, is correct, the Pastons' rise in the fifteenth century was positively meteoric. According to this document, Clement Paston was a 'good plain husband[man], and lived upon his land that he had in Paston, and kept thereon a plough all times in the year. . . . Also, he had in Paston a five score or a six score acres of land at the most, and much thereof bond-land to Gemyngham Hall, with a little poor water mill running by the river there, as it appeareth there of old time. Other livelihood nor manors had he none there, nor in none other place' (Davis xli–xlii, translation Bennett, *Pastons* 1). With his father-in-law's help he found the money to send his son William Paston to school and later to London where he was a student in one of the Inns of Court (Bennett, *Pastons* 2). Clement's investment apparently paid off; William's rise to prominence was rapid. He was appointed Steward to the Bishop of Norwich. In 1421 he became a sergeant of the Court of Common Pleas and eight years later was raised to the bench. He began to purchase land around Paston, eventually making himself the major landowner there (Bennett, *Pastons* 2). He married Agnes, daughter and heiress of Sir Edmund Berry. The marriage settlement brought William the manor of East Tuddenham in Norfolk and Agnes inherited several other manors from her father. William and Agnes had five children: John I, Edmund, Elizabeth (later Poynings and Browne), William II and Clement. By the time of William's death, the Pastons were major landholders in Norfolk and a force to be reckoned with, but their good fortune was beginning to arouse the jealousy of their neighbours (Bennett, *Pastons* 3).

John Paston I inherited the family properties on his father's death. He was only twenty-two or twenty-three at the time and faced the considerable challenge of protecting his family's interests and properties against challenges by their enemies. This he did, like all parvenus of the time, through every means at his disposal, including law, patronage, marriage, and the placement of his children in the households of great landowners, nobility or even of the king (Bennett, *Pastons* 4).[28] John I married Margaret, the daughter and heiress of John Mauteby of Mauteby, Norfolk, acquiring several new properties in the bargain. Margaret is by far the most prolific of the Paston letter-writers and her letters document many of the difficulties the family faced in maintaining control of their scattered properties. She relentlessly pursued the interests of her new family, even defending those properties from physical assaults. Margaret bore seven children: John II, John III, Edmund II, Margery (later Calle), Anne (later Yelverton), Walter and William III. John II became head of the family on his father's death, but both John II and John III are shown to be actively pursuing family interests throughout their adult years. John II was knighted at about the same time he was placed in the king's household. Despite several courtships which are described in the letters, he never married. John III married Margery Brews; given the calculating descriptions of other family marriages this one can only be described as a love match (Bennett, *Pastons* 46–7).[29]

Sir John seems to have presided over the decline of the family fortune. He was much less interested than his father or grandfather in the legal and business affairs incumbent on property owners. He spent much of his time in London, leaving the affairs in Norfolk to his mother and younger brother. Letters from this period show the family hard pressed for money. For instance, in a letter to her son John III, Margaret Paston begs him to get money from his elder brother so she can repay a debt she incurred for him:

> My cousin Clere hath sent to me for the 100 marks that I borrowed of her for your brother. It fortuned so that a friend of hers lately has lost better than 300 marks, and he sent to her for money, and she had none that she might come by and therefore she sent to me for the said 100 marks. And I k[n]ow not what to do therefore, by my troth, for I have it not nor I can not make shift therefore and I should go to prison. Therefore commune with your brother hereof and send me word how he will make shift therefore in haste. For I must else needs sell all my woods, and that shall disavail him more than 200 marks if I die, and if I should sell them now there would no man give for them nearly as much as the 100 marks they are worth because there are so many wood sales in Norfolk at this time. (vol. 1 353)[30]

Other letters suggest that John spent most of his time in London enjoying the fruits of his position rather than defending it from encroachment. When he writes to John III describing his participation in a tournament at Eltham, he says 'I would that you had been there and seen it, for it was the goodliest sight that was seen in England this forty year' (Bennett, *Pastons* 22). His brother replies somewhat less enthusiastically: 'I had rather see you once in Caister Hall than to see as many king's tourneys as might be between Eltham and London' (Bennett, *Pastons* 22). Most of the lands the Pastons inherited from Sir John Fastolf were lost at this time and Sir John was forced to sell off other properties to maintain himself and his family, as Margaret fears.

When John II died unmarried and without heir, his brother John III took over the family affairs. His keener business sense enabled him to restore the family fortunes. The end of the fifteenth century found him a knight, Sheriff of Norfolk, and 'right well beloved counsellor' of the Earl of Oxford (Bennett, *Pastons* 26). Over the ensuing two centuries, the family continued to flourish and extend its influence. In 1679 a descendent of the family, Robert Paston, became Earl of Yarmouth. His son, the second earl, died without issue; the male line and the title died with him (Davis li–lii).

Letters from four Paston women survive, as well as letters from many other female relatives and acquaintances. In the first generation, there are thirteen letters from Agnes Paston. The second generation is represented by Elizabeth Paston (later Poynings) and the prolific Margaret Paston. Six of Margery Paston's letters survive among third-generation letters. Scholars often downplay these women's authorship of their letters since none of their letters is indisputably in the author's own hand. Whatever is of value in them is attributed to the often anonymous clerks or scribes who did the actual writing. Davis concludes from the evidence of the letters' handwriting that, because the Paston women appear not to have written their own letters, the Paston women were either totally or nearly illiterate. Even though Agnes Paston concludes one letter to her husband conventionally 'written at Paston in haste . . . for default of a good secretary', Davis argues that 'if she could write as well as this she would surely not have had her other letters written by clerks', concluding that 'the point of the closing words is therefore obscure' (Davis 26). If Davis were to admit that Agnes might have meant in her closing remark that she wrote this letter hastily and did not have a secretary at hand then he would also have to admit that she wrote out at least part of a draft of one of her husband's letters, which is in the same hand (Davis 13). However, as Diane Watt has argued, the evidence is far more ambiguous (Watt 124). The evidence of handwriting alone finally can tell us very little about individuals' literacy or their mastery of the rhetorical skills of composition, since dictation was as common among the great and learned as it was among the illiterate. That the Paston women had their letters written for them by clerks may be merely a sign that they were wealthy enough to afford such a luxury; it does not necessarily mean they were not responsible for those letters' contents and style.

The best-known women's letters in the Paston correspondence demonstrate how significant marriage was in the life of a fifteenth-century Englishwoman, especially if she were a member of a family as ambitious as the Pastons. A 1449 letter to John I from his niece Elizabeth Clere concerns a potential match between Elizabeth Paston and Stephen Scrope, the stepson of a family friend and patron, Sir John Fastolf. The Fastolf connection was extremely important to the Pastons. John I became connected with Fastolf, a wealthy and influential veteran of the French wars, through his marriage to Margaret Mautby. By 1450 John was acting for Fastolf in several matters of business; by 1456 he was named a trustee of Fastolf's holdings in Norfolk and Suffolk. In Fastolf's 1459 will he was named as one of his executors. Paston claimed, however, that before his death, Fastolf had made a nuncupative, or oral, will leaving Paston lands in Norfolk, including the manor of Caister (Davis xliv). Paston spent the rest of his short life trying to defend the disputed properties against the claims of the other executors and his sons carried on after him. But in 1449, a potential marriage between Fastolf's fifty-year-old widowed stepson and John's eighteen-year-old sister must have seemed ideal even if, as Scrope himself says, he was 'disfigured in my person and shall be whilst I live' (Bennett, *Pastons* 29). The marriage is alluded to favourably in one of Agnes Paston's letters to her son:

> My cousin Clere has written to me that she spoke with Scrope after he had been with me at Norwich, and he told her what welcome I had given him; and he said to her he liked well the welcome that I gave him. He said to my cousin Clere that unless you gave him encouragement and words of comfort at London he would no more speak of the matter [the proposed marriage]. My cousin Clere thinks that it were folly to forsake him unless you knew of another as good or better, and I have assayed your sister and found her never so willing to any as she is to him, if his land stands clear. (Davis, vol. 1, 30; translation mine)

Agnes describes Elizabeth as amenable to the marriage, but only if it is clear that any children of the marriage would stand clear to inherit his property, and not the daughter of his first marriage. Agnes certainly conceives of this marriage as a property transaction between the Paston family and Scrope's, complete with indentures outlining the terms of the settlement.[31] Elizabeth Clere's letter describes the negotiations over the proposed marriage from a very different perspective in her letter to John I. Clere's letter relates Scrope's willingness to disinherit his own daughter from a previous marriage, leaving her '1 mark and no more' (vol. 2, 32). In this letter, however the daughter seems far less compliant and the mother determined to have her way:

> She has since Easter, for the most part been beaten once a week or twice, and sometimes twice in one day, and her head broken in two or three places. Wherefore, cousin, she hath sent to me by Friar Newton in great council and prays me that I would send to you a letter of her heaviness and pray you to be her good brother, as her trust is in you. (vol. 2, 32)

Lest we be tempted to romanticize this as Elizabeth's resistance to a miserable arranged and loveless marriage, we ought to note that Clere goes on to convey a message from Elizabeth that makes her seem both as calculating as her mother and every bit the dutiful daughter:

> And she says that if you may see by his evidences that his children and
> hers may inherit, and she to have reasonable jointure [a sum of money
> or property settled on a woman by her husband], she hath heard so much
> of his birth and his condition that, if you will, she will have him whether
> her mother will or not, notwithstanding she is told that his person is
> simple. (vol. 2, 32)

Since only three letters by Elizabeth survive, all written after her 1459
marriage to Robert Poynings, it is impossible to tell whether these words
reflect her own feelings or those of her mother after she had beaten her
daughter into submission. The earliest letter of Elizabeth's is dated about a
year after her marriage to Poynings and is a request directed to her mother
to pay the hundred marks she had promised her husband upon their marriage. Her attitude toward the husband she was finally given seems less than
enthusiastic: 'And as for my master, my best beloved as you call him, and
I must needs call him so now, for I find no other cause, and as I trust Jesus
never shall; for he is full kind to me, and is as busy as he can to make me
sure of my jointure' (vol. 1, 206). She seems at best resigned to making the
most of the bargain, entering into the financial spirit of the game.

For this reason, the courtship twenty years later of John Paston III and
Margery Brews seems intimate by comparison. In a letter written before
their marriage, Margery writes:

> Right reverent and worshipful and my right well-beloved Valentine, I
> recommend me to you full heartily, desiring to hear of your welfare, . . .
> And if it pleases you to hear of my welfare, I am not in good health of
> body nor of heart, nor shall be until I hear from you.
>
> For no creature knows what pain I endure,
> And even on pain of death I dare it not disclose.[32]
>
> And my lady my mother has belaboured the matter to my father full
> diligently, but she can get no more than you know of, for which God
> knows I am full sorry.
> But if you love me, as I trust truly that you do, you will not leave me
> for that reason. Even if you had but half the livelihood you have, I would
> not forsake you even if I had to do the greatest labour that any woman
> alive might. (Davis vol. 1, 662)

This love match, which was encouraged by the mothers,[33] was apparently
not lucrative enough for John's father and elder brother. In a subsequent,
and more practical, letter, Margery suggests that her father will not offer
any more money than he already has, even though his offer falls far short of
what the Pastons expected (Davis vol. 1, 663). Despite these obstacles to
true love, the marriage did finally take place in 1477 and the affection
between the two appears to have endured. While most of Margery's letters
to John begin with the conventional formal salutation used above – 'Right

reverent and worshipful sir' – at least one, dated 1481, addresses John as 'My own sweetheart' (vol. 1, 665).

Perhaps the most spectacular marriage story told in the letters concerns Margaret's youngest daughter Margery, who defied her mother and brothers and scandalously betrothed herself to the family bailiff, Richard Calle. The narrative as it emerges from three correspondents offers both touching romance and juicy gossip, flying, as it does, in the face of the usual family procedures for arranging marriages, which involved extensive and protracted financial negotiations which were about as passionate as a tax audit. The family battles as fiercely in law to retain control over this rebellious daughter's marriage as they do to protect their various properties. John III writes to his brother, 'if my father, whom God pardon, were alive and had consented thereto, and my mother and you both, he should never have my good will to make my sister sell candle and mustard in Framlingham' (Davis vol. 1, 541). Calle writes to Margery reproving her for showing his letters to her family, which resulted in two years of enforced separation. He begs her to burn his letter and show it to no one (which she obviously neglected to do). But mostly he reminds her of how binding their promises are:

> My own lady and mistress, and before God very true wife, I with heart full sorrowful recommend me unto you as he that cannot be merry nor never shall be until it be otherwise with us then it is yet; for this life that we lead is neither a pleasure to God nor to the world, considering the great bond of matrimony that is made betwixt us. (Davis vol. 2, 48)

According to Calle, he and Margery had contracted a lawful marriage. The plighting of troth between two people was as binding a marriage as any; no witnesses nor ceremony were required beyond the recitation of the appropriate words (see above pp. 45–7). Calle urges her to make this clear to her family.

Apparently she did so, judging from the anger displayed in Margaret Paston's letter of 10 or 11 September 1469 detailing to John II the steps she has taken to have the marriage annulled. The matter was taken before the Bishop of Norwich and Margaret's account of the examination illustrates nicely the methods courts used to determine whether a disputed marriage was valid or not. Margaret attempts to get the Bishop to delay the proceedings until John II and her husband's other executors could be present, but the Bishop refuses. Margaret and her mother-in-law Agnes, speaking for the family, deny that there has been any legal marriage between the two: 'My mother and I informed him that we never understood by what she said that they were bound to each other . . . but that they might both choose' (vol. 1, 342). The Bishop then examines Margery and Calle separately to determine what exactly they had said and when they had said it. He needs to know the exact words they had exchanged to determine if a valid marriage existed: 'and therefore he bade her be right well advised how she did, and said that he would understand the words that she had said to him, whether it made matrimony or not' (vol. 1, 342). Margery's response shows considerable defiance, at least as Margaret reports it: 'And she rehearsed what she had said, and said if those words made it not sure . . . that she would make it sure before she went thence' (vol. 1, 342). The Bishop then examines Calle to determine if their stories agree both on the words spoken and the time and place where they were spoken. Even after this examination the judge equivocates, postponing his decision to look for other impediments to the marriage. At this point Margaret, in her wrath, disowns her daughter. She refuses to receive her and sends word she is not to be admitted to the house. She advises her son, 'I pray you and require you that you do not take it so hard for I know well it goes right near your heart, and so it does to mine and to others. But remember, and as I do, that we have lost here but a worthless person, and set it the less to heart; for if she had been good it should not have been as it is. Even if he [Calle] were dead at this hour, she should never be at my heart as she was' (343).

Eventually Calle and Margery were allowed to marry, so presumably the Bishop was unable to find any impediments to the unseemly marriage. Furthermore, Calle had proved himself so invaluable that the Pastons had to retain his services as bailiff, though it is likely that he was never received as a member of the family. It is possible that Margaret relented somewhat from the position she articulates in this letter, as her will bequeaths £20 to Margery's eldest child John (vol. 1, 388).

The Paston women, however, did not merely concern themselves with such domestic, and therefore stereotypical female, matters as love, marriage, childbearing and rearing, supervising servants and provisioning the household. Indeed, Margaret would hardly be anyone's candidate for mother of the year. She seems decidedly cool toward her children. In 1470 she writes to her son, John III, and asks him to find a place for her daughter Anne: 'Therefore I pray you commune with my cousin Clere in London and find how he is disposed toward her, and send me word, for I shall be loathe to send for her and with me she shall but waste time; and, although she will be better occupied, she shall often times move me and put me in great discomfort' (vol. 1, 348).

Margaret's letters demonstrate that women of the landowning class had duties and interests that went far beyond the domestic sphere. If Margaret is, like Chaucer's Wife of Bath, calculating in her assessment of potential family marriages, she is also like the Wife of Bath in her zest for business affairs. Most likely so many of Margaret's letters survive because her husband was frequently in London defending the family's interests in the courts. In his absence, Margaret remained behind in Norfolk to manage the family's estates and defend them, even against violence. Her letters keep her husband informed about events at home, ask questions about how to handle various affairs, report decisions she has made. They may have been saved as evidence for legal proceedings. The letters show her exercising considerable authority within the family. Though Margaret deferred to the conventional authority of her husband, at times even apologizing for her behaviour – 'By my troth it is not my will neither to do nor say anything that should cause you to be displeased' (vol. 1, 251), John's frequent absences left her considerable latitude to exercise her own judgement.

In Margaret, John found a capable, loyal and resourceful business ally. The dispute with the Lord Molyns over the property at Gresham demonstrates her capabilities, even if it does end with Margaret being expelled in humiliation from Gresham. In 1448 Margaret writes to John requesting some crossbows and various other weapons in preparation for an attack on that property (vol. 1, 226). In his petition to the king for redress of the wrongs Molyns had done him, John describes his wife's role in the attack on Gresham that finally came in January of 1449:[34]

> the said lord [Molyns] sent to the said mansion a mob of at least one thousand people, . . . arrayed in manner of war . . . so came into the said mansion, the wife of your said petitioner at that time being therein, and twelve persons with her, the which persons they drove out of the said mansion and mined down the wall of the chamber wherein the wife of your said petitioner was, and bore her out at the gates and cut asunder the posts of the houses and let them fall, and broke up all the chambers and coffers within the said mansion, and rifled and in the manner of thieves bore away all the stuff, array, and money that your said petitioner and his servants had there. (vol. 1, 52)

In 1465, at Hellesdon, one of the Fastolf manors, Margaret was once again called upon to defend her husband's property, this time against attacks by the Duke of Suffolk.

If, as wives, the Paston women were required to stand in for their husbands' interests, as widows they were often themselves involved in litigation to maintain property that was rightfully theirs. For instance, after her husband's death, Agnes Paston found herself being sued by a Carmelite friar over her right to land in Oxnede which her husband had settled on her (even though technically friars were not supposed to own land). Margaret writes to her husband, 'He [the friar] said plainly that he shall have Oxnede, and that he has my lord of Suffolk's good lordship. . . . There was a person warned my mother within these two days that she should beware, for they said plainly she was like to be served as you were served at Gresham within right short time' (vol. 1, 30 1, 233 4). Though eventually the friar's patron died and Agnes was able to maintain her hold on her property, the incident demonstrates that the women of the Pastons' class were just as likely as men to maintain their lands, and fight for them in court, even in the face of violent attack.

After her husband's death, Margaret continued to dominate family affairs, advising her sons, directing them, criticizing, and sometimes even manipulating them. In a 1472 letter to his elder brother, John III expresses the frustration of a nearly thirty-year-old man living in the same house with his mother:

> Many quarrels are picked to get my brother E. [Edmund] and me out of her house. . . . All that we do is ill done, and all that Sir James and Pekok do is well done. Sir James and I are at odds. We fell out before my mother with 'Thou proud priest' and 'Thou proud squire', my mother taking his part, so I have almost beshit my boat as for my mother's house. . . . My mother proposes to make an account of all her lands and upon that account to make her will. . . . And in this anger between Sir James and me she has promised me that my part shall be nought; what yours shall be I can not say. (vol. 1, 353)

Margaret seems to have no qualms about using the property and authority she has acquired during her marriage to keep her grown sons in line. Her letters and those of her sons suggest that she remained active in family affairs until her death in 1484.

The letters of the Paston women are interesting not only for what they can tell us about the lives of Englishwomen in the second half of the fifteenth century. They are of considerable literary interest as well. Norman Davis has already demonstrated the importance of the Paston Letters to our understanding of the development of English prose. Diane Watt has examined the women's letters, and especially those of Margaret Paston, for their most conspicuous rhetorical features. Her analysis of letter 129, which describes an attack on the family chaplain, James Gloys, by John Wymondham, shows Margaret to be a deft storyteller who draws instinctively upon the features of oral narrative with dramatic effects (131–2). We can see Margaret's use of the looser syntax of spoken language (not surprising if she dictated her letters) in the postscript to the same letter in which she warns her husband to beware of Wymondham:

> When Wymondham said that James should die I said to him that I supposed that he should repent him if he slew him or did to him any bodily harm; and he said nay, he should never repent him nor have farthing worth of harm though he killed you and him both. And I said yes, and [if] he slew the least child that belonged to your kitchen, and if he did he were like, I suppose, to die for him. (vol. 1, 225)

In this passage, as in the prose of most of the letters, the connections between ideas are paratactic rather than hypotactic, additive rather than logical. In her indignation, Margaret's report of the words between herself and her chaplain's attacker slides between indirect discourse (in the first period) to direct discourse or quasi-direct discourse (in the second and third periods).[35] Margaret's reported response to Wymondham in the second sentence merits closer examination for its failed attempt to muster the rhetorical devices of the threat. The sentence begins with two conditional clauses, the first beginning with a suppressed 'if' ('and he below be lest chylde'), creating the expectation that Margaret will offer in the final clause some dire threat of retaliation. But instead of building up to the threat, the sentence falls away in anti-climax, the force of Margaret's indignation expended by the parenthetical 'I suppose' which undercuts her rage with a hint of uncertainty. In its failure to deliver an adequate threat, in fact, the sentence beautifully conveys what Margaret must have frequently felt when her husband left her in a position of authority to make decisions for her household, but often lacking the power to back those decisions with appropriate physical force.

The portrait of Margaret Paston that emerges from the Paston Letters offers us another remarkable medieval Englishwoman to put alongside Chaucer's fictional Wife of Bath and Margery Kempe's account of her own life. Together these portraits – fictional and non-fictional – of ambitious, shrewd and outspoken women challenge stereotypical views of medieval women as docile and submissive. Given the violent and often lawless world in which he lived, John Paston would have been a fool to pass over the formidable Margaret Mautby for a more conventionally compliant and tractable wife.

CHRISTINE DE PIZAN IN ENGLAND

Though there is no evidence that the Franco-Italian poet Christine de Pizan ever set foot on English soil, she is a fitting figure with whom to end this investigation of medieval women writers for several reasons, not the least of which is that she is the most prolific woman writer of the Middle Ages: her works, were they ever collected, would fill several large volumes and include most of the major genres of medieval literature: narrative poetry, lyric, prose, allegory, dream visions, history, biography, autobiography and hortatory epistles. While she wrote many works, she is perhaps best known for her *Book of the City of Ladies*, a long prose allegory which attempts to refute medieval misogyny by rewriting history from a woman's perspective, or, to use her own allegorical conceit, to construct a tradition of great women – a city of ladies. But Christine is important to the history of both women's writing and English letters for other reasons as well. Christine's works – and surprisingly not primarily the *City of Ladies* – were well known in England, especially among the aristocracy. Several translations of her works appear both in manuscript and in print during the fifteenth century. Furthermore, the media in which those translations appear and the purposes they serve, point to several key developments in English culture occurring during this period. Translations of her works participated in the conversion from manuscript to print culture and they figure in some of the earliest expressions of British nationalism.

Most of what we know about Christine comes to us from her own writing, especially from *Lavision Christine* (1405), a lengthy lamentation against Fortune in the tradition of Boethius' *Consolation of Philosophy*. Though this narrative was perhaps not intended as an autobiography, it does provide most of the significant details of the poet's life. She was born in Venice around 1364 after her father, Tommasso di Benvenuto da Pizzano, an astrologer-physician, had gone there to marry the daughter of a friend. While there, he received an offer of employment from Charles V of France – perhaps the age's most remarkable patron of learning – and eventually went to Paris to Charles's court. There, Tommasso was 'most graciously received and honored by the said King Charles the Wise who, having seen his [Tommasso's] erudition and knowledge, appointed him soon thereafter his special, private, and valued counselor' (108).[36] While *Lavision Christine* blames the family misfortunes on the vicissitudes of Fortune, the text sheds much more light on the vicissitudes of the patronage system by which royal retainers were recruited and rewarded. The king promises 'wealth, revenues, and pensions' to maintain Tommasso's position in Paris, to which he brought his family in 1368. And for a while his royal patron was able to make good his promises: 'During the lifetime of the said good and wise King Charles, Fortune was most favorable to us; and since every loyal servant is naturally delighted to see the prosperity of his good master . . . time then advanced toward the passage of my said father into the service of the King, governed partly, especially in warfare, by his wise counsel administered in accordance with the science of astrology' (108).

Around 1380, at about fifteen ('the age when young girls are customarily assigned husbands', 109), Christine was married to Étienne de Castel. In the same year, however, the fortunes of Christine's family began to wane as the death of the king meant the loss of the royal patronage they had enjoyed. In an economic system governed by patron/client relationships, the client's employment is dependent not on contractual arrangements, but on the favour of a single individual – the patron – and on the client's willingness to remind the patron of his debt. Christine is quite specific in spelling out the losses her family suffered after the death of their patron:

> at the time, my father's large pensions disappeared. He was no longer fully paid 100 francs a month with his books and gifts, which were hardly worth less, as he learned. And as for the hope that the good King had given of settling 500 livres of land on him and his heirs, the untimely death and the failure to remind the king prevented the realization of this and other promised benefits, even though he was retained by some of the governing princes at wages sorely reduced and infrequently paid. (110)

We might wonder about the purpose of such exact accounting in a genre (the consolation) that is generally quite abstract and philosophical; it reminds a patron or potential patron of the extent of financial loss when promises are not kept. It perhaps violates one of the essential features of patronage relationships – that the transaction between patron and client be disguised as a gift – and may suggest the extent to which wage transactions are becoming at least conceivable, even within the royal household. When Charles died, Tommasso was forced to seek new patrons; however, the new king, Charles VI, had little of the reputation for learning that his father had.

In 1389, both Tommasso and Castel died, leaving Christine a twenty-five-year-old widow with 'three small children and a large household' (111). Though her father and husband left her some small inheritance, they also left her with debts and (as we have already seen above in the Paston Letters) the legal complexities inheritances involved, which usually required many years of expensive litigation to settle. In her complaint, Christine does not sound all that different from Agnes or Margaret Paston: 'From everywhere impediments rose before me and since this is widow's fare, lawsuits and legal actions surrounded me' (112). Fortunately Christine's father had given her some education, although *Lavision* recounts the difficulties women experienced in pursuing education (bear in mind she was married and bearing her own children at the age of fifteen): 'For although I was naturally inclined to scholarship from my birth, my occupation with the tasks common to married women and the burden of frequent childbearing had deprived me of it to employ me there' (117).

Christine turned to writing and scholarship to support her family. From 1399 until her death in 1429 she wrote several volumes in prose and verse which she presented to members of the French court, relying on their patronage to maintain her household. Around 1400 she completed her first major work, *L'Epistre d'Othéa la déese a Hector* (*Epistle of Othea*) which she initially dedicated to Louis of Orléans (Charles VI's brother). In 1404 she got her first large commission from Philip the Bold of Burgundy (another of the king's brothers) to write a biography of Charles V. *The City of Ladies* was completed in 1405, along with *Lavision Christine* and *Le Livre de Faits d'Armes et de Chevalrie (The Book of Deeds of Arms and Chivalry)*. In 1406 she completed *The Book of Three Virtues* and the *Treasury of the City of Ladies*. She died shortly after completing the *Ditié de la pucelle*, a poem about Joan of Arc.

Christine's patrons included Charles VI, his wife Isabeau of Bavaria (to whom she dedicated a magnificent two-volume deluxe edition of her works, now British Museum MS Harley 4431), Philip and John of Burgundy, Louis of Orléans, and John of Berry. That Christine was widely read in France is suggested by the sheer number of manuscripts of her works that have survived: 40 of the *Epistle of Othea*, 25 of *City of Ladies*, and 17 of *The Book of Three Virtues*. That these manuscripts range from deluxe, highly and skilfully illuminated volumes to crude and cheaply made texts suggest that Christine appealed to a wide variety of readers, not all of them wealthy or aristocratic.

Her popularity in England is also well attested. Indeed, Christine herself refers to it in *Lavision* in a passage that is well worth quoting at length:

> Around the time when the French king's daughter was married to King Richard of England, a noble count named Salisbury [Sir John Montague] came from there to France. And since this gracious knight loved poems and was himself a courteous poet, after what he had seen of my poems he begged me so that I agreed – albeit unwillingly – that my oldest son, a very clever and charming child of thirteen [Jean of Castile], might go with him to England to be a companion to one of his own sons of the same age; for this said count conducted himself quite nobly and generously toward my child and promised more for the future. I believe he would not have disappointed in these matters since he was powerful enough to bring them about; certainly the promises he made me were not revealed to be lies. (120)

Yet, once again, patronage proves – even with the best intentions – to be a capricious means of support. Not long after, King Richard was deposed by his cousin Henry Bolingbroke and the Earl of Salisbury was beheaded for supporting Richard in a civil conflict that eventually became the Wars of the Roses. Her son was left virtually abandoned in England:

> Still a child in a foreign land at the time of the great pestilence, he must have been justifiably terrified. But when King Henry, who had stolen the crown, happened to see these books and poems – several of which I had already sent being eager to please the said count – and knew everything about it, he joyfully brought my child to his court and held him dear and in high rank. In fact, by two of his heralds . . . he actually sent for me to come, beseeching me in earnest and generously promising great benefits if I might go there. (121)

But Christine refuses his offer and has to resort to a bit of deceit to get her son back:

> Seeing how things were there, I was not tempted by this in any way, and I concealed my feelings until I might have my son, thanking the King profusely and saying that I was fully at his command. To be brief, I did so many things – not without great forfeit, it cost me several of my manuscripts – that I obtained leave for my son to come and fetch me to lead me there, [a place] I still have not seen. And so I refused the bequest of Fortune for my son and myself because I could not believe a traitor would come to a good end. (121)

Christine might have been an English poet after all. However, refusing the patronage of the English king, Christine remained a staunch French royalist all her life, despite the insanity and ineptitude of Charles VI and the contentiousness of his barons, and despite France's losses to England during the early years of the Hundred Years War.

Notwithstanding her political views, her works continued to circulate in England and in the latter half of the fourteenth century were frequently translated. Which works got translated and by whom tells us a great deal about how fifteenth-century English readers received Christine. As twentieth-century readers, we read Christine as a 'woman writer', not only a writer who happened to be a woman but a woman who wrote about women and their concerns. This, however, does not appear to have been how fifteenth-century English readers valued her works. All of the translations of her works were done by men and their interest appears to have been primarily in her military, political and didactic works. Of all Christine's work to be translated into English in the fifteenth century only Thomas Hoccleve's unacknowledged 'Letter to Cupid' (an English version of 'L'Epitre de Cupid') deals with the courtly love tradition as we understand it.

The survival of British Library MS Royal 18. B. xxii, entitled the *Boke of Noblesse*, provides us with the best evidence of Christine's reception among fifteenth-century English readers, at the same time providing some clue to the complex web of relationships that link the translations of her works. *The Boke of Noblesse* is a long epistle, addressed to Edward IV. In his prologue, the writer identifies his purpose to whip up the English outcry against recent losses in France and to encourage the king to renew the hostilities, 'to encourage and comfort the hearts of the English nation' (f. 1; translation mine). This curious text was written around 1475 by someone connected with the household of Sir John Fastolf, a prominent Norfolk landowner and Knight of the Garter who, in the words of William Caxton in his 'Tully of Old Age', exercised 'the wars in the realm of France and other countries by forty years enduring'.[37] Fastolf may have had good reasons for commissioning such a work. He benefited enormously from the wars in

France, being appointed, with the Duke of Exeter, governor of Harfleur after that battle, distinguishing himself at Agincourt, and in 1422 becoming master of the household of the Duke of Bedford who was then regent of France. He also suffered from English losses, chiefly at the hands of Joan of Arc. Fastolf was even accused in some quarters of being responsible for the loss of the king's French inheritance through cowardice or treachery. *The Boke of Noblesse* may be a response to these accusations, accusations which were to persist and find their way into Shakespeare's characterization of him in *Henry VI*. Though Fastolf himself died in 1460, the text appears to have been originally written in 1451 and later revised for the occasion of Edward's immanent invasion of France in 1475; the colophon does state that the present text was made 'under correction'.

The *Boke of Noblesse* is a remarkably polyglot text. Abstract philosophical speculation on the morality of war is juxtaposed with historical narratives which tend to be vague and exemplary for the ancient Romans, but quite detailed, if idealized, for more contemporary accounts like that of Henry V. Exhortations to the king to reclaim his rightful lands rubs up against the minutiae of Fastolf's own campaigns in Harfleur, supplied in excruciating detail by William Worcester, Fastolf's secretary, who heavily annotated the present manuscript. Despite the singularity of the author's purpose, the text views history from many perspectives, not all of them congruent with his purpose.

Of most interest for our purposes, however, is the author's incorporation into his epistle exhorting the King of England to attack France and reclaim his rightful inheritance, of several passages from Christine's *Livre des faits d'armes*. The *Boke of Noblesse* offers valuable evidence of how Christine was being read in fifteenth-century England. The passages are not just silently cribbed from Christine, as Hoccleve had done in his 'Letter to Cupid'; she is not simply being appropriated by a male author. Rather she is cited as an authority on the proper conduct of war; she is given prominence equal to that of other great authorities both classical and contemporary. As with the other authorities cited, passages from her work are always announced by phrases like 'which Dame Cristyn makithe mencion of' or 'the said Dame Cristin in the xiiii chapter seieth'.

This attribution of so much authority to a woman, however, could not help but provoke anxiety among the manuscript's earliest readers and indeed, the marginal annotations and accounts of the manuscript signal those anxieties, providing still more evidence of Christine's conflicted English reception. A Latin annotation in a hand that has been identified as that of William Worcester suggests that Christine must be understood not as the author of the text, but as its patron, a situation we know from her own account in *Lavision Christine* to be unlikely.[38] Given her own financial dependence, it is unlikely that Christine could have offered patronage to anyone. This characterization of Christine as a kind of medieval religious *salonière* suggests that Christine's autobiographical texts were unavailable in England for a very long time after her death. It persists well into the nineteenth century when John Gough Nichols, the *Book of Noblesse*'s first and only editor, decisively claimed that Christine could not have been the author of the interpolated passages. Indeed Nichols goes so far as to deny that Christine could have even written the *Faits d'armes*. In discussing Caxton's translation he writes, somewhat patronizingly: 'Now Christina de Pisan was a poetess: and it is not likely that she had more to do with this treatise in the art of war than the "dame Christine" of our present author had with the *Arbre des Battailles*. Indeed it is probable that the two mis-appropriations are connected in their origins' (*Book of Noblesse* vi). It was left to William Blades, editor of the facsimile edition of Caxton's *Fayttes of Armes*, to point out Nichols's error.[39]

The *Boke of Noblesse* may not be notable for its literary merit and even its historical interest must be slight, but it does illuminate the relationships among the English translations of Christine de Pizan in the last half of the fifteenth century, all of which emanate from two centres: the household of John Fastolf and William Caxton's workshop. In the 1450s, *The Epistle of Othea* was translated into English by Stephen Scrope, son-in-law of Sir John Fastolf, the same Stephen Scrope who was nearly married off to the eighteen-year-old Elizabeth Paston. In 1478 Caxton published an edition of Christine's *Moral Proverbs* which had been translated by Anthony Woodville, Lord Rivers, the queen's brother. In 1489 Caxton published his own translation of *Fayttes of Armes and of Chivalrye* which he dedicated to his patron, Henry VII. Curiously it is not until 1521 that a copy of *The City of Ladies* (the work for which Christine is best remembered) is published by Henry Pepwell. The translation was done by Brian Anslay, a yeoman of the wine cellar to Henry VIII.

All of these translators have patronage connections to key figures in the interrelated politics of the War of the Roses and the Hundred Years War with France. The latter half of the fifteenth century in England was largely shaped by these two conflicts – the one a civil contest between the Lancastrians and Yorkists over the succession to the throne, the other a long and intermittent foreign war with France. The works of Christine chosen for translation tend to speak to the political concerns raised by those conflicts. Taken as a group these translations illuminate two major developments in fifteenth-century material culture that would give rise to the particular character of the English Renaissance. The first was the transition from a manuscript to a print culture; the second was the creation of a specifically English nationalism. These two developments (along with the discovery of the 'new world' and the Protestant reformation) would distinguish the sixteenth century from those that came before it, though the rupture must seem more obvious to us with the benefit of hindsight than to those living through it and commenting on it.

Nationalism, as Benedict Anderson has argued, is not a natural or inevitable ideology; it has not always existed. Rather it is the outcome of a series of historical and imaginative processes. Nationalism requires a communal perception of an imagined community in which all the members of the nation, though they may never meet, are bound by horizontal, rather than vertical ties. The two great conflicts of the fifteenth century – the one civil, the other foreign – seemed unintentionally to provide the raw material for representations of the nation which the Tudor monarchs in the sixteenth century were able to forge into a coherent image of the English nation. This perhaps explains why Shakespeare's only cycle of plays on English history focus on this period. The St Crispin Day speech in *Henry V* is a good an example of the representation of these emerging horizontal ties of nationalism: 'We few, we happy few, we band of brothers'. However, for individuals to develop a sense of imagined community there must be some mechanism for disseminating representations of that imagined community, since it is through representation that members of the state, who could never meet and know all other members of the state, are united. Printing was admirably suited to this task, since it enabled a wide distribution of identical texts, which was impossible with manuscripts. Instead of a single patron for whom one customized the text being copied, printing made it possible to reach a wider audience of mostly anonymous readers, all of whom would be reading the same text and would be able to identify with representations of national identity carried by those texts, and in doing so would identify with each other.

Stephen Scrope's translation of the *Epistre Othea* (which may have been written at roughly the same time as the earliest version of the *Boke of Noblesse*, i.e. 1451) epitomizes the way in which the Middle Ages used manuscripts and the sort of imagined community encouraged by a manuscript culture. *Othea* seems less a text for public consumption than an artifact to be possessed by a single individual, an observation that holds both for the original French manuscripts and Scrope's English translation. The book, in a manuscript culture, is not a means of disseminating knowledge widely; rather it is a means for delivering up control of that knowledge to a unique individual. The *Epistre Othea* (written around 1400), presented initially to Louis of Orléans and, at various other times, to Isabeau of Bavaria, Charles VI, and the Dukes of Berry and Burgundy, is an epistolatory allegory. It purports to be a letter from the goddess Othea to a fifteen-year-old Hector. While Hector was a well-known Trojan hero identified with the ideals of knighthood and chivalry, the goddess Othea cannot be identified with any particular character from Greek mythology. One possible gloss for the name is etymological. O plus the Greek 'thea' for goddess would yield 'O goddess'. This was an epithet Homer often used to refer to Athena. In Christine's poem Othea is identified with prudence. Christine writes that 'Othea, according to the Greek, can be taken for the wisdom of women.'[40] Most scholars have understood the *Othea* to be a conduct book or courtesy manual, illustrating proper courtly behaviour. This may indeed be how its English translators, both Scrope and, in the sixteenth century, Anthony Babyngton, understood it when they referred to it as *The Duke of Knyghthode*. And Scrope's reading of the text's contents is not inaccurate: it is, he says, 'grounded first upon the .iiii. Cardinal Virtues: Justice, Prudence, Strength, and Temperance . . . which teach and counsel how a man should be a knight principally for the world' (Buhler 122).[41]

Recently, however, Sandra Hindman has offered a convincing reading of the *Othea* as a political allegory of French royal politics during the reign of Charles VI. Her reading is dependent on understanding not only the text, but the relationships between the visual and literary aspects of the work, including text, layout and illuminations. One of the earliest manuscripts in which the *Othea* is preserved is BM Harley 4431 whose production Christine oversaw herself. A lavish volume such as this one was produced for a single individual (Isabeau of Bavaria); it is a unique event. In this manuscript, *Othea* is clearly a picture poem, with 101 illuminations which illustrated the 100 'textes' of Othea's letter to Hector. (Of the 130 illuminations in Harley 4431, 101 illustrate the *Epistre Othea*.) Each of the 'texts', usually a four-line poem, was accompanied by an illustration, a gloss which contains a moral lesson for Hector, and an allegory which contains a spiritual lesson. Later manuscript and printed editions (of which there were many) vary a great deal in the layout of these elements, which makes each manuscript unique. The manuscript is much more like a work of art in this regard than a book. It does not necessarily presume more readers than the immediate patron and its possession becomes a sign of the patron's power. Without the illuminations which partly explain it (both the English translations and modern editions of the *Othea* omit the visual material), the text becomes more abstract and less interesting, perhaps accounting for one editor's judgement that the poem is not Christine's most skilful work (Buhler, *Epistle of Othea* xi). With the loss of the illuminations much, if not all, of the specific political allegory – and hence the text's interest – is lost.

Hindman argues that Christine wrote the *Othea* as a means of advising the French monarchy and aristocracy during a period of particularly acute social conflict (Hindman, *Painting and Politics* 139, 143–4). For Christine, Charles's father and predecessor, Charles V, was the ideal monarch, 'a good wise king [who] restored France from the state of ruin into which it had fallen before' (*Christine's Vision* 108).[42] Charles VI could only have been a disappointment to her. He came to the throne as a minor and his regency was controlled by his uncles, the dukes of Berry and Burgundy. During his reign he was for much of the time incapacitated by insanity. The ensuing struggle for power between Charles's queen Isabeau, his brother Louis of Orléans and his uncles, all of whom had their own ambitions, led to considerable social instability. The allegory of *Othea's* visual programme is made to carry quite specific political meanings. By means of decorative symbols – such as the signs of chivalric orders or coats of arms – that refer to specific political actors in the Valois court worked into the design of the illuminations and by the juxtaposition of the contemporary figures alluded to by those symbols with the mythological figures in the text, Christine was able to give advice to the royal family about their responsibility to rule wisely in a way that was discrete and inoffensive (Hindman, *Painting and Politics*).

The intimacy that marked the patronage relations that subsidized manuscript production could produce magnificent works of art, but these were more suited for partisan politics of early fourteenth-century France than for creating the imagined community required by nationalism. *Othea*, however much it may have pleased its patrons, was not likely to become a means of building the imagined community of the French nation. But it appears to have been a popular text and was frequently recopied (there are 43 extant manuscript copies of the French text alone). Those copies would have treated the text in many different ways. As the original political allegory was lost, new meanings could be attached to it.

The Duke of Bedford must have acquired Harley 4431 from the royal library in the Louvre when he was regent of France. But Bedford was not the only member of the English army that plundered France during the first half of the fifteenth century to demonstrate an interest in books. John Fastolf must have acquired his Christine manuscripts through purchase or looting during his campaigns in France. Bodleian MS Laud. Misc. 570 contains a French copy of the *Epistre d'Othea* which was made in England for Fastolf. It contains only the first six illuminations whose workmanship, attributed to the Fastolf master, while not rivaling that of Harley 4431, is still quite skilful. If this manuscript was not the text that Scrope used for his translation (Chesney, 'Two Manuscripts' 35–41), it is close enough to suggest that both had a common parent which Fastolf must have brought back from France when he returned in 1439. Scrope's translation, which was most likely completed some time between 1440 and 1459, appears originally to have been a gift to his stepfather, a patron who had much misused his stepson by withholding his mother's inheritance from him, keeping him dependent on him for much of his adult life. In the Paston Letters Fastolf is described as 'hot tempered, arbitrary, and rapacious, harsh and mean to his dependents, an exacting creditor and rancorous litigant' (Warner, *Epistle of Othea* xxxi). Scrope says he translated the *Othea* 'by the sufferance of [Fastolf's] noble and good fatherhood and by your commandment' (122). The knight, he says, is now sixty years old and, 'at this time of age and feebleness', it is appropriate to leave off 'the exercising of deeds of chivalry' and 'to occupy the time of your age and feebleness in body in ghostly chivalry of spiritual deeds of arms, in contemplation of moral wisdom and in exercising of spiritual works that may cause you to be called to the order of knighthood that shall perpetually endure and increase in endless joy and worship' (121).[43] Despite the references in his dedication to Fastolf which suggest he understood this text as a guide to the moral development of the individual knight, Scrope also recognizes the political implications of Christine's work for 'policie gouernaunce' or wise government (122). In writing of the Duke of Berry, the dedicatee of the French manuscript Scrope was translating, he describes the three 'knightly labours' chivalry requires. The first is care for the welfare of the soul. But 'one was in victories, deeds of chivalry and of armies, in defending the said Realm of France from its enemies; the second was in using great policy, great counsels and wisdom, giving the same for the conservation of justice and tranquillity and also peace keeping for all the common welfare of that noble Realm' (123). He also recognizes the political significance of the document when he dedicates a later version of the work (MS H.5, St John's College, Cambridge) to Humphrey Stafford, the Duke of Buckingham, that 'excellent prince of wisdom' (3).[44]

The manuscript dedicated to Buckingham (the St John's manuscript) contains six illuminations which exactly parallel the six illuminations included in Fastolf's French manuscript (Laud. Misc. 570). They include an illustration of Scrope presenting his work to the duke, Othea presenting her letter to Hector (which is taken as a representation of the cardinal virtue of prudence), and illustrations of the texts about the other cardinal virtues: temperance, Hercules (strength), Minos (justice). The final illumination illustrates Perseus. While the iconography of these illuminations is consistent with that of other manuscripts of the *Othea*, what makes them unique is their incorporation of *grisaille* – a technique of monochromatic painting in which black and white pigments are used to create shades of grey – into all but the first illumination.[45] The grisaille figures set against a background executed in colour makes the illuminations seem ghostly. Since the first illumination is the only one which includes no grisaille and it is also the only one to portray historical individuals (Scrope and Buckingham, the patron and client), it is possible that the grisaille figures were intended to call attention to the allegorical or 'ghostly' status of the text, to the fact that the mythical figures represented (Minos, Hercules, Perseus) depict 'truth [hidden] under the cover of a fable'.

Christine's mythography, interpreted as it is through a system of glosses and allegorical explanations, is designed to promote those virtues and skills most necessary to good government, something rather sadly lacking both in fifteenth-century France and England. Her use of gloss and allegory is designed to ensure that her readers do not miss rather cryptic morals of some of the 'texts'. For instance, Text XXX's invocation to 'Delight thee greatly in the cunning/ Of Io', who was seduced by Jupiter and later turned into a cow, would seem, on the surface, a story not terribly relevant to an analysis of good government. However, the gloss explains that Io invented letters and 'as, it may be that Jupiter loved her, that is to understand, by the virtues that were in her she became a cow, or as a cow gives milk, which is sweet and nourishing, so she by the letters that she discovered gave nourishing to understanding. . . . Therefore it is said that the good knight should greatly love Io, by which may be understood the letters and writings and stories of good people, which the good knight should hear told gladly and read' (40–1). What is striking about this gloss, besides the twisted attempt to make sense out of the rather grotesque image of Io being transformed into a cow, is its focus on importance of literacy as a means of creating stable government and the role women have played in creating and sustaining literacy.

Christine attempted, throughout her career, to use her writing to advise the French royal family against the disastrous political infighting which brought the monarchy to the brink of civil war. It is not surprising that, given the political turmoil and civil strife that characterized the War of the Roses in fifteenth-century England, these works should appeal to English translators of that period, especially when they too were clients of a royal family. Another of Christine's political works, the *Body of Policy* or *Le Livre de Corps de Policie*, written in 1406 for the fourteen-year-old heir to throne, Louis of Guyenne, may have been translated in 1470, perhaps by Anthony Woodville, Lord Rivers, the brother-in-law of the Yorkist Edward IV. In this treatise, Christine likens the 'thre gendres of estate' (the three estates) to

a living body . . . of which the prince or the princes hold the higher place of the head in as much as they should and ought to be sovereigns and from them should come the particular institutions just as out of the understanding of men springs forth the deeds that the limbs achieve. The knights & the nobles hold the place of the hands and arms. For as the arms of a man are strong to endure labour and pain so they ought to have the charge to defend the rights of the prince and the commonwealth. And they also are compared to the hands for as the hands put away the annoying things, so they should put away all things that are evil and unprofitable. The third estate of the people are like the belly, the feet, and the legs. For as the body receives all things that comfort the head and the limbs, likewise the exercise of the princes and nobles ought to return to the public good . . .

and as the legs and feet bear the weight of a man's body, so the labourers
sustain all other estates. (a.i–a.i^v)[46]

Though extremely conservative, Christine's view of government differs from
the traditional medieval understanding of the three orders – those who fight,
those who pray, those who work the land – in that it is entirely secular
(Duby, *The Three Orders*). Furthermore, it understands the various estates as
a single unified entity. While hierarchy still dominates the relations between
the estates, individuals are encouraged to see themselves as vital parts of
a whole, as horizontally as well as vertically bound with the others. The
metaphor of the body, drawn from medieval representations of the Church,
but secularized, is designed to remind the reader that the nation is one
entity which requires the health of all its members to function properly:
'For just as the body of a man is defective and deformed when he lacks any
of his members, likewise the body of the Polity may not be perfect or
entire if these estates are not well joined and assembled all in one so that
each of them holds the others' (m.v).

Towards the end of the treatise Christine writes about the different kinds
of governments that have been known throughout history and argues that
of all these France's form of government accords best to the principles
outlined above.

> Because we reside in France, even though the writing of books and,
> especially books that teach manners & doctrine, ought to be general and
> relate to those who dwell in all countries (in as much as books are
> profitable & are carried in to divers countries & regions), it will suffice for
> our purposes to address our words & instruction to the people of France,
> though these words & instructions may generally serve as a good example
> to all other regions, if they will understand it was intended.

Here France becomes the model for all good government; its appropriation
by other peoples simply reinforcing its exemplary status as a nation. Christine,
while allowing that she might have readers who are not French, assumes that
what binds the readers of this particular text together is their identification
with 'France' as an entity, a literal 'body', in which all parts or 'estates' are
connected. The act of reading the treatise becomes a potential mechanism
for establishing the imagined community of the nation in ways that the
Othea's more general and abstract calls for just government could not.

The Boke of Noblesse's recontextualization of Christine's treatise on warfare against the backdrop of English history surely suggests something of
these first rumblings of English nationalism – of an imagined community of
Englishmen – especially in its adaptation of the medieval practice of genealogy to bind its readers not only across space, but across time as well. As
a unique manuscript, however, it was not well suited to disseminating this
sense of national identity. Indeed there is no evidence that the manuscript

ever left Fastolf's household during the fifteenth century, no evidence that it even reached its addressee, the king. But William Caxton's establishment of a printing press in Westminster in 1476 would provide the mechanism necessary to dissemination of the representations of national identity.

In 1489 Caxton published his own translation of Christine's *Faits d'armes* under the title *The Fayttes of Armes and of Chyualrye*. In his epilogue he relates how he was asked to translate into English Christine's book by 'the most Christian king & redoubted prince, my natural & sovereign lord King Henry the vii king of England & of France' from a book in the king's possession which was delivered to him by the Earl of Oxford. The king commissioned the publication so that 'every gentleman born to arms & all men of war, captains, soldiers, vitallers & all other should have knowledge of how they ought to behave in the deeds of war & of battles' (Oxford Bodleian MS Douce 180, H ii^v; translation mine).

The Fayttes of Armes is quite literally an instructional manual on warfare, encompassing everything one needed to know to wage war in the fifteenth century. The first two books combine philosophical speculation on the justice of warfare with advice on how to prepare for war, how to finance wars, how to train soldiers, and how to arrange troops on the battlefield, as well as practical instructions on such technical matters as how to use siege engines, how to defend against a siege, how to undermine a castle, how to defend against the mining, and even how to fight naval battles. The advice is sprinkled with copious examples drawn both from contemporary wars, particularly the French wars with England (of particular interest is the description of Charles V's conflict with England and his sending of ambassadors to John of Gaunt, then Duke of Lancaster [I. 5]), and from ancient accounts of war, particularly those of Rome.

The final two books take the form of a dialogue between Christine and her 'master', Honoré de Bonet, whose *L'Arbre des Batailles* (*Tree of Battles*) is a major source for the last part of the *Fayttes of Armes*. She encounters Bonet in a dream vision after she has fallen asleep from 'the heavy weight of the labour' of the previous two books. The dialogue enables Christine to pose a series of hypothetical situations that clarify the rules of war. For instance, 'suppose that an earl or a baron of the realm of France / held certain lands of the king of Aragon or of some other king and that it happened that the said two kings of France and Aragon / sent for the said earl or baron to help them in their wars / which of these two kings shall he then obey / For it is impossible to be in two places at once' (198–9).[47] The answer: he should go and serve under the king from whom he holds the most land and send some of his men to serve under the other king. Precedent suggests that this solution holds even if the two kings are fighting one another, though Bonet holds this to be a less than satisfactory solution since 'If he should do so, then his own men must be against him.' His solution is to choose one and forfeit the lands held of the other (199).

Besides enabling Christine to elucidate the rules of war by means of concrete examples, however, the dialogue with Bonet also enables her to mitigate some of her own anxieties about her authorship and to distance herself from her 'master'. The very first question she asks of Bonet is whether 'any rebuke could be cast on her work' (190) because, to paraphrase Bonet, she has gathered flowers from other writers' gardens (189). Bonet answers that the practice is common among great writers, giving the example of Jean de Meun's use of Guillaume de Lorris in the *Romance of the Rose*:

> Dear love, to this I answer thee / that the more a work is witnessed and approved of by folk, the more it is authorized and made more authentic . . . it is a common use among my disciples to give to one another the flowers that they take diversely out of my gardens. (190)

But I think plagiarism is not the real issue for Christine in this passage. Rather I think it has much to do with her own anxiety about her authority as a woman writing about such subjects as warfare and policy. Why should anyone believe that a mere woman could have anything to say on such subjects? And indeed we have seen that at least two of her translators – William Worcester and Stephen Scrope – were all too willing to believe that Christine did not really write either the *Fayttes of Armes* or the *Othea*, and how easily such beliefs were picked up by later editors like Richard Pynson, who attributed the *Moral Proverbs* to Chaucer, or John Gough Nichols, who simply refused to believe that Christine might have written about warfare.

Despite the popularity of her work and despite her obvious ability to support herself as both a writer and publisher, Christine had good reason to be anxious about the reception of the work of a woman writer, especially when she is writing about what have been traditionally thought of as male subjects. She often expresses these anxieties in the prefaces to her work. In *Body of Polycye*, for instance, she begins

> If it is possible that virtue might grow from vice, it will please me well to be as passionate as a woman, since many men hold the opinion that it is in the nature of women to be unable to keep silent the abundance of their courage. Now come boldly and be shown the many clear rivers and crystal springs and the inexhaustible fountains of my courage which cannot be hidden to cast out the desire for virtue. (a.i; translation mine)

Christine always casts these doubts about the wisdom and virtue of her gender in circumspect terms, employing a torturous syntax full of elaboration, subordination and metaphor. This high rhetorical style is one that feels to the twentieth century reader unnaturally stilted and excessively wordy, but

Christine is sometimes able to use it to good effect, as in this sentence where she is literally turning the vice of her sex into a virtue.

Another example occurs in the preface to the *Fayttes of Armes* where her irony is so subtle that the inattentive reader might easily miss it. She begins by contrasting her own inadequacies with the importance of the material she has to treat, referring to 'the insignificance of my person / which I know is neither dignified nor worthy to treat of such high matter' (5). Yet despite these inadequacies she is encouraged to continue by her own literary success: 'Then moved not by arrogance in foolish presumption, / but admonished by the affection and good will of noble men in the service of arms, / after my previous writings, / I was exhorted (as he who has previously beaten down many strong edifices / is bolder to take upon himself to beat down a castle or fortress when he feels himself equipped with suitable arms /) then to speak in this present book of the right honorable service of arms & of Chivalry' (5–6). The metaphor she has chosen to justify her writing is drawn from the very subject she proposes to write about, the storming of a castle. Christine promises that she will treat her subject more by 'diligence and wit / than by subtleties of polished words' (6). She understands that the wits of those who might read it could well be even smaller than hers. Considering 'that those who are practised and expert in the art of chivalry are not commonly clerks nor instructed in the science of language', she promises to write only 'the plainest and comprehensible language' (6). The claim that one is speaking plainly and not trying to obfuscate through the dazzling jargon of rhetoric is no doubt a common claim among writers, but Christine seems to be having a small joke here at the expense of her male readers, especially those belonging to the audience Caxton has in mind – the gentlemen born to arms, the captains, soldiers and vitallers (see Barratt, *Women's Writing* 139). Through an impressive display of verbal gymnastics, she suggests that if her wits are small because of her sex, her readers' are smaller still because of their occupation. War may not be a subject fit for a woman, 'who commonly do nothing but spin & occupy themselves in household matters' (7), but language is an alien subject to those who are expert in the art of warfare.

When Christine reminds her readers it was a woman, Minerva, the goddess of arms and chivalry, who first invented armour, we catch a glimpse of the Christine of *City of Ladies*, the Christine who argues that nothing is an unfit subject for women, that women have always participated in their cultures for good and ill; if they are capable of building cities (as Semiramis and Dido did), they are also capable of destroying them. The dialogic interanimation I have explored between Christine, the Franco-Italian poet, and those luminaries like Henry IV, John of Bedford, Sir John Fastolf,

Stephen Scrope, Anthony Woodville, Edward IV, Henry VII and William Caxton, who made both British history and letters in the fifteenth century, is exemplary of the dialogic relations between women's writing and the hegemonic culture, suggesting the power of the hidden transcript to challenge our assumptions about women's silence and uncover the histories of their participation in culture. Women were not silent in the Middle Ages; misogyny was only one among several discourses through which women might fashion themselves. The women whose writing I have examined in this chapter deserve to be included in any account of the English language, English history or English literature, alongside of the men who are usually credited with the development of English culture. These women's work, as I have tried to show, engages dialogically with patriarchy, sometimes resisting it, sometimes sustaining it. It would, however, be shortsighted to treat these 'major authors' as if they were isolated geniuses who had transcended the limits of their sex; indeed the isolation of the major author from the culture that produced her may itself be part of the ideology that perpetuates the belief in women's silence. True, these writers are not part of a 'tradition' of women's writing in the sense that these writers knew of the others and could model themselves on their predecessors. However, throughout this study, I have emphasized women's active participation in communities of readers – both male and female, secular and religious. Their participation in these intellectual communities granted them access to the cultural capital not just to write, but to become *auctores*, authorities in their own right. For every Jean Gerson who deplored the education of women (see above p. 68), there was a Hugh of Fleury who wrote to Adela of Blois that 'members of the female sex should not be deprived of knowledge of deep things, for great industry of mind and the elegance of most upright morals have always existed among women' (Ferrante, *Glory of her Sex* 97). The writing of medieval women that has survived, however meagre and fragmentary, provides insight into a hidden transcript of women's resistance to the narratives of male domination and female inadequacy that are part of our inherited culture.

NOTES

1. Though the evidence for dating is extremely tenuous, scholars have put the date of the *Lais* between 1155 and 1170, the *Fables* between 1160 and 1190, and St Patrick's Purgatory after 1189

2. For a summary of the various identifications of Marie see Finke and Shichtman, forthcoming.
3. See the discussion of the opening of *City of Ladies*, pp. 5–7.
4. For an analysis of the concept of intellectual property before the development of copyright law see Long 1991; see also Finke and Shichtman, forthcoming.
5. Much of the charm of Marie's Anglo-Norman octosyllabic couplets is lost in trying to translate them, as Spiegel does, into English couplets, which easily lapse into doggerel.
6. Ferrante and Hanning differ from Spiegel (p. 4) in their rendering of Marie's line 'ki en sun tens pas ne s'oblie'. While recognizing the ambiguity of the French, their text translates the line as a reference to Marie, 'who does not forget her responsibilities when her turn comes' (p. 30).
7. On the theory and practice of translation, see Beer, *Translation Theory* and Bassnett-McGuire, *Translation Studies*.
8. On the large surplus population of bachelor knights see Duby, 'Les "jeunes"' 835–46. On the plight of bachelor knights see Crouch, *William Marshal* 26–8.
9. Although *Equitan* and *Bisclavret* offer a slightly different view of unhappy marital relations.
10. All references to Marie's *lais* are from the translation by Hanning and Ferrante. Citations will be noted parenthetically by line numbers.
11. The text does pay some lip service to the dishonour Eliduc seems to be courting: 'he would not pursue the love/that would dishonor her /because of the faith he owed his wife/and because he served the king' (473–5). Yet the tale raises the spectre of dishonour only to dismiss it. Eliduc plunges right in and abducts Guilliadun.
12. All quotations are from the translation, *The Revelations of Divine Love*, by Clifton Wolters. Julian's Middle English is not terribly difficult, even for the beginning student of Middle English. I recommend Georgia Ronan Crampton's excellent 1993 edition entitled *The Shewings of Julian of Norwich*, which conveys Julian's prose style, vocabulary and diction better than any translation could.
13. One of these manuscripts, BL MS Sloane 3705, may have been copied by Anne Clementine Cary, the founder of the Paris convent at which the copy was made (Crampton, *Shewings* 16).
14. On the life of anchoresses see above pp. 40–2.
15. On the distinction between constative and performative speech acts see Austin, *How To Do Things With Words*.
16. I will examine more fully the dilemma mystics posed to the Church's struggle to maintain its right to authorize doctrine when I examine Margery Kempe's heresy trials below.
17. See Modleski, *Feminism*, for a critique of male appropriation of the feminine and Bynum, *Fragmentation and Redemption*, for an analysis of medieval gender play.
18. The conflation of Christ's blood with milk may have seemed less strange in the Middle Ages, when natural philosophy taught that breast milk was transmuted blood, than it might to us in the late twentieth century (see Bynum, *Holy Feast* 270).
19. Compare this with the more traditional assertion in *Piers Plowman* that 'even the just man sins seven times daily' ('sepcies in die cadit Iustas', Passus VIII, ll. 21–2).

20. All citations to *The Book of Margery Kempe* are taken from the translation by Barry Windeatt. The standard Middle English edition was prepared by Sanford Meech and Hope Emily Allen.

21. For a description of the difficulties of travelling from England to distant places like Rome and Jerusalem in the fifteenth century, see Louise Collis, *Memoirs of a Medieval Woman.* Sharan Newman's highly entertaining mystery, *Strong as Death,* documents the arduous route across the Pyrenees to Santiago de Compostella, the popular shrine of St James in Spain.

22. For analyses of the proem see Lochrie, *Margery Kempe* 97–105; Staley, *Dissenting Fictions* 11–38; and Finke, *Feminist Theory* 98–107. For an analysis of medieval authorship see Minnis, *Medieval Theories.*

23. See, for instance, Lochrie's analysis of the Latinity of Kempe's text, 114–27.

24. On the relation between speech and writing and the necessary failure of such claims to logocentrism see Derrida. A later addition to the *Shewings* of Julian of Norwich attempts to exert the same kind of control over the instability writing introduces into revelatory speech with the following warnings: 'I pray God almighty that this book shall fall only into the hands of those who intend to be his lovers, and who are willing to submit to the Faith of Holy Church. . . . For this revelation contains deep theology and great wisdom, and is not meant for those who are enslaved by sin and the Devil. Beware of selecting only what you like, and leaving the rest. That is what heretics do' (213).

25. The trials in hagiographies of early Christian martyrs are quite different from the examinations for heresy represented in Kempe's narrative. The saints in these narratives need not prove the orthodoxy of their Christian beliefs; rather the trial serves as a forum for their proclamation of a faith that is never in question.

26. For discussions of Lollardy and the *Book of Margery Kempe* see Lochrie, *Margery Kempe* 102–12; Staley, *Dissenting Fictions* 5–11; and Atkinson, *Mystic and Pilgrim* 105–13. The notes in Windeatt's translation are helpful in detailing Margery's connections with well-known opponents of Lollardy.

27. William Sawtrey was burned at Smithfield (*Kempe* 308).

28. John placed his second son, John III, in the household of the Duke of Norfolk, hoping to strengthen the family hold on the manor of Caister and other properties. He placed his eldest son, John II, in the king's household, but he was apparently not as successful as his younger brother because his uncle Clement complains in one letter 'it were best for him to take his leave and come home, until you have spoken with somebody to help him forth, for he is not bold enough to put himself forth' (Bennett, *Pastons* 83).

29. One can get a sense of how calculated such marriages were in this letter in which Margaret Paston, speculating on a potential marriage for one of her daughters, writes to her husband, 'I was at my mother's [presumably Agnes Paston], and while I was there there came in one Wrothe, a kinsman of Elizabeth Clere, and he saw your daughter and praised her to my mother, and said that she was a goodly young woman. And my mother prayed him to get for her some good marriage if he knew any. And he said he knew one that should be of 300 mark per year, which is Sir John Cleyson that is chamberlain to my lady of York; and he is xviij years old. If you think it worth speaking of, my mother thinks that it could be gotten for less money now in this world than it should be hereafter, either that one or some other good marriage' (vol. 1, 207).

30. All citations to the Paston Letters will be from the edition by Norman Davis and will be noted parenthetically in the text; translations mine.

31. In fact, included in Agnes's correspondence is a draft of a proposed indenture for another marriage for Elizabeth, this time with William Clopton (about 1454), which, like the Scrope marriage, eventually fell through.

32. In the Middle English, this couplet rhymes: 'For ther wottys no creature what peyn that I endure, / And for to be deede I dare it not dyscure.'

33. In a letter to Elizabeth Brews, Margery's mother, Margaret writes 'I know well you have not forgotten the extensive communication that diverse times we have had touching the marriage of my cousin Margery, your daughter, and my son John, of which I have been as glad, and now lately as sorry, as ever I was for any marriage in my life. And where or in whom the default of the breach is, I have no knowledge; but, madam, if it be in me or any of mine, I pray you assign a day when my cousin your husband and you think to be at Norwich near Salle, and I will come thither to you, and I think before you and I depart there the default shall be known where it is, and also that, with your advise and help and mine together, we shall find some way that it shall not break' (Davis vol. 1, 378).

34. This petition was not, of course, written in John's own hand, but by his clerk James Gloys who ironically also wrote many of Margaret's letters. No one, to my knowledge, has ever questioned John's authorship on this basis (Davis, vol. 1, 51).

35. For a discussion of the stylistic uses of direct and indirect discourse see Vološinov, *Marxism* 125–40.

36. All references to *Lavision Christine* will be from the translation of Glenda K. McLeod and will be noted parenthetically in the text.

37. The identification of the manuscript with the Fastolf household is suggested by several peculiarities about the manuscript: the mention of 'myn autour [John] Fastolfe' on several occasions, marginal references to Fastolf's account books, two letters, probably addressed to Fastolf, bound up in the fly-leaves of the manuscript, and most convincingly, lengthy marginal annotations in a hand identified as that of William Worcester who was Fastolf's secretary. Fastolf was a close friend of John Paston and is mentioned in several of John's letters. Paston was one of the executors of his will. See *Book of Noblesse* i–iv.

38. As the same mistake is repeated in Stephen Scrope's introduction to his translation of the *Epistle* of *Othea* it is not unreasonable to suppose that the misattribution originated in Fastolf's household, perhaps even with Fastolf himself. Scrope writes: 'And this seyde boke, at the instavnce and praer off a fulle wyse gentylwoman of Frawnce called Dame Cristine, was compiled and grounded by the famous doctours of the most excellent in clerge the nobyl Vniuersity of Paris.'

39. In a letter to Nichols dated 28 March 1862 which is included along with other research papers and correspondence in the British Library's copy of his edition, Blades writes: 'I beg to return herewith the "Boke of Noblesse" which you were kind enough to lend me. I have taken great interest in its perusal, altho as you know I think you underrate somewhat Sir John Fastolf's literary character and treat Christine de Pise still worse in decrying her authorship of her "fais d'Armes".'

40. The French reads 'sagesse de femme'; Scrope modifies this line, equating Othea with 'the wisdom of man or woman' (Buhler, *Epistle of Othea* 6)

41. Hindman argues that the first four illustrations of the poem – Othea, Temperance, Hercules and Minos – which are among the six images reproduced in the manuscripts of Scrope's translation – are supposed to represent the four cardinal virtues.

42. Perhaps even more significant for Christine's situation, while Charles V was a sophisticated patron who continually commissioned lavishly illuminated manuscripts to be housed in the newly constructed royal library in the Louvre, Charles VI had little interest in patronizing the arts and sciences. Christine (and other French writers) were required to secure patronage elsewhere.

43. All references to Scrope's translation of *Othea* are from Buhler's edition; translations are mine.

44. Like Christine, Scrope dedicated his work at different times to several patrons (each of the three extant manuscripts is dedicated to a different patron), scrambling to secure whatever rewards he could for his 'little labour'.

45. Grisaille became popular in fifteenth-century manuscript painting; the incorporation of grisaille figures in illuminations in which other areas are executed in colour was popular in the court of Charles V, see Brown, *Understanding Illuminated Manuscripts* 63.

46. Citations of the Middle English *Body of Polycy* are from the 1524 edition by John Scot; translations are mine.

47. All citations from *Fayttes of Arms* are from the edition by A. T. P. Byles unless otherwise noted. Translations are mine.

Chronology

Date	Historical Events	Literary Events	Women Writers
43	Roman Invasions		
60	Boudicca's rebellion		
425–600	Anglo-Saxon Invasions		
500–70		Gildas, *De Exidio Britanniae*	
597	Augustine's mission to Kent		
627	Conversion of King Edwin of Northumbria		Conversion of Hild
663	Synod of Whitby	Caedmon's Hymn	Hild, abbess at Whitby
7–8 centuries	Northumbrian Renaissance		
716–57		Boniface Correspondence	Eadburga's letter to Boniface
719–22			Eangyth's and Bugga's letter
731		Bede	
732		*History of the English Church and People*	Leoba's Letter
778			Hugeberc, *Hodoeporicon of St Willibald*
787–865	First Danish Invasions		
868		Nennius, *Historia Britonum*	

Date	Historical Events	Literary Events	Women Writers
871–90	Reign of Alfred the Great		
892		*Anglo-Saxon Chronicle*	
978	Second Danish Invasions		
960–90		*Exeter Book*	'Wulf and Eadwacer' 'Wife's Lament'
1016–35	Reign of Canute	*Beowulf*	
1042–66	Reign of Edward the Confessor		
1066	Norman Conquest		
1066–87	Reign of William the Conqueror		
1086		*Domesday Book*	
1087–1100	Reign of William Rufus		
11th–12th c.			Latin Trotula texts
1100–35	Reign of Henry I		
1132		Abelard, *Historia Calamitatum*	
1135–54	Anarchy of King Stephen	*Peterborough Chronicle*	
1120–36		*Mabinogion*	
1136			Gwenllian ferch Gruffudd d.
1138		Geoffrey of Monmouth, *History of the Kings of Britain*	
1152	Henry marries Eleanor of Aquitaine		
1154–89	Henry II		
1155		Wace's *Brut*	
1158–65	Welsh Wars		
1150		*Lay of Horn*	
1166		Aelred of Rievaulx d.	
1160–1215			Marie de France, *Lais*, *Fables*
1170	Murder of Becket	Hywel ab Owein Gwynedd d.	

Date	Historical Events	Literary Events	Women Writers
1175–84	Henry's wars with his sons		
1150–1250			*Trobairitz*
1180		*Ormulum*	
c. 1180–1200			Clémence of Barking, *Life of St Catherine* Gwenllian ferch Rhirid Flaidd
1189		Layamon's *Brut*	*St Patrick's Purgatory*
1189–92	Third Crusade – Acre taken 1191		
1189–99	Richard Coeur de Lion		
1192–4	Richard in Germany		
1199–1216	John		
1204	Loss of Normandy, Anjou, Maine, and Touraine		
1215	Magna Carta		
c. 13c			Marie, *Life of St Audrey*
c. 13c			*Life of St Edward the Confessor* by an anonymous nun of Barking
1170–1221	St Dominic		
1182–1226	St Francis		
1216–72	Henry III		
1216–19	Regency of Wm Marshal		
1220		*Owl and Nightingale*	
1220–4	Friars come to England	*King Horn*	
1225	Henry III marries Eleanor of Provence	*Ancrene Wisse*	
1254	Henry renounces claim to Continental possessions except Aquitaine and Gascony		

Date	Historical Events	Literary Events	Women Writers
1258	First proclamation in English The Mad Parliament		
1260	Balliol College founded		
1285		*Havelok the Dane*	
1263	Wars with Barons		
1264	Taking of Amiens Battle of Lewes		
1265	Parliament of Simon de Montfort Battle of Evesham		
1274	Council of Lyon		
1272–1307	Edward I		
1276–84	Annexation of Wales		
1276	Statute of Mortmain		
1280–90		*South English Legendary*	
1290	Expulsion of Jews		
1291	Last of Christian possessions in Palestine abandoned		
1291–8			Mechtild, *Liber Spiritualis Gratiae*
1292	Balliol becomes King of Scotland		
1294	Wars in France and Scotland		
1295	First 'perfect' Parliament		
1296	Capture of Berwick		
1297	Revolt of Scots under Wallace		
1298	Battle of Falkirk		
1296–1306		*The Harrowing of Hell*	Marguerite Porete, *Mirror of Simple Souls*
1294			Mechtild of Hackborn d.
c. 1301		*Cursor Mundi*	Gertrude the Great d.

Date	Historical Events	Literary Events	Women Writers
1303		Robert Mannyng, *Handlying Sin*	Bridget of Sweden b.
1305	Wallace executed		
1306	Bruce crowned		
1304–21		*Divine Comedy*	
1307–27	Edward II		
1309–77	Popes at Avignon		
1310			Marguerite Porete executed
1312	Order of Knights Templars dissolved		
1315		Dafydd ap Gwilym b.	
1321	The Despensers exiled		
1325		*Sir Orfeo*	
1327	Edward deposed and murdered		
1330		Auchinleck MS	*Lay le Freine*
1327–77	Edward III Regency of Isabella and Mortimer		
1333	Battle of Halidon Hill		
c. 1336			Elizabeth of Hungary, *Revelations*
c. 1340		Chaucer b.	
1342			Julian of Norwich b.
c. 1345			Bridget founds Order of St Saviour
1346	Hundred Years' War begins		
1347			Catherine of Siena b.
1349	Black Death	*The Cloud of Unknowing*	
1349		Richard Rolle d. Dafydd ap Gwilym d.	
1350		White Book of Rhydderch	
1358–77			Katherine of Sutton, Barking plays

Date	Historical Events	Literary Events	Women Writers
1360	Treaty of Bretigny		
1361	Black Death		
1364			Christine de Pisan b.
1369	Black Death	Geoffrey Chaucer, *The Book of the Duchess*	
1370		*Alliterative Morte Arthure* John Lydgate b.	Bridget of Sweden, *Liber Celestis*
1373			Bridget of Sweden d.
c. 1373			Julian of Norwich, *Short Version of Shewings* Margery Kempe b.
1376	Death of Black Prince	Barbour's *Bruce*	
1376–87		Langland, *Piers Plowman*	
1376	The Good Parliament		
1377–99	Richard II		
1380		Wycliffe's Bible	Catherine of Siena, *Il Dialogo*
1381	Wat Tyler's revolt		
1380–1400		*Pearl*	
1384		John Wycliffe d.	
1384		*House of Fame*	
1385–7		*Troilus and Crisedye*	
1388	Merciless Parliament		
1390		*Sir Gawain and the Green Knight*	
1387–1400		*Canterbury Tales*	
1390–3		Gower, *Confessio Amantis*	
1391			St Bridget canonized
1393			Julian of Norwich, Long Version of *Shewings*
1398	Henry Bolingbroke banished		
1399	Richard deposed Henry IV crowned		
1399–1413	Henry IV		

Date	Historical Events	Literary Events	Women Writers
1400		Chaucer d. Chestre, *Sir Launfal* Red Book of Hergest	Christine de Pisan, *Epistle of Othea*
1401	*De haeretico comburendo*		
1403	Battle of Shrewsbury		
1405			*Body of Policy* *Lavision Christine*
1406			*Faits d'Armes*
1413–22	Henry V		
1415	Battle of Agincourt		Syon Abbey founded
1414–17	Oldcastle rebellion		
c. 1420			Eleanor Hull, *Meditations of the Days of the Week*
1422			*Revelations Shown to a Holy Woman*
1422–61	Henry VI		
1429			*Ditié de la pucelle* Christine de Pisan d.
1431	Joan of Arc executed		
1436–8			*Book of Margery Kempe*
1440			John Paston m. Margaret Mautby
1449		Lydgate d.	
c. 1450	Jack Cade's Rebellion		Hull, *Seven Psalms* *Faits and Passions of Our Lord Jesu Christ*
1456		John Shirley d.	
1460			Eleanor Hull d.
c. 1460	Duke of York claims throne		Juliana Berners, *Book of Hunting*
1460–70		Malory, *Morte Darthur*	
1461	Accession of Edward IV		
1462–1500			Gwerful Mechain
1464	Edward IV m. Elizabeth Woodville		
1469			Margery Paston m. Richard Calle

Date	Historical Events	Literary Events	Women Writers
c. 1470	Henry VI restored to throne		Anthony Woodville tr. *Body of Policy*
1471	Battle of Tewkesbury		
1471–83	Edward IV		
1475		*Boke of Noblesse*	
1476		Caxton establishes a printing press at Westminster	
1477			John Paston m. Margery Brews
1478			Caxton pub. *Moral Proverbs of Christine*
1483–5	Richard III		
1483	Anthrony Woodville executed		
1484			Margaret Paston d.
1485	Battle of Bosworth Field		
	Henry VII crowned		
1486	Henry VII m. Elizabeth of York		
1489			Caxton pub. *Fayttes of Arms*
c. 1500		*Everyman* *Wakefield Cycle*	Margaret Beaufort, *Mirror of Gold, Imitation of Christ*
1503			Pynson publ. *Imitation of Christ*
1506			Pynson publ. *Mirror of Gold* Margaret Beaufort d.

Bibliography

WOMEN WRITERS

Anglo-Norman hagiographies by women

Editions

CLÉMENCE OF BARKING, *The Life of St Catherine*, William McBain, ed., Oxford: ANTS, 1964.

La Vie d'Edouard Le Confesseur, Östen Södergard, ed., Uppsala: Almqvist & Wiksells, 1948.

MARIE, *La Vie Seinte Audrée*, Östen Södergard, ed., Uppsala: Lundqvistska Bokhandeln, 1955.

Studies

WOGAN-BROWNE, Jocelyn, '"Clerc u lai, muïne u dame": Women and Anglo-Norman Hagiography in the Twelfth and Thirteenth Centuries' in Meale, pp. 61–85.

Margaret Beaufort

Texts

Imitation of Christ, London: Richard Pynson, 1503.
The Mirror of Gold, London: Richard Pynson, 1506.

Middle English Translations of the De Imitatione Christi, J.K. Ingram, ed., New York: Kraus rpt, 1975; EETS es 63, 1893.

Juliana Berners

Manuscripts and texts

The Book of Hunting, Bodleian Library MS Rawlinson poet. 143.
Book of Hunting, London: Richard Pynson, 1486.
'Book of Hunting', G.M. London, trans. Wynkyn de Worde, 1595.

Facsimiles

The Boke of Saint Albans by Dame Juliana Berners with an Introduction by William Blades, London: Elliott Stock, 1881.
English Hawking and Hunting in 'The Boke of St Albans', Rachel Hands, ed., Oxford: Oxford University Press, 1975.

Studies

HANDS, Rachel, 'Juliana Berners and The Boke of St Albans', *Review of English Studies* n.s. 18 (1967): 373–86.

Boniface

Editions

The Letters of St Boniface, Ephraim Emerton, trans., New York: Columbia University Press, 1940.
Die Briefe Des Heiligen Bonifatius und Lullus, Michael Tangl, ed., Berlin: Weidmannsche Buchhandlung, 1916.

Bridget of Sweden

Manuscripts

Revelations, Bodleian Library MS Rawlinson c. 41.
Liber Celestis, British Library MS Cotton Claudius B i.
The Rule of Saynte Saviour, Cambridge University Library MS Ff.6.33.

Editions

Liber Celestis of St Bridget of Sweden: the Middle English Version in British Library MS Claudius B i, Together with a Life of the Saint from the Same Manuscript, Roger Ellis, ed., Oxford: EETS, no. 291, 1987.
The Revelations of St Birgitta, William Patterson Cumming, ed., London: EETS, os 178.

Catherine of Siena

Orcherd of Syon, British Library MS Harley MS 3432.
The Orcherd of Syon, P. Hodgson and G.M. Liegey, Oxford: EETS os. 258, 1966, 2 vols.

Christine de Pizan

Manuscripts

The Boke of Noblesse, British Library MS Royal 18. B. xxii.
Epistle of Othea, Stephen Scrope, trans., St Johns College, Cambridge MS H. 5.
Epistre d'Othea, Bodleian Library MS Laud. Misc. 570.
Epistre d'Othea, British Museum MS Harley 4431.

Early printed books

Body of Polycye, London: John Scot, 1524.
Book of Fayttes of Armes and of Chyualrye, William Caxton, trans., London: Caxton, 1476. Oxford Bodleian Library Douce 180.
The City of Ladies, Brian Anslay, trans., London: Henry Pepwell, 1529.
Morall Proverbes of Christyn, Anthony Woodville, Lord Rivers, trans., in *Works of Chaucer*, London: Richard Pynson, 1526.

Editions

The Book of the Body Politic, Kate Langdon Forhan, trans., Cambridge: Cambridge University Press, 1994.

The Book of the City of Ladies, Earl Jeffrey Richards, trans., New York: Persea Books, 1982.

The Book of Fayttes of Armes and of Chyvalrye, A.T.P. Byles, ed., Oxford: EETS no. 189, 1932.

The Boke of Noblesse, John Gough Nichols, ed., London: Roxburghe Club, 1860.

Christine's Vision (Lavision Christine), Glenda K. McLeod, trans., New York: Garland, 1993.

Epistle of Othea to Hector, or the Boke of Knighthode, Stephen Scrope, trans., George F. Warner, ed., London: Roxburghe Club, 1904.

The Epistle of Othea, Stephen Scrope, trans., Curt F. Buhler, ed., Oxford: EETS 264, 1970.

Studies

BRABANT, Margaret, ed., *Politics, Gender, and Genre: The Political Thought of Christine de Pizan*, Boulder, CO: Westview Press, 1992.

CHESNEY, Kathleen, 'Two Manuscripts of Christine de Pisan', *Medium Aevum* 1 (1932): 35–41.

HINDMAN, Sandra, *Christine de Pisan's 'Epistre d'Othea': Painting and Politics at the Court of Charles V*, Toronto: Pontifical Institute, 1986.

LAIDLAW, J.C., 'Christine de Pizan, the Earl of Salisbury and Henry IV', *French Studies* 36 (1982): 129–43.

QUILLIGAN, Maureen, *The Allegory of Female Authority: Christine de Pizan's Cité des Dames*, Ithaca: Cornell University Press, 1991.

TEAGUE, Frances, 'Christine de Pisan's Book of War', *The Reception of Christine de Pisan from the Fifteenth to Nineteenth Centuries*, Glenda McLeod, ed., Lewiston: Edwin Mellon Press, 1991.

ZIMMERMANN, Margarete, and Dina DE RENTIIS, eds, *The City of Scholars: New Approaches to Christine de Pizan*, Berlin: Walter de Gruyter, 1994.

Elizabeth of Hungary

Revelations of St Elizabeth, Cambridge University Library MS Hh.1.11.

Devotional treatises

Feites and Passion of Our Lord Jhesu Crist, 1450, Bodleian Library MS Holkenham Misc. 11.

Drama

COTTON, Nancy, *Women Playwrights in England, c. 1363–1750*, Lewisburg, PA: Bucknell University Press, 1980.

FAULKNER, Ann, 'The Harrowing of Hell at Barking Abbey and in Modern Production', *The Iconography of Hell*, Clifford Davidson and Thomas H. Seiler, eds, Kalamazoo, Mich.: Medieval Institute Publications, 1992.

Floure and Leafe and *Assembly of Ladies*

Edition

The Floure and Leafe, The Assembly of Ladies, and the Isle of Ladies, Derek Pearsall, ed., Kalamazoo, Mich.: TEAMS, 1990.

Studies

BARRATT, Alexandra, ' "The Flower and the Leaf" and "The Assembly of Ladies": Is There a (Sexual) Difference?', *Philological Quarterly* 66 (1987): 1–24.

CHANCE, Jane, 'Christine de Pizan as Literary Mother: Women's Authority and Subjectivity in "The Floure and Leafe" and "The Assembly of Ladies" ', in Zimmermann and De Rentiis, 245–60.

MARSH, G.L., 'Sources and Analogues of *The Flower and the Leaf*', *Modern Philology* 4 (1906–7): 121–68, 281–328.

STEPHENS, John, 'The Questioning of Love in the Assembly of Ladies', *Review of English Studies* 24 (1973): 129–40.

Gertrude the Great

Visions of St Matilda, British Library MS Egerton 2006.

The Book of Ghostly Grace, Theresa Halligan, ed., Toronto: Pontifical Institute, 1979.

Dame Eleanor Hull

The Seven Psalms and *Meditations Upon the Seven Days of the Week*, Cambridge University Library MS KK 1. 6.

Julian of Norwich

Manuscript

Showings (short text), British Library MS Add. 37790: ff. 97–136.

Editions

Revelations of Divine Love, Clifton Wolters, trans., New York: Penguin, 1966.
The Shewings of Julian of Norwich, Georgia Ronan Crampton, ed., Kalamazoo, Mich.: Medieval Institute Publications, 1993.

Studies

LEVERTOV, Denise, *Breathing the Water*, New York: New Directions, 1984.
STONE, Robert Karl, *Middle English Prose Style: Margery Kempe and Julian of Norwich*, The Hague: Mouton, 1970.

Margery Kempe

Manuscript

Book of Margery Kempe, British Library MS Add. 61823.

Editions

The Book of Margery Kempe, Sanford Brown Meech and Hope Emily Allen, eds, Oxford: Oxford University Press. EETS o.s. 212, 1940.
The Book of Margery Kempe, B.A. Windeatt, trans., New York: Penguin, 1985.

Studies

ATKINSON, Clarissa W., *Mystic and Pilgrim: The Book and the World of Margery Kempe*, Ithaca: Cornell University Press, 1983.
COLLIS, Louise, *Memoirs of a Medieval Woman: The Life and Times of Margery Kempe*, New York: Crowell, 1964.
LOCHRIE, Karma, *Margery Kempe and the Translations of the Flesh*, Philadelphia: University of Pennsylvania Press, 1991.

STALEY, Lynn, *Margery Kempe's Dissenting Fictions*, University Park, PA: Pennsylvania State University Press, 1994.

The Mabinogion

The Mabinogi and Other Medieval Welsh Tales, Patrick Ford ed., Berkeley: University of California Press, 1977.

Marie de France

Translations

Fables, Harriet Spiegel, trans. and ed., Toronto: University of Toronto Press, 1987.

The Lais of Marie de France, Robert Hanning and Joan Ferrante, trans., Durham, N.C.: Labyrinth, 1978.

Studies

BURGESS, Glyn, 'Social Status in Marie de France', *The Spirit of the Court: Proceedings of the Fourth Congress of the International Courtly Literature Society*, Robert A. Taylor, Alan Deyermond, Dennis Green, Beryl Rowland, and Glyn Burgess, eds, Dover, N.H.: Brewer, 1985: 69–78.

FINKE, Laurie A., and Martin B. SHICHTMAN, 'Magical Mistress' Tour: Patronage, Intellectual Property, and the Dis-Semination of Wealth in the *Lais* of Marie de France', *Signs* (forthcoming).

KINOSHITA, Sharon, 'Two for the Price of One: Courtly Love and Serial Polygamy in the *Lais* of Marie de France', *Arthuriana* 8 (1998): 33–55.

Paston Letters

Editions

Paston Letters and Papers of the Fifteenth Century, Norman Davis, ed., 2 vols, Oxford: Clarendon, 1976.

The Paston Letters 1422–1509, J. Gardiner, ed., Westminster: A. Constable and Co., 1900–1.

Studies

BENNETT, H.S., *The Pastons and their England*, Cambridge: Cambridge University Press, 1932.

WATT, Diane, '"No Writing for Writing's Sake": The Language of Service and Household Rhetoric in the Letters of the Paston Women', in Cherewatuk and Wiethaus, 122–38.

Marguerite Porete

Manuscripts

Myrrour of Symple Soules, Bodleian Library MS Bodley 505.
Myrrour of Symple Soules, British Library MS Add. 37790: ff. 137–215v.

Revelations of Purgatory

Manuscript

Revelation Shown to a Holy Woman, Bodleian Library MS Eng. theol. c. 58.

Stonor Letters

Edition

The Stonor Letters and Papers, 1290–1483, C.L. Kingsford, ed., London: Offices of the Royal Historical Society, 1919.

Trotula

Manuscripts

Knowing of Women's Kind in Childyng, Bodleian Library MS Douce 37.
Liber Trotuli, British Library MS Add. 34111. 1450. ff. 197–217.
Of the Diseases of Women, British Library MS Sloane 421a.

Studies

BENTON, John F., 'Trotula, Women's Problems, and the Professionalization of Medicine in the Middle Ages', *Bulletin of the History of Medicine* 59 (1985): 30–53.

WOMEN'S LIVES AND WRITING: PRIMARY TEXTS

BARRATT, Alexandra, *Women's Writing in Middle English*, London: Longmans, 1992.

BLAMIRES, Alcuin, ed., *Woman Defamed and Woman Defended: An Anthology of Medieval Texts*, with Karen Pratt and C.W. Marx, Oxford: Clarendon Press, 1992.

BOGIN, Meg, *The Women Troubadours*, New York: Norton, 1980.

GOLDBERG, P.J.P., *Women in England, c. 1275–1525: Documentary Sources*, Manchester: Manchester University Press, 1995.

The Life of Christina Markyate, C.H. Talbot, ed. and trans., Oxford: Clarendon Press, 1987.

MCSHEFFREY, Shannon, *Love and Marriage in Late Medieval London*, Kalamazoo: TEAMS, 1995.

Orders and Constitutions of the Nuns of Syon, British Library MS Arundel 146.

PETROFF, Elizabeth, ed., *Medieval Women's Visionary Literature*, Oxford: Oxford University Press, 1986.

RADICE, Betty, ed. and trans., *The Letters of Abelard and Héloise*, London: Penguin, 1974.

WILSON, Katherina M., ed., *Medieval Women Writers*, Athens: University of Georgia Press, 1984.

OTHER PRIMARY TEXTS CITED

ARISTOTLE, *Generation of Animals*, A.L. Peck, ed., Loeb Classical Library, Cambridge, Mass.: Harvard University Press, 1963.

BACON, Francis, *The Advancement of Learning*, William Aldis Wright, ed., 1st edn, Oxford: Clarendon Press, 1926.

BARTLETT, Anne Clark, and Thomas BESTUL, eds, *Cultures of Piety*, Ithaca: Cornell University Press, forthcoming

BEAUMANOIR, Philippe de, *Coutumes de Beauvaisis*, F. R. P. Akehurst, trans., Philadelphia: University of Pennsylvania Press, 1992.

BEDE, *A History of the English Church and People*, Leo Sherley-Price, trans., revised by R.E. Latham, Baltimore: Penguin, 1968.

Beowulf, E. Talbot Donaldson, trans., New York: Norton, 1966.

BRADLEY, S.A.J., *Anglo-Saxon Poetry*, London: Dent, 1982.

BROWN, Carleton, *Religious Lyrics of the Fourteenth Century*, 2nd edn, revised G.V. Smithers, Oxford: Clarendon Press, 1965.

CAXTON, William, *The Prologues and Epilogues of William Caxton*, W.J.B. Crotch, ed., London: EETS vol. 176, 1928.

CHAUCER, Geoffrey, *The Canterbury Tales*, David Wright, trans., New York: Vintage, 1964.

———, *The Riverside Chaucer*, 3rd edn, Larry D. Benson, ed., Boston: Houghton Mifflin, 1987.

GALEN, *On the Usefulness of Parts of the Body*, Margaret Tallmadge May, trans., Ithaca: Cornell University Press, 1968.

GARBÁTY, Thomas J., ed., *Medieval English Literature*, Lexington, Mass.: D.C. Heath, 1984.

GOLDIN, Frederick, ed., *Lyrics of the Troubadours and Trouvères*, Garden City, N.Y.: Anchor Books, 1973.

GORDON, R.K., trans. and ed., *Anglo-Saxon Poetry*, London: J.M. Dent, 1937.

LAYAMON, *Brut*, Rosamund Allen, trans., New York: St Martin's Press, 1992.

PEARSALL, Derek, and I.C. CUNNINGHAM, *The Auchinleck Manuscript: National Library of Scotland Advocates' MS. 19.2.1*, London: The Scolar Press, 1977.

WILLIAM OF MALMESBURY, *Chronicle of the Kings of England*, J.A. Giles, trans., London: H.G. Bohn, 1847, rpt. New York: AMS Press, 1968.

SECONDARY TEXTS

Women's writing

BARTLETT, Anne Clark, *Male Authors, Female Readers: Representation and Subjectivity in Middle English Devotional Literature*, Ithaca: Cornell University Press, 1995.

BLOCH, R. Howard, *Medieval Misogyny and the Invention of Western Romantic Love*, Chicago: University of Chicago Press, 1991.

BOFFEY, Julia, 'Women Authors and Women's Literacy in Fourteenth- and Fifteenth-Century England', in Meale, 159–82.

BREEZE, Andrew, *Medieval Welsh Literature*, Dublin: Four Courts Press, 1997.

CAZELLES, Brigitte, *The Lady as Saint: A Collection of French Hagiographic Romances of the Thirteenth Century*, Philadelphia: University of Pennsylvania Press, 1991.

CHEREWATUK, Karen, and Ulrike WIETHAUS, eds, *Dear Sister: Medieval Women and the Epistolary Genre*, Philadelphia: University of Pennsylvania, 1993.

DELANY, Sheila, *Writing Woman: Women Writers and Women in Literature, Medieval to Modern*, New York: Schocken Books, 1983.

DESMOND, Marilynn, 'The Voice of Exile: Feminist Literary History and the Anonymous Anglo-Saxon Elegy', *Critical Inquiry* 16.3 (1990): 572–90.

DRONKE, Peter, *Women Writers of the Middle Ages: A Critical Study of Texts from Perpetua (c. 203) to Marguerite Porete (c. 1310)*, Cambridge: Cambridge University Press, 1984.

FERRANTE, Joan M., *Woman as Image in Medieval Literature, from the Twelfth Century to Dante*, New York: Columbia University Press, 1975.

——, *To the Glory of Her Sex: Women's Role in the Composition of Medieval Texts*, Bloomington: Indiana University Press, 1997.

FINKE, Laurie A., *Feminist Theory, Women's Writing*, Ithaca: Cornell University Press, 1992.

FRADENBURG, Louise O., '"Fulfild of fairye": The Social Meaning of Fantasy in the Wife of Bath's Prologue and Tale', in Beidler, 205–20.

FRESE, Dolores Warwick, '*Wulf and Eadwacer*: The Adulterous Woman Reconsidered', *Religion and Literature* 15 (1983): 1–22.

HUNEYCUTT, Lois L., '"Proclaiming Her Dignity Abroad": The Literary and Artistic Network of Matilda of Scotland, Queen of England 1100–1118', in McCash, 155–74.

JAMBECK, Karen K., 'Patterns of Women's Literary Patronage: England, 1200–c. 1475', in McCash, 228–65.

KRUEGER, Roberta L., *Women Readers and the Ideology of Gender in Old French Verse Romance*, Cambridge: Cambridge University Press, 1993.

LLOYD-MORGAN, Ceridwen, 'Women and their Poetry in Medieval Wales', in Meale, 183–201.

McCASH, June Hall, ed., *The Cultural Patronage of Medieval Women*, Athens: University of Georgia Press, 1996.

McLEOD, Glenda, '"Wholly Guilty, Wholly Innocent": Self-Definition in Héloise's Letters to Abelard', in Cherewatuk and Wiethaus, 64–86.

MEALE, Carol M., ed., *Women and Literature in Britain, 1150–1500*, Cambridge: Cambridge University Press, 1993.

MEALE, Carol M., '". . . alle the bokes that I haue of latyn, englisch, and frensch": Laywomen and their books in late medieval England', in Meale, 128–58.

MILLETT, Bella, 'English recluses and the development of vernacular literature', in Meale, 86–103.

REMLEY, Paul, '*Muscipula Diaboli* and Medieval English Antifeminism', *English Studies* 1 (1989): 1–14.

RIDDY, Felicity, '"Women talking about the things of God": A Late Medieval Sub-Culture', in Meale, 104–27.

SKEAT, W.W., 'The Authoress', *Modern Language Quarterly* 3 (1900): 111–12.

STANBURY, Sarah, 'Regimes of the Visual in Premodern England: Gaze, Body, and Chaucer's *Clerk's Tale*', *New Literary History* 28 (1997): 261–90.

SULLIVAN, Karen, 'At the Limits of Feminist Theory: The Architectonics of the Querelle de Rose', *Exemplaria* 3 (1991): 435–66.

Women's history

BYNUM, Caroline Walker, *Jesus as Mother: Studies in the Spirituality of the High Middle Ages*, Berkeley: University of California Press, 1982.

——, *Holy Feast and Holy Fast: The Religious Significance of Food to Medieval Women*, Berkeley: University of California Press, 1987.

——, *Fragmentation and Redemption: Essays on Gender and the Human Body in Medieval Religion*, New York: Zone Books, 1991.

——, *The Resurrection of the Body*, New York: Columbia University Press, 1995.

CADDEN, Joan, *Meanings of Sex Difference in the Middle Ages: Medicine, Science, and Culture*, Cambridge: Cambridge University Press, 1993.

CROSS, Clair, ' "Great Reasoners in Scriptures": the Activities of Women Lollards', Derek Brewer, ed., *Medieval Women*, Oxford: Blackwell, 1978: 359–80.

DALARUN, Jacques, 'The Clerical Gaze', in Klapisch-Zuber, 15–42.

DE HAMEL, Christopher, *Syon Abbey: The Library of the Bridgettine Nuns and their Peregrinations*, London: Roxburghe Club, 1991.

DUBY, Georges, *The Knight, the Lady, and the Priest: The Making of Modern Marriage*, Barbara Bray, trans., New York: Pantheon, 1983.

ECKENSTEIN, Lina, *Women Under Monasticism: Chapters on Saint-Lore and Convent Life Between A.D. 500 and A.D. 1500*, New York: Russell and Russell, 1963.

ELKINS, Sharon K., *Holy Women of Twelfth-century England*, Chapel Hill: University of North Carolina Press, 1988.

FELL, Christine, with Cecile CLARK and Elizabeth WILLIAMS, *Women in Anglo-Saxon England and the Impact of 1066*, Bloomington: Indiana University Press, 1984.

GILCHRIST, Roberta, *Gender and Material Culture: The Archaeology of Religious Women*, London: Routledge, 1993.

GOLDBERG, P.J.P., *Women in England, c. 1275–1525*, Manchester: Manchester University Press, 1995.

GREEN, Monica, 'Women's Medical Practice and Health Care in Medieval Europe', *Signs* 14 (1989): 434–73.

KELLY, Joan, *Women, History and Theory: the Essays of Joan Kelly*, Chicago: University of Chicago Press, 1984.

KLAPISCH-ZUBER, Christiane, ed., *A History of Women in the West: Silences of the Middle Ages*, Cambridge, Mass.: Belknap, 1992.

LEYSER, Henrietta, *Medieval Women: A Social History of Women in England, 450–1500*, New York: St Martin's Press, 1995.

L'HERMITE-LECLERCQ, Paulette, 'The Feudal Order', in Klapisch-Zuber, 202–49.

McSHEFFREY, Shannon, *Gender and Heresy: Women and Men in Lollard Communities*, Philadelphia: University of Pennsylvania Press, 1995.

NEWMAN, Sharan, *Strong as Death*, New York: Forge, 1996.

OPITZ, Claudia, 'Life in the Later Middle Ages', in Klapisch-Zuber, 267–318.

PAGELS, Elaine, *Adam, Eve, and the Serpent*, New York: Random House, 1988.

PARSONS, John Carmi, 'Of Queens, Courts, and Books: Reflections on the Literary Patronage of Thirteenth-Century Plantaganet Queens', in McCash, 175–201.

THOMASSET, Claude, 'The Nature of Woman', in Klapisch-Zuber, 43–69.

WALKER, Sue Sheridan, 'Widow and Ward: The Feudal Law of Child Custody in Medieval England', *Women in Medieval Society*, Susan Mosher Stuard, ed., Philadelphia: University of Pennsylvania Press, 1976.

WEMPLE, Suzanne Fonay, 'Women from the Fifth to the Tenth Century', in Klapisch-Zuber, 169–201.

General works on medieval literature

BARRATT, Alexandra, 'Works of Religious Instruction', in Edwards, 413–32.

BEER, Jeanette, ed., *Translation Theory and Practice in the Middle Ages*, Kalamazoo, Mich.: Medieval Institute Publications, 1997.

DEIDLER, Peter G., ed., *The Wife of Bath*, Boston: Bedford Books, 1996.

BLOCH, R. Howard, *Etymologies and Genealogies: A Literary Anthropology of the French Middle Ages*, Chicago: University of Chicago Press, 1983.

CARRUTHERS, Mary, 'The Wife of Bath and the Painting of Lions', *PMLA* 94 (1979): 209–22.

CHAMBERS, R.W., *On the Continuity of English Prose from Alfred to More and His School*, Oxford: Oxford University Press, 1932.

CRANE, Susan, *Insular Romance: Politics, Faith, and Culture in Anglo-Norman and Middle English Literature*, Berkeley: University of California Press, 1986.

DURLING, Nancy Vine, 'Hagiography and Lineage: The Example of the Vie de Saint Alexis', *Romance Philology* 40 (1987): 451–69.

EDWARDS, A.S.G., ed., *Middle English Prose: A Critical Guide to Major Authors and Genres*, New Brunswick, N.J.: Rutgers University Press, 1984.

FELLOWS, Maldwyn Jennifer, and Carol Meale Mills, eds, *Romance in Medieval England*, Cambridge: D.S. Brewer, 1991.

GREEN, Richard Firth, *Poets and Princepleasers: Literature and the Court in the Late Middle Ages*, Toronto: University of Toronto Press, 1980.

JOLLIFFE, P.S., *Check-List of Middle English Prose Writings of Spiritual Guidance*, Toronto: Pontifical Institute, 1974.

JORDAN, Robert M., *Chaucer and the Shape of Creation: The Aesthetic Possibilities of Inorganic Structure*, Cambridge, Mass.: Harvard University Press, 1967.

LAGORIO, Valerie, 'Problems in Middle English Mystical Prose', in *Middle English Prose: Essays on Bibliographic Problems*, A.S.G. Edwards and Derek Pearsall, eds, New York: Garland Press, 1981.

LEGGE, M. Dominica, *Anglo-Norman in the Cloisters*, Edinburgh: Edinburgh University Press, 1950.

LEWIS, C.S., *Allegory of Love*, Oxford: Oxford University Press, 1936.

MATTHEWS, William, ed., *Later Medieval English Prose*, New York: Appleton, Century, Crofts, 1963.

MEHL, Dieter, *The Middle English Romances of the Thirteenth and Fourteenth Centuries*, New York: Barnes and Noble, 1969.

MINNIS, A.J., *Medieval Theories of Authorship: Scholastic Literary Attitudes in the Later Middle Ages*, Philadelphia: University of Pennsylvania Press, 1984: 86–103.

PAINTER, George D., *William Caxton: A Quincentenary Biography of England's First Printer*, London: Chatto & Windus, 1976.

PATTERSON, Lee, '"Experience woot well it is noght so": Marriage and the Pursuit of Happiness in the Wife of Bath's Prologue and Tale', in Beidler, 133–54.

PEARSALL, Derek, ed., *Studies in the Vernon Manuscript*, Woodbridge, Suffolk: D.S. Brewer, 1990.

RUTTER, Russell, 'William Caxton and Literary Patronage', *Studies in Philology* 84 (1987): 469–70.

SALTER, Elizabeth, *English and International: Studies in the Literature, Art and Patronage of Medieval England*, Derek Pearsall and Nicolette Zeeman, eds, Cambridge: Cambridge University Press, 1988.

SARGENT, Michael G., 'Minor Devotional Writings', in Edwards, 147–75.

SEATON, Ethel, *Sir Richard Roos: Lancastrian Poet*, London: Rupert Hart-Davis, 1961.

General medieval history

ABU-LUGHOD, Janet L., *Before European Hegemony: The World System A.D. 1250–1350*, New York: Oxford University Press, 1989.

ALEXANDER, Michael Van Cleave, *The Growth of English Education, 1348–1648: A Social and Cultural History*, University Park: Pennsylvania State University Press, 1990.

BAUGH, Albert C., and Thomas Cable, *A History of the English Language*, 3rd edn, Englewood Cliffs, N.J.: Prentice-Hall, 1978.

BIRRELL, T.A., 'English Catholic Mystics in Non-Catholic Circles', *The Downside Review* 94 (1976): 60–81, 99–117, 213–31.

BROWN, Michelle P., *Understanding Illuminated Manuscripts: A Guide to Technical Terms*, Los Angeles: The Paul J. Getty Museum, 1994.

BRUNDAGE, James A., *Law, Sex, and Christian Society in Medieval Europe*, Chicago: University of Chicago Press, 1987.

CARPENTER, Christine, 'The Religion of the Gentry of Fifteenth-Century England', *England in the Fifteenth Century: Proceedings of the 1986 Harlaxton Symposium*, Daniel Williams, ed., Woodbridge, Suffolk: Boydell & Brewer, 1987: 53–74.

CROUCH, David, *William Marshal: Court, Career and Chivalry in the Angevin Empire, 1147–1219*, London: Longman, 1991.

DAVIS, Natalie Zemon, *Society and Culture in Early Modern France*, Stanford: University of Stanford Press, 1975.

DUBY, Georges, 'Au XIIe siècle: les "jeunes" dans la société aristocratique', *Annales* 19 (1964): 835–46.

——, *The Early Growth of the European Economy: Warriors and Peasants from the Seventh to the Twelfth Century*, Howard B. Clarke, trans., Ithaca: Cornell University Press, 1974.

——, *The Three Orders: Feudal Society Imagined*, Arthur Goldhammer, trans., Chicago: University of Chicago Press, 1980.

——, *William Marshal: Flower of Chivalry*, New York: Pantheon Books, 1985.

——, *A History of Private Life: Revelations of the Medieval World*, Arthur Goldhammer, trans., Cambridge, Mass.: The Belknap Press, 1988.

Eco, Umberto, *Travels in Hyperreality*, William Weaver, trans., New York: Harcourt Brace Jovanovich, 1983.

Hollister, C. Warren, *The Making of England, 55 B.C. to 1399*, Lexington, Mass.: D.C. Heath, 1971.

Le Goff, Jacques, *The Birth of Purgatory*, Arthur Goldhammer, trans., Chicago: University of Chicago Press, 1984.

Long, Pamela O., 'Invention, Authorship, "Intellectual Property," and the Origins of Patents: Notes Toward a Conceptual History', *Technology and Culture* 32 (1991): 846–84.

Parkes, M.B., 'The Literacy of the Laity', *The Mediaeval World*, David Daiches and Anthony Thorlby, eds., London: Aldus Books, 1973: 555–77.

Pollock, Frederick, and F.M. Maitland, *The History of English Law Before the Time of Edward I*, 2 vols, Cambridge: Cambridge University Press, 1968.

Stock, Brian, *The Implications of Literacy: Written Language and Models of Interpretation in the Eleventh and Twelfth Centuries*, Princeton: Princeton University Press, 1983.

Talbot, C.H., *The Anglo-Saxon Missionaries in Germany*, New York: Sheed & Ward, 1954.

Thompson, James Westfall, *The Literacy of the Laity in the Middle Ages*, Berkeley: University of California Press, 1939.

Thrupp, Sylvia, *The Merchant Class of Medieval London, 1300–1500*, Ann Arbor: University of Michigan Press, 1962.

Underhill, Evelyn, *Mysticism: A Study in the Nature and Development of Man's Spiritual Consciousness*, London: Methuen, 1930, rpt. 1967.

Vaneigem, Raoul, *The Movement of the Free Spirit*, New York: Zone Books, 1994.

Voigts, Linda Ehrsam, 'Medical Prose', in Edwards, 315–35.

Warren, Ann, *Anchorites and their Patrons in Medieval England*, Berkeley: University of California Press, 1985.

Wolf, Eric, *Europe and the People without History*, Berkeley: University of California Press, 1982.

Theoretical

Anderson, Benedict, *Imagined Communities: Reflections on the Origins and Spread of Nationalism*, 2nd edn, London: Verso, 1991.

Austin, J.L., *How To Do Things With Words*, Cambridge, Mass.: Harvard University Press, 1962.

BAKHTIN, M.M., *The Dialogic Imagination*, Michael Holquist and Caryl Emerson, trans., Austin: University of Texas Press, 1984.

——, *Problems of Dostoevsky's Poetics*, Caryl Emerson, ed. and trans., Minneapolis: University of Minnesota Press, 1984.

BARTHES, Roland, 'From Work to Text', in *Textual Strategies: Perspectives in Post-Structuralist Criticism*, Josué V. Harari, ed., Ithaca: Cornell University Press, 1979: 73–81.

BASSNETT-MCGUIRE, Susan, *Translation Studies*, London: Methuen, 1980.

BERGER, John, *Ways of Seeing*, London: Penguin Books, 1972.

BOURDIEU, Pierre, *Outline of a Theory of Practice*, Richard Nice, trans., Cambridge: Cambridge University Press, 1977.

DE CERTEAU, Michel, *Heterologies: Discourse on the Other*, Brian Massumi, trans., Minneapolis: University of Minnesota Press, 1986.

DERRIDA, Jacques, *Dissemination*, Barbara Johnson, trans., London: Athlone Press, 1981.

EAGLETON, Terry, *Literary Theory: An Introduction*, Minneapolis: University of Minnesota Press, 1983.

EISENSTADT, S.N., and Luis RONIGER, *Patrons, Clients, and Friends: Interpersonal Relations and the Structure of Trust in Society*, Cambridge: Cambridge University Press, 1984.

FOUCAULT, Michel, *Discipline and Punish: The Birth of the Prison*, Alan Sheridan, trans., New York: Pantheon, 1977.

——, 'What is an Author?' *Textual Strategies: Perspectives in Poststructuralist Criticism*, Josué V. Harari, ed., Ithaca: Cornell University Press, 1979: 141–60.

——, *Power/Knowledge: Selected Interviews and Other Writings by Michel Foucault, 1972–1977*, Colin Gordon, ed., New York: Pantheon, 1980.

——, 'Sexuality and Solitude', *On Signs*, Marshall Blonsky, ed., Baltimore: The Johns Hopkins University Press, 1985: 365–72.

GIDDENS, Anthony, *The Constitution of Society: Outline of the Theory of Structuration*, Berkeley: University of California Press, 1984.

IRIGARAY, Luce, *Speculum of the Other Woman*, Gillian Gill, trans., Ithaca: Cornell University Press, 1985.

KAMUF, Peggy, *Fictions of Feminine Desire: Disclosures of Héloise*, Lincoln, Nebraska: University of Nebraska Press, 1982.

KRISTEVA, Julia, *The Powers of Horror: An Essay on Abjection*, Leon S. Roudiez, trans., New York: Columbia University Press, 1982.

LACAN, Jacques, *Female Sexuality: Jacques Lacan and the École Freudienne*, Juliet Mitchell and Jacqueline Rose, eds., New York: Norton, 1982.

LAKOFF, George, and Mark JOHNSON, *Metaphors We Live By*, Chicago: University of Chicago Press, 1980.

MODLESKI, Tania, *Feminism Without Women: Culture and Criticism in a Post-feminist Age*, London: Routledge, 1991.

MORSON, Gary and Caryl EMERSON, *Mikhail Bakhtin: The Creation of a Prosaics*, Stanford: Stanford University Press, 1990.

NORRIS, Christopher, *Derrida*, Cambridge: Harvard University Press, 1987.

POOVEY, Mary, *The Proper Lady and the Woman Writer: Ideology as Style in the Works of Mary Wollstonecraft, Mary Shelley, and Jane Austen*, Chicago: University of Chicago Press, 1984.

RUSS, Joanna, *How to Suppress Women's Writing*, Austin: University of Texas Press, 1983.

SCOTT, James, *Domination and the Arts of Resistance: Hidden Transcripts*, New Haven: Yale University Press, 1990.

SHOWALTER, Elaine, 'Feminist Criticism in the Wilderness', *Critical Inquiry* 8 (1981): 179–205.

SPINGARN, J.E., ed., *Critical Essays in the Seventeenth Century*, vol. 1, Oxford: Clarendon Press, 1908.

VOLOŠINOV, V.N., *Marxism and the Philosophy of Language*, Ladislav Matejka and I.R. Titunik, trans., Cambridge, Mass.: Harvard University Press, 1976.

WOOLF, Virginia, *A Room of One's Own*, New York: Harcourt Brace Jovanovich, 1957.

Index

244